CANADIAN CANONS

Essays in Literary Value

Which works of Canadian literature are the most important? What makes them valuable? And who decides?

Such innocent-sounding questions – such hotly debated answers. The establishment of the Canadian canon or canons (those works that form the recognized foundation, or foundations, of our national literature) is a subject of intense controversy today, touching on a wide range of political and social issues.

Robert Lecker has brought together the first collection of essays to focus on Canadian literary canons. Its twelve essays on English and French criticism, fiction, poetry, and drama are written by accomplished scholars from across the country who share a desire to answer the fundamental questions raised above.

They are concerned less with identifying a Canadian canon and more with examining the forces that shape canonical activity in Canadian literature and criticism. By engaging in this process they also try to account for shifts in taste, differing ideas about the appropriateness of genre, the relationship between politics and literary value, and the impact of canonical choices on marginalized groups that have traditionally been excluded from the canon.

These essays explore a central component in Canadian cultural history. Inevitably contentious, they will fuel debate on a host of contemporary cultural issues, not limited to literature but touching on all the arts and beyond, as Canadians struggle with the increasingly urgent questions of who we are and what we value.

ROBERT LECKER is Professor of English at McGill University, and the author of *An Other I: The Fictions of Clark Blaise*. He is also co-editor, with Jack David, of the journal *Essays on Canadian Writing* and *The Annotated Bibliography of Canada's Major Authors*.

Canadian Canons: Essays in Literary Value

Edited by Robert Lecker

UNIVERSITY OF TORONTO PRESS

Toronto Buffalo London

© University of Toronto Press 1991
Toronto Buffalo London
Printed in Canada

ISBN 0-8020-5826-4 (cloth)
ISBN 0-8020-6700-x (paper)

Printed on acid-free paper

Canadian Cataloguing in Publication Data

Main entry under title:

Canadian canons : essays in literary value

Includes index.
ISBN 0-8020-5826-4 (bound)
ISBN 0-8020-6700-x (pbk.)

1. Canon (Literature).
2. Canadian literature – History and criticism.
I. Lecker, Robert, 1951–

PS8061.C35 1991   C810.9   C91-094869-0
PR9184.3.C35 1991

75064

This book has been published with the help of a grant from the
Canadian Federation for the Humanities, using funds provided by
the Social Sciences and Humanities Research Council of Canada.
Publication has also been assisted by the Canada Council and
Ontario Arts Council under their block grant programs.

Contents

Contributors

CAROLINE BAYARD is associate professor of French at McMaster University. She has published many works on literary theory, including *The New Poetics in Canada and Quebec: From Concretism to Post-Modernism*.

DONNA BENNETT teaches at the University of Toronto. She has published numerous essays on literary theory and is the co-editor of *Anthology of Canadian Literature in English*. Her current work on literary canons received a Toronto Arts Council Award.

CAROLE GERSON is a member of the Department of English at Simon Fraser University. Her recent publications include *A Purer Taste: The Writing and Reading of Fiction in English in Nineteenth-Century Canada* and many articles and reviews.

RICHARD PAUL KNOWLES is Chair of the Department of Drama at the University of Guelph. His works on Shakespeare and on Canadian theatre have appeared in numerous publications. He is the editor of *Theatre in Atlantic Canada* and the author of a play entitled *From Fogarty's Cove*.

ROBERT LECKER teaches at McGill University. He is co-editor of *The Annotated Bibliography of Canada's Major Authors, Canadian Writers and Their Works,* and the critical journal *Essays on Canadian Writing*. His recent studies include *An Other I: The Fictions of Clark Blaise*.

LAWRENCE MATHEWS is associate professor of English at Memorial University of Newfoundland. He has published articles on a number of Canadian writers, including Margaret Avison, Matt Cohen, Mavis Gallant, Hugh Hood, Norman Levine, Alice Munro, and Leon Rooke.

DERMOT MCCARTHY teaches in the Department of English at Huron College. He has published widely on the topic of Canadian poetry and criticism and is the author of several volumes of poetry. His most recent critical work is *Poetics of Place: The Poetry of Ralph Gustafson*.

LUCIE ROBERT teaches Quebec literature at the Université du Québec à Montréal. Her award-winning *L'Institution du littéraire au Québec* was published in 1989. She is currently working on a history of eighteenth- and nineteenth-century Quebec literature.

DENIS SALTER teaches at McGill University, where he is currently director of the Drama and Theatre Program. His recent publications include a number of works on Canadian cultural nationalism and on Canadian theatre history.

STEPHEN SCOBIE teaches Canadian literature at the University of Victoria. His many volumes of poetry include *McAlmon's Chinese Opera*, which won the Governor General's Award in 1981. He has also written critical works on Leonard Cohen, Sheila Watson, bpNichol, and Jacques Derrida.

SHERRY SIMON teaches in the Département d'études françaises at Concordia University. She is co-editor of the journal *Spiral* and of *Mapping Fiction: The Art and Politics of Translation*. She is the author of *L'Inscription social de la traduction au Québec* and co-author of *Fictions de l'identitaire au Québec*.

LEON SURETTE teaches in the Department of English at the University of Western Ontario. He has published widely on the poetry and criticism of Ezra Pound, including a study entitled *A Light from Eleusis: A Study of the Cantos of Ezra Pound*.

LORRAINE WEIR teaches in the Department of English, University of British Columbia. She has published widely on Canadian literature, modern literature, and literary theory. She co-edited *Margaret Atwood: Language, Text, System* and is the author of *Writing Joyce: A Semiotics of the Joyce System* and of *Jay Macpherson and Her Works*.

ACKNOWLEDGMENTS

I am grateful to the following people who assisted me in preparing this book for publication: Ken Lewis, for his efficient and exacting copy-editing; Don McLeod, for his meticulous indexing; Holly Potter, for her patience and assistance in putting so many things together; and the contributors to the volume, who helped me at every turn. My special thanks go to Gerry Hallowell, for his enthusiasm and support.

CANADIAN CANONS

ROBERT LECKER

Introduction

A canon is commonly seen as what other people, once powerful, have made and what should now be opened up, demystified, or eliminated altogether.

Robert von Hallberg, *Critical Inquiry* 10 (1983), iii

This is the first collection of essays to focus on Canadian literary canons. Its deliberately plural emphasis on canons reflects the multiple and shifting forms of recent canonical debate. The contributors are not so much concerned with identifying *a* Canadian canon as they are with interrogating the forces that constitute and determine canonical activity in Canadian literature and criticism. Such interrogations are inevitably contentious. They investigate, and frequently undermine, the discursive and ideological forces comprising 'the hierarchy of what we value.'[1] They testify to some wide-ranging differences in the perception of literary merit. And they question the structures that invest certain texts and authors with canonical authority. In short, this book cannot avoid becoming a field of contestation both within and outside its covers, for canonical enquiry is deliberately aimed at destabilizing authority through its analysis of the intermingling structures that uphold the political, economic, social, and cultural institutions that house the prevailing versions of literary history, tradition, form, and taste. Any analysis of canons must consider the status of these institutions. Who rejects them? Who sees them crumbling? Who feels locked out? Who feels locked in and can't leave? Who loves their shape and size? Who is determined to remodel? Who holds their keys?

These complex questions have been addressed by conflicting theories of inclusion and exclusion that delineate the evolution of canonical debate. Canonical theories recognize that the very existence of art forms called 'masterpieces' must be put in grave doubt, and that perhaps the value of literary forms must also be put in doubt. At the same time, they recognize that not everyone is ready to engage in these destabilizing activities: arguments in favour of a great tradition filled with masterpieces that have pleased many and pleased long still abound, while the values associated with canonical inheritance continue to have power and influence over what is written, what is published, and how it is transmitted or taught. For this reason, the ideal examination of any canon would include an analysis of market forces; of the publishing and bookselling industry; of curriculum development in schools and universities; of government attempts to patronize a national literature and its supporters; of the dissemination of literary value in newspapers, magazines, scholarly journals, and books. As one product of the economic forces that helped to shape the Canadian canon, this book cannot fully encompass this ideal; space remains a function of cost. But the essays collected here do make a concerted attempt to address these forces and to resolve some central questions. Why do we read the books we read? What ideologies inform our choices? How do these ideologies embody codes of authority and subordination? Whose canonical values does a book entitled *Canadian Canons* undermine, promote, provoke?

Canonical interrogations were originally inspired by post-structuralist views about the relationship between interweaving modes of discourse and the deconstruction of authority, and by such European theorists as Althusser, Derrida, Foucault, and Macherey, who examined the impact of cultural ideologies on canonical thought. These writers 'rejected assumptions on which any literary history must rest: namely, the significance of original meaning and value.'[2] Further, they argued against humanist assumptions about the validity of self, text, and consciousness. The assault on these assumptions was assisted by other cultural historians who maintained that criticism had created literature in its own image, an image fundamentally aligned with various forms of liberal individualism. Today, canonical theory continues to focus on how literature is the product of ideological forces that remain largely unexamined, even though these forces have created the values aligned with works called good or pronounced to be worthy of study. The influence of these views appears in studies by several British and

American critics. In Britain, one thinks of the work of Belsey, Eagleton, Fowler, Kermode, and Williams, and of the contributors to an important collection of essays edited by Widdowson. In the United States, there is a very active enquiry into the nature of literary value associated with a number of theorists including Altieri, Baym, Guillory, Herrnstein Smith, Hohendahl, Kolodny, Lauter, and Tompkins; a special issue of *Critical Inquiry* on canons appeared in 1983.

At the centre of canonical theory is a paradox described by Paul Lauter. He observes that any discussion of canons necessarily involves the recognition of a historical paradox, because 'certain historical constructs gave importance to a body of texts, while the weight attributed to the texts sustained the very credibility of received versions of history.' For this reason, Lauter says, 'we have come to realize not only the need to construct new versions of history – social as well as literary – but the need to reconstruct our standards of excellence, our understanding of form, indeed our ideas about the function of literature. The question of the canon, in short, affects all the structures of literary study.'[3]

John Guillory extends Lauter's comments by further identifying the relation between the 'delegitimation crisis' and a growing scepticism about conventional notions of history and tradition:

In recent years the formation of the literary canon has emerged as an arena of struggle over questions of a more systemic nature than the rise and fall of individual reputations. The canon has become the site of a structural fatigue, where pressures conceived to be extrinsic to the practice of criticism seem to have shaken literary pedagogy in fundamental ways. Nor does the recollection that canon-formation has always responded historically to pressures that are now represented as extrinsic or social alleviate this fatigue; in fact ... the unveiling of the canon as an institutional construction has had so demystifying an effect upon the ideology of tradition as to bring about a legitimation crisis with far-ranging consequences.[4]

Because the debate about canons has become a debate about the nature of history, society, and culture, it is appropriate to include in the above list of canonical theorists several new historicists who argue these 'key assumptions' as they are identified by H. Aram Veeser:

1. that every expressive act is embedded in a network of material practices;
2. that every act of unmasking, critique, and opposition uses the tools it condemns and risks falling prey to the practice it exposes;
3. that literary and non-literary 'texts' circulate inseparably;

4. that no discourse, imaginative or archival, gives access to unchanging truths nor expresses inalterable human nature;
5. finally ... that a critical method and a language adequate to describe culture under capitalism participate in the economy they describe.[5]

To act on these assumptions is to become involved in questions about how literary history is produced and who has managed its production. It is also to become involved in discussions about how critical discourse encodes various notions of truth, validity, and power. In *The Canadian Postmodern*, Linda Hutcheon observes that 'literary history ... can never be separated from other forms of history. The canon, whether formed deliberately or inadvertently, will always reflect the discourses out of which it derives: social, cultural, ideological.' Contemporary analyses of these discourses have allowed postmodern theories of language and feminist thought to work together 'in their related challenges to the canon (to the "eternal" "beauty" and "truth" of the "universally" agreed-upon "great tradition") and to the borders that conventionally divided fiction from non-fictional forms.'[6]

Hutcheon's words may suggest that the preoccupation with canonical issues so evident in European and American theory is paralleled by a similar preoccupation in Canada. This is not the case. Although there are scattered essays on these issues, along with two important feminist studies,[7] the voluminous discussion of Canadian literature over the past three decades has produced no sustained enquiry into Canadian canons. While we do hear calls for evaluative and ideologically self-conscious criticism, we seldom find criticism that investigates the values we have enshrined. We have shied away from theorizing about why certain Canadian authors or texts are 'major,' or 'minor,' or seldom mentioned at all. Although the evaluation of these texts is based on strong political and cultural assumptions, few Canadian critics have examined these assumptions or determined how they influence their own choices and theoretical perspectives. As Frank Davey notes in the introduction to his own ideologically self-conscious *Reading Canadian Reading*: 'Most criticism published in Canada still seems unaware that every critical act, no matter how naive or unpretentious, assumes at least one theory of criticism'; and 'Even in books in which critics have displayed an awareness of theoretical issues, they have frequently been blind to the implications of their own approaches.'[8]

To some extent, the contributors to this volume remain guilty of Davey's charge, as does its editor, for in seeking to display and explore a Canadian canon or canons, we have also sought to make the subject of our enquiry understandable, accessible, and therefore, safe. In doing so, we prove that every comment about a canon becomes a contribution to it and a further inscription of its authority. But we also suggest that by ordering and de-ordering the subject, we can see it from new angles, even if those new angles can never be free of the biases and politics imposed by any analysis.

We are condemned to be political and to act out our theoretical choices. Yet the question remains: what explains the lack of attention to both the French- and English-Canadian literary canons? In the case of French texts, the answer may lie in the realization that history is too far away: the radical changes in Québécois literature since the Quiet Revolution have provoked much analysis of recent shifts in value, perhaps at the expense of a broader picture that takes account of a value-laden, but now suppressed, version of canonical history. The study of English-Canadian literature poses the opposite problem: history is too close, or has been made to feel too close.

One effect of this English-Canadian longing for historical proximity is the creation of an order – inevitably canonical in orientation – called tradition. This notion of a single literary tradition is a canonical misconception. Traditions and canons are always in the process of being made and unmade, and whatever has been constructed shares its space with all that has been destroyed. There are no constant or prevailing values, no unadulterated inheritances, and no clear-cut lines of descent; canons thrive in flux. But as so many of the contributors to this volume observe, the interests of academics, pedagogical concerns, government intervention, and marketing strategies all conspire to create the impression of a stable canon and to promote a set of critical assumptions that congregate around this impression. The congregation promises safe haven to believers; it is invitingly safe. Its members are often reluctant to question what Louis Montrose calls the 'unproblematized distinctions between "literature" and "history," between "text" and context,'[9] or to consider how the 'range of aesthetic possibilities within a given representational mode' is tied to 'the complex network of institutions, practices, and beliefs that constitute the culture as a whole.'[10]

If literary canons have begun to decompose in the face of current ideology and theory, it is because the 'fantasies of orthodoxy' enshrined in these institutions have also begun to decay, while the forces accounting for exclusion and 'difference' have replaced orthodoxy and become a 'central critical category.'[11] In Annette Kolodny's words, the delegitimation crisis 'asserts as its central critical category not commonality but *difference*.'[12] Only when we begin to focus on the forces of exclusion, difference, and defamiliarization can we finally 'stand before the vast array of texts – canonical and non-canonical alike – and view them as more or less complex assemblages of rhetorical and stylistic devices whose meanings and value have been variously constituted over time by changing audiences' (Kolodny, 303).

An awareness of delegitimation as defamiliarization 'empowers us to understand that the critic's nagging obsession to locate any and every text within a graded, evaluative hierarchy, irrespective of history, is no more (and no less) than one facet of an ongoing process by which competing interest groups vie for cultural hegemony, in part by defining what shall be invested with merit' (Kolodny, 303). The same awareness empowers us to reformulate our notion of literary value in terms proposed by Jane Tompkins, terms that ask us to determine 'how and why specific texts "have power in the world" (or do not attain power, as the case may be) at any given moment' (Kolodny, 304). These current theories about literary value, or about what Barbara Herrnstein Smith describes as 'a more general rethinking of the concept of value,'[13] now appear 'to bracket the majority of theoretical problems over which criticism has not unfruitfully labored, among them the problem of literary language.'[14] As Montrose observes, they encourage us to 'resituate canonical literary texts among the multiple forms of writing ... while, at the same time, recognizing that this project of historical resituation is necessarily the textual construction of critics who are themselves historical subjects.'[15]

The preceding comments are designed to place this volume in relation to some of the issues and contexts informing recent discussion about canons and the value systems they promote. It should also be placed in relation to the Canadian studies that have been part of this discussion. Along with the essays collected here, these works represent the bulk of recent analysis devoted to canonical questions posed in Canadian terms. (The names I list are those of writers who deliberately situate their commentary in relation to canonical questions or ideological issues such as institutional control of interpretation; the values embodied in literary history-making; the effect of the educational system on assumptions about gender, quality, and taste; the relationships among ideology, representation, and privileged discursive acts; the notions of inclusion, exclusion, and marginalization; or the production of literary consensus as a function of economic conflict or interest.) In French criticism, there have been studies by Andrès, Belleau, Giguère, Hayne,

Landry, Lemire, Michon, Robert, and Simon.[16] In English criticism, canonical issues have been discussed (sometimes with less intensity or sophistication than in Quebec) by Barbour, Cude, Davey, Fee, Fry, Gerson, Greenhill, Hjartarson, Hutcheon, Jasen, Keith, Lecker, Lister, MacLaren, Mathews, Metcalf, Pache, Ross, Staines, Tippett, Ware, and Weir.[17] Some of these English studies (particularly those by Jasen, Metcalf, and Weir) seem to have fallen on deaf ears, despite the fact that they offer challenging insights into the values underlying the 'tradition' of Canadian literature and criticism. Two recent volumes, which are part of a larger series to appear on 'a history of the literary institution in Canada,' make important contributions to the canonical debate; they contain essays by some of the critics I mention above.[18] Perhaps the concerted efforts of the contributors to this book will allow us some new insights into how Canadian literary history has been formed and deformed in response to powerful ideologies accounting for the nature of *réception*, or for what English-Canadian writers refer to as canonical standards, judgments, taste.

The volume opens with Leon Surette's identification of 'some of the principles that have governed canon-formation for English-Canadian literature.' For Surette, as for several of the other contributors, the evolution of canonical value projects a displaced expression of nationalist ideology. From this perspective, Canadian criticism becomes 'an enterprise in which the central purpose was the discovery of the Canadian-ness of the literature written in this country.' Such a discovery involves more than the assertion that a text is faithful to the established values of its milieu and more than the belief that 'topocentrism' (to use Surette's term) is a canonical end in itself. Surette argues that the valorization of nationalist thought in criticism was synonymous with the valorization of Canadian history. To find the literature was to find the country, and to find successive works of literature that embodied the nationalist ideal was, in effect, to discover the solidity of the nation's existence in time. Surette speaks of how the critical alignment with this notion of historical solidity led to canonical solidity – an affirmation of 'continuity' over 'breach' – or the potential victory of 'Ghibelline' over 'Guelph' forces. But Surette is careful to note that this potential victory is far from won, for the texts we value, like the prominent theories of Canadian culture, tend to wobble between the anti-imperial Burckhardtian notion of 'spiritual continuity' and the imperial Arnoldian belief in 'cultural appropriation and acculturation.' While he recognizes this form of oscillation in Canadian critical value, Surette suggests that the texts we currently call worthy are those which embody the desire 'to find a reprise of European literary history in Canada' and the consequent belief that 'Canadian literature should ground itself in myth before attempting the more "advanced" form of epic.' Surette's argument is fertile, for it provides an initial basis for explaining why texts that do not 'internalize' and resolve the conflict between Guelph and Ghibelline consciousness 'have a very difficult time legitimating themselves as genuinely Canadian.'

Surette's deliberate attempt to situate canonical value in relation to historical understanding anticipates Dermot McCarthy's assertion that 'in the Canadian situation ... no challenge to the contemporary canon can be complete, or achieve a level of subversion sufficient to bring about any serious structural damage, which does not address the canon both theoretically ... and concretely, in relation to its full historical development as a structure.' Neither of these critics pretends to offer a definitive assessment of this historical development; and they disagree as to the kind of text that has been validated by the nationalist impulse. But both support the view, articulated in this case by McCarthy, that 'the writing of Canadian literary history has been organized around the extra-literary concept of the "nation" and has structured itself through the use of various metaphor-systems of organic growth or natural process.' For McCarthy, the history of Canadian literary value is the history of '(con)fusing aesthetic form and national coherence.' By demonstrating that the selections and rhetoric associated with numerous anthologies masked the ongoing assumption that 'literary history and canon are conceived as instruments of national unity,' McCarthy illustrates – perhaps with Hayden White in mind – how the '(con)fusing' history becomes a con, a 'discursive fabrication' that reveals more about its speaker than the historicized text. Because he emphasizes that 'the function of literary history and the canon is to show how the literary development mimes the social, political, and cultural progress of the nation' (a progress that is necessarily 'coherent and cohesive'), his essay complements the argument voiced by Lorraine Weir in her 'Strategies of Containment' (see note 17), as well as the assertions by other contributors to this volume concerning what McCarthy calls 'the topocentric fusion of place, identity, authenticity, and authority in the process of Canadian canon-formation.'

Carole Gerson's essay is also concerned with questions of 'authenticity and authority,' but from a feminist perspective. For her, the 'contours of a canon' are the product of 'national, aesthetic, and sexual politics' that allow those in power to determine what is read. Gerson shows that the forms of textual certification that emerged in Canada during the post-Victorian era were those aligned with the values of male 'publishers, editors, and English professors' who 'formed a loose "invisible college" ' that was 'distinctly masculine in gender and taste.' In many ways, the unarticulated consensus that governed textual selection 'during the critical canon-forming decades between the wars' was that good books were 'male modernist' books. The same valorization of male modernism, in Gerson's model, influences the canonical choices made today, despite the 'comforting claim,' made by some feminist writers, that women have always contributed to this influence. What the early canonizers wanted was what many contributors to this volume say they got: a milieu in which 'literary history and canon are conceived as instruments of national unity' (in McCarthy's words), a masculine canonical institution whose members 'shared a self-conscious awareness of their role as cultural arbiters and shapers of their country's literary destiny' (Gerson's perspective).

If it is true that Canadian modernism comprises a fundamentally male-oriented ideology of literary value, this may help to explain the curious paradoxes that Stephen Scobie identifies in his analysis of the canonical and non-canonical careers of Phyllis Webb and Leonard Cohen. Scobie frames his discussion with the assertion that modernism, and especially late modernism, enshrines 'the canonical mainstream of contemporary Canadian literature.' How, then, can we account for the canonization and continuing popularity of Cohen – an apparent postmodernist – and for the non-canonization of Webb – an apparent modernist? Scobie's answer seems to support Gerson's observations about earlier modernist values in Canada, for he argues that Cohen embodies an ideological stance that allows him to be seen 'as a modernist in the trappings of postmodernism,' while Webb may be excluded from the canon because she is 'a postmodernist in the trappings of modernism.' In this paradoxical context, the 'real' modernist turns out to be (inevitably?) male; the 'real' postmodernist (Webb) is excluded not only by virtue of her formal and generic interests, but also by gender. Perhaps it is a misreading of Scobie's essay to suggest that this paradox may account for the historical exclusion of women from the canon: to be not-modern, or postmodern, was to embrace an implicitly unmale form (Scobie acknowledges that 'much feminist writing ... seems more closely allied to the postmodernist canon'). Conversely, to be a modern, to be a male, was to be in history, in the nation that history was making, and in the institution that controlled the history-making.

Although every national canon embodies a nationalist ideal, many of the contributors to this volume suggest that in both French and English Canada nationalist values occupy centre stage. Denis Salter makes this case in 'The Idea of a National Theatre,' which proceeds from the central assumption that 'agitation for a distinctively *Canadian* kind of national theatre begins as early as the nineteenth century and ... remains unabated even now.' In words that reinforce the opinions of McCarthy, Knowles, and Robert, Salter identifies the governing 'cultural and political orthodoxy' behind the theatrical canon: a belief 'that the theatre should be obliged to commit itself to the never-ending task of building a sense of national destiny.' Salter's detailed tracing of the evolution of this orthodoxy provides a fascinating narrative about the history of Canadian theatre, one that remains aware of the historical construction it engenders through its deliberate act of deconstruction. Although the author might recoil from such a description of his project, he demonstrates throughout his essay a willingness to undo the implications of his own participation in the idea of a national theatre that, he admits, is 'potentially self-defeating and potentially dangerous.' He also suggests, along the lines of McCarthy, Mathews, and Weir, that the creation of the canon involves an act of duplicitous self-projection into an historical arena that is fictionalized rather than found. In Salter's essay, the canon is revealed to be a con job that is 'endlessly deferred,' just as the 'the very idea of "Canada"' is deferred, 'no matter which theatrical (dis)guises it decide[s] to adopt.'

Richard Paul Knowles also offers a wide-ranging deconstruction of the assumptions and values behind the dramatic canon. For Knowles, this deconstruction provides an essential challenge to a conservative theatrical institution that has 'neutralized and muffled' the 'subversive' and 'marginal' forms promoted by 'feminist, "ethnic," or regional playwrights and theatre companies.' By examining the choices made by editors in prominent anthologies of Canadian drama, Knowles demonstrates that the canonized dramatic forms are those that have been assimilated, systematized, classified, and neutralized; 'controversial works are avoided' or are explained into safety (a process described in pointed fashion in Lorraine Weir's essay). Even the 'experimental' work, infrequently accepted by the canon through a gesture towards difference, loses its once-questionable status by virtue of its assimilation. Knowles agrees with most of the contributors to this volume when he argues that canonical value in Canada affirms what is 'centralized, hierarchical, and nationalistic.' This affirmation is responsible for producing a structure that is conservative, self-congratulatory, and static, because the solidification of the canon 'necessarily restricts any experimentation or change that does not evolve in a linear way out of existing forms.' The only way out of such restriction, Knowles suggests, would be through a thorough, self-conscious re-evaluation of what drama gets published, how theatre companies are structured, and how drama – among other literature – gets taught.

Lucie Robert's examination of the new Quebec theatre suggests that the self-examination Knowles recommends has been crucial to the development of dramatic production outside English Canada. While the canonical process described by Knowles and Salter involves normalization and the affirmation of existing structures, the history Robert traces is one of increasing subversion and breach. She observes that various challenges to the dramatic canon in Quebec are simultaneously challenges to a worn-out institutional bias in favour of a 'grand theatre' based on the myth of continuity with, and allegiance to, a federalist or European ethos. The new Quebec theatre works against the Canadianization of culture that prevailed during the 1950s and 1960s. Its conscious departure from the established models – in terms of its use of language, setting, and characters – is part of a wider need to recognize an indigenous Québécois culture. As Robert says, the object is to discover an autonomy that is represented in the totality of theatrical signs: political, cultural, and institutional – all at once. Robert traces the evolution of this ideal as it appears in crucial changes embodied in recent theatre in Quebec: colloquial diction – 'langue populaire' – became central to expression; parody undermined traditional models; carnivalization and 'collective creation' put in question the 'traditional hierarchy.' Although these subversive elements did transform theatre in Quebec and signal a radical break both with English-Canadian theatre and with Continental forms, the break was bound to be absorbed by a new canonical order. Robert concludes her essay by observing that ' "new Quebec theatre" has ceased to be new. It has become canonical, attained hegemony.' In this sense, it has been normalized in the same way as English-Canadian avant-garde theatre has been normalized: by becoming a recognized object of enquiry, the property of academics, the subject of a scholarly essay in a volume on canons published by a university press.

While most of the contributors to this collection differentiate between literature and criticism and choose to examine the effect of one form on the other, Caroline Bayard makes no such distinction. Her essay rests on the crucial assumption that canonical values are so embedded within critical discourse that theory *is* the canon in Quebec culture. For this reason, her essay focuses exclusively on canonical developments in Quebec criticism. What it demonstrates is that the allegiances in Quebec thought are European and contemporary in origin. But because Quebec theorists are trying to restructure their own institutions in hope of articulating 'a new discourse for French Canada,' they find themselves caught in 'a dialectical movement between imported structuralism, on the one hand, and a separatist, historical Marxist-inspired discourse on the other.' In the hands of the most canonized Quebec theorists, this discourse 'challenged textual, political, and syntactical order,' therefore consciously, or even unconsciously, putting forward a 'liberationist philosophy.'

While discussions about canonicity in Quebec often focus on discourse and discourse theory, there is little parallel discussion in English Canada. Instead, critics tend to focus on value as a function of representation. We have seen that the canon is frequently viewed as representing a dream of national unity, hierarchical tradition, or centralist notions of coherence and order. The assumption behind this reading of the canon is that representation itself is a value. Although many contemporary theorists would challenge the notion that it is possible to 'represent' the world (since representation is a construct of discourse rather than a mimesis of reality), this conventional understanding of mimesis prevails as a locus of value and highlights a concern with *what* is represented and *how* the representation is effected. Many of the critics in this volume argue that the chief representational preoccupation in English-Canadian criticism is with depicting the nation through various forms of mimesis. In other words, the vehicle of value is genre, and the appropriate genre is mimetic in orientation.

The connection between value and genre is the subject of extended analysis in the essays by Donna Bennett and Lawrence Mathews, both of whom position their discussions in relation to the 1978 Conference on the Canadian Novel at the University of Calgary. Certainly this conference provides a good testing ground for any canonical theory, for its proceedings record the first Canadian attempt to identify the top novels in the country and to discuss why these novels were chosen. Bennett and Mathews draw our attention to the fact that the conference privileged one genre – 'an aesthetics based in fiction' – and that it did so explicitly in relation to questions of literary value. For Mathews, the predisposition on the part of academic critics to realistic narratives was a displaced expression of an elitist desire to remain in control: 'The texture of the realism ... discourages the reader from questioning suspiciously simple presuppositions about character or theme. This is how the world is, these novels tell us.' Bennett argues that the conference demonstrated how discussions of the canon frequently confuse merit and genre. For her, 'failure to maintain a distinction between genre-definition and canonical evaluation has contributed to the inherent instability of the canon' in Canada. The conference revealed that 'genre-definition' was the key issue for conference participants. While allegiance to specific genres may shift over time, the 'aesthetic history' that informs our views may well be organized around generic distinctions that need to be better defined.

In her essay on the novel and criticism in Quebec during the 1980s, Sherry Simon provides some of these generic distinctions and shows how they can be related to an analysis of cultural shift (and drift). Simon begins from the assumption – shared by every contributor to this volume – that critical activity is a function of 'the articulation of the link between representation and value, between literary and social configurations.' While this assumption seems to support a distinction between creative and critical expression, Simon makes it clear that the boundaries between author and critic have broken down: so-called 'critical' works are as revealing in their representation of value as the texts they comment on. As Simon says by way of quoting René Payant: ' "The postmodern condition is the ... disappearance of stable and absolute frames of reference." ' Simon finds one expression of this disappearance in the contemporary criticism of Pierre Nepveu, whose work reacts to ' "ideological exhaustion," ' to ' "the loss of meaning of history," ' to ' "the problematic nature of reality itself," ' to ' "the fragmentation of the territory of culture." ' Because he 'accepts the difficult paradoxes of texts (and worlds) devoid of centre,' Nepveu may provide a telling example of how criticism can embody a new conception of culture that emphasizes 'increasing hybridization and pluralism.' In contrast, the criticism of Patricia Smart, also eminently conscious of its social arena, is grounded in a problematic of difference focused on alterity. While Nepveu's and Smart's critical projects are both important variations on a venerable Quebec tradition which gives an identical form to literature and society, they differ in their conceptualization of this social space – primarily binary for Smart, fragmented and plural for Nepveu. Although Simon's comparison of Smart and Nepveu is designed to illustrate two ways of representing contemporary fiction and criticism in Quebec, her model can fruitfully be applied to the analysis of any national literature in which questions of identity, difference, and pluralism are important.

The concluding essay by Lorraine Weir confronts these tensions on several fronts. Although Weir's study has a very particular focus – a critique of how Linda Hutcheon's postmodern poetic 'converts danger into safety, the marginalized into the mainstream, the non-referential into the referential' – it would be a misreading of Weir and of her deconstructive strategies to see this as purely a response to one critic. Such a misreading would normalize Weir's arguments and make her 'attitude' acceptable (after all, controversy is worthwhile, and academic infighting is to be expected). It would also provide proof of the assertion that many Canadian critics share the normalizing values Weir finds in Hutcheon's work: a desire to reinscribe 'a hermeneutics of word and world'; an affirmation of 'progress as strategy of control, containment'; a 'legitimation of what might otherwise disrupt the hegemonic balance of a *Realpolitik* founded on good taste and liberal-humanist assumptions about the correct construction of the world, the text, and their points of interface.'

If Weir is correct in saying that Hutcheon's work is symptomatic of 'the great Canadian attempt to normalize the subject through sheer force of decorum and civility,' then Canadian criticism needs to undo itself now. By remaining conscious of how powerfully cultural value is inscribed in critical history and pronouncement, the contributors to this volume commit themselves to this necessary process of undoing. They also realize that their commentary paradoxically augments the value of whatever canons are undone. The double bind of canonical enquiry may be inescapable. But remaining conscious of it is a rewarding start.

LEON SURETTE

Creating
the Canadian Canon

Perfection, as culture conceives it, is not possible while the individual remains isolated. The individual is required, under pain of being stunted and enfeebled in his own development if he disobeys, to carry others along with him in his march towards perfection.

Matthew Arnold, *Culture and Anarchy* (1869)

Canadian literary criticism has always been an enterprise in which the central purpose was the discovery of the Canadian-ness of the literature written in this country. 'The search for English-Canadian literature'[1] has encountered perennial criticism as a provincial and anti-aesthetic program offending the Enlightenment axiom of the universality of cultural values. But that Enlightenment axiom has itself now come under very broad attack from relativists of all stripes. In particular, studies of canon-formation have made us all aware that the Arnoldian and New Critical claims that the canon consists of the best that has been thought and written are not easily supported. In the light of these new attitudes it might be interesting to try to identify some of the principles that have governed canon-formation for English-Canadian literature.

It seems natural to begin with one of the first theorists of canonicity, Matthew Arnold. However, it is his theory of culture as expressed in *Culture and Anarchy*, rather than the 'touchstone' theory of canonicity expressed in 'The Study of Poetry,' that is most relevant to the formation of the Canadian canon. Arnold was prompted to write *Culture and*

Anarchy by an act of the British Parliament passed in 1867; the bill in question was not the British North America Act, but the Second Reform Act, which established universal male suffrage. Nonetheless, Arnold's articulation of his faith in the power of top-down acculturation to ennoble and unify a heterogeneous population expresses a doctrine that has been an unquestioned article of faith for English-Canadian nationalists from as early as the emigration of the Moodies and Traills to the backwoods of Ontario in 1820s and 1830s. The shared belief of Arnold, the Moodies, and the Traills in the power of acculturation belongs to Toryism in that the inculcation of approved cultural values must be paternalistic and elitist. And, more importantly for my argument, the perception expressed in the epigraph – that cultural values are a collective rather than an individual possession – is *echt* Tory, for in Tory theory, culture is the expression and possession of a community, as opposed to a capricious collection of the inspirations of brilliant individuals – as it is in Whig or Enlightenment theories of culture. Arnold's cultured community is implicitly opposed to the free, untrammelled individual of Lockean Whiggism, most familiarly exemplified by such anarchic figures as Cooper's Natty Bumppo, Twain's Huckleberry Finn, and Walt Whitman's Walt Whitman. At the same time, Arnold's theory retains a measure of Puritan and Methodist self-improvement, as the epigraph reveals.

The problem confronting the Canadian cultural theorist, however, is quite different from Arnold's. He feared the consequences of egalitarian democracy in a nation divided, as he thought, into a barbarian aristocracy, a philistine middle class, and an ignorant populace. Arnold's solution was to homogenize the classes through the inculcation of pan-European cultural values. He described those values as 'Hellenic,' but they were essentially Enlightenment values tinged with Romantic spiritualism and Tory collectivism. The Canadian cultural problem at first was how to formulate our relation to a parent culture – whether English or French. English Canada has leaned towards a theory requiring a strenuous maintenance of links with the parent culture, while French Canada favours the notion of a severed fragment pursuing its own separate destiny in North America.

I cannot discuss the relations between the two linguistic communities in the brief compass I am allowed, but these two contrary paradigms of our cultural destiny – continuity and breach – operate simultaneously *within* English-Canadian cultural theory as well as *between* English and French Canada, and also between English Canada and the United States. The first formulation of the fragment theory of transatlantic culture is also contemporaneous with the birth of the Canadian state. It is found in Jacob Burckhardt's lectures given at the University of Basel and later published as *Force and Freedom* (1943).

Burckhardt's cultural theories grow out of the same mix of Enlightenment and Romantic ideas as Arnold's, but Arnold was writing from the heart of the British Empire, and Burckhardt from the intersection of the decaying Austro-Hungarian Empire, the emerging Italian state, and the expanding Second German Reich. Burckhardt could hardly adopt a paternalistic and hegemonic theory of culture like Arnold's. His problem was to preserve Swiss political independence in the face of pan-Germanic pressures. His solution was to postulate a 'spiritual' continuity with the past as a carrier of culture distinct from both language and the state.[2]

Burckhardt enjoined his Swiss students to remember 'all we owe to the past as a spiritual *continuum* which forms part of our supreme spiritual heritage.' There are, he says, only two peoples who 'renounce that privilege': first, the 'barbarians, who, accepting their cake of custom as preordained, never break through it. They are barbarians because they have no history, and vice versa.' Second, the Americans (of both continents), who 'renounce history,' are peoples of 'unhistorical cultures who cannot quite shake off the old world.'[3] Burckhardt's 'spiritual heritage' is quite distinct from Arnold's 'best that has been thought and said,' for the latter is a specific historical – and therefore capricious – continuity, while the former is a rational selection.

Arnold's influence on Canadian cultural theorizing hardly needs demonstration, but Burckhardt's influence is less apparent. Clearly the Swiss did and do face difficulties somewhat analogous to those faced by Canadians. But we need not rely on analogy. Burckhardt's principle of continuity appears prominently in the fragment theory of the American political philosopher Louis Hartz. Hartz argues that the Americans cut themselves off from Europe by their revolution, that the American 'fragment' froze ideologically in the Enlightenment phase of Lockean liberalism, and that, as a consequence, adherence to Lockean liberal ideology became the touchstone for American patriotism.'[4] Hartz thus accepts Burckhardt's assessment that the Americans renounced history, and then accounts for their powerful patriotic sentiments by the fact of that renunciation.

Hartzian-Burckhardtian analysis was adapted to Canada by Gad Horowitz in a 1966 article ('Conservatism, Liberalism, and Socialism in Canada: An Interpretation') which has become a canonical study for the interpretation of Canadian political culture. Horowitz accepts the

Burckhardt-Hartz notion of a fragment culture cut off from its 'spiritual heritage' but argues that Canada's frozen ideological baggage is Toryism rather than Lockean liberalism, and for that reason Canadian political culture is less hostile to collectivism – whether right- or left-wing – than is American political culture. In a recent attack on the Horowitz thesis, H.D. Forbes expresses puzzlement at the great success of Hartzian analysis in Canada compared to its relative obscurity in the United States – particularly since it is, in Forbes's view, empirically unsupportable. Horowitz defends himself by arguing that the ideologies in question do not *produce* the political cultures of the two nations in a causal way, but rather formulate climates of legitimation for political action. In this defence, Horowitz adopts an Arnoldian position which permits – indeed requires – a component of choice in the formulation of culture.[5]

Whatever the merits of the Hartz-Horowitz thesis, its success in Canada is good evidence that Burckhardt's notion of spiritual continuity is alive and current – at least among Canadian political scientists. It seems to me that Canadian cultural theorizing tends to wobble between the Arnoldian and Burckhardtian positions – both of which would fairly be characterized as Tory or conservative. At the risk of terminological overkill, we might label Arnoldian Toryism 'Ghibelline' since it sees centralized political authority as the executive instrument guaranteeing the maintenance of an appropriate cultural homogeneity. Burckhardtian Toryism could be called 'Guelph' since it regards local and variegated *historical* continuities as the best guarantors of cultural health and authenticity, and as a desirable alternative to cultural unity achieved by the hegemonic power of a distant capital. The appropriateness of both postures to the Canadian situation is obvious enough.

The Italian Ghibellines of the late Middle Ages looked to the distant emperor as a balance against the power of the nearby pope. Canadian cultural Ghibellines similarly look to distant Britain as a balance against the cultural pressures of the nearby American juggernaut. Early Canadian Ghibellines were all Imperialists and Loyalists. On a Ghibelline model Canada would remain forever British. Canadian Ghibellines believed that only through the Imperial connection could this outpost of British culture survive. Just as Arnold's Hellenism was to unify the three British classes, so British culture – seen from this side as already unified – would homogenize and unite English, Scottish, Welsh, Irish, German, Italian, Ukrainian, Jewish, and all other immigrants. It was also hoped at the beginning that the already settled French of Quebec could be absorbed by British culture. (The Acadians had already been deported, and the native Amerindians were safely set aside in wilderness ghettos.)

Arnold was far too Ghibelline to entertain the possibility of a division of 'Hellenic' culture into provincial branches as Canadian Ghibellines required. He asked his readers to 'imagine the face of Philip or Alexander at hearing of a Primer of Macedonian Literature: are we to have a Primer of Canadian Literature too, and a Primer of Australian?'[6] Arnold's contempt for the local and provincial has been an embarrassment for Canadian Ghibellines. They have been forced – somewhat inconsistently – to invoke Burckhardt's Guelph principles of a 'spiritual heritage' and an 'historical continuity' in order to legitimate some local cultural and political autonomy.[7]

This revisionist application of the Burckhardtian principle of cultural continuity – unhappily from a Ghibelline perspective – legitimates a Balkanization of English-Canadian culture. The Italian Guelphs looked to the Vatican for nurture and protection. Canadian Guelphs look to Ottawa, and its cultural institutions – the CBC, the CRTC, the Canada Council, and Canada Pension. The analogy with the medieval Italians must be bent a little here, for Canadian Guelphs and Ghibellines both perceive the United States as a threat to our cultural and political integrity, and therefore both support Confederation and the degree of centralization that it entails.

Indeed some Canadian Guelphs still view British cultural hegemony with greater alarm than they do the apprehended American threat to our political integrity and are out of sympathy with old-style Ghibellines like George Grant and Robertson Davies. The purest Canadian Guelphs are Westerners, who tend to regard Ontario rather than Britain or the United States as the hegemonic power threatening domination of their imaginative lives parallel to its political, economic, and cultural domination of the nation.

Canadian Guelphs do indeed argue for a Burckhardtian continuity with the past, but they do so in a peculiarly strained manner. As good Burckhardtians, they wish to maintain cultural ties with the past – whether that be Britain, Europe generally, or even Ontario – but at the same time they are conscious that they are not British, or European, or often even Ontarian. Like the German-speaking Swiss of Burckhardt's time, contemporary Canadians belong to a greater linguistic and cultural community – in our case made up of a declining British and an established American empire. Like the Swiss we hope to maintain some political and cultural independence from both. But, unlike the Swiss, we cannot easily claim some mystical continuity with either our 'spiritual heritage' or our history because neither protects us from either British or American domination. Our 'spiritual heritage' is as much American as British – and must include our ethnic diversity as well. And, unlike the Swiss, our history is richer in internal quarrels and rebellions than in heroic resistance of foreign intruders.

French-Canadian nationalism is in a very different position. It is not torn by a conflict between Arnoldian notions of paternalistic acculturation and Burckhardtian theories of organic continuity. Instead, it is Herderian. Johann Gottfried von Herder, the father of modern ethnic nationalism, expressed his theory most fully – just as the French Revolution was taking place – in *Ideen zur Philosophie der Geschichte der Menschheit* (Thoughts on the philosophy of the history of mankind) (1784–91). He argued that any people who shared a language and a historical tradition constituted a *Volk* or nation. He thought that the natural state should be the political expression of a homogeneous *Volk*, but that the *Volk*, not the state, was the nation. French Canada's perception of itself as a nation even though it is not a state is pure Herderianism.[8]

Burckhardt, in *Force and Freedom*, was self-consciously resisting a Herderian justification of the Second Reich's expansionism. And we all know that Hitler used the same arguments to legitimate the expansionism of the Third Reich. However, even if Herderian nationalism had not acquired an odour of evil, it could hardly serve the interests of English-Canadian nationalists as it does French Canadians. It is much more likely to serve the interests of American expansionists and their Canadian supporters.

Even though Burckhardt was hostile to pan-Germanic arguments derived from Herder, he follows Herder in the high status he gives to language and literature: 'languages are the most direct and specific revelation of the spirit of the nations, their ideal image, the most perdurable material in which they enclose the content of their spiritual life, especially in the sayings of their great poets and thinkers.'[9]

On Herderian grounds English Canadians and Americans form a single *Volk*, and we are very sensitive to that apparent fact.[10] Canadian Ghibellines – most articulately Gad Horowitz – counter this Herderian perception with a Burckhardtian riposte: the insistence on our continuity with British culture, in contrast to the American rupture. That claim is obviously valid for political culture, but it is increasingly unconvincing for either popular culture – which is entirely American – or indigenous high culture, which looks much more to New York, Chicago, and

Los Angeles than to London, Oxford, or Edinburgh. A trivial example is the staffing of our universities. They used to be staffed to a large extent by British emigrés, but the British are now greatly outnumbered by American emigrés.

The decline of British cultural hegemony and the concomitant rise of that of America have greatly enhanced the success of Guelphism within Canada. For if it is a cultural fragment, Canada is free to develop its own history and to forge its own spiritual continuity with a past that begins *here* in our part of North America. But in order to do so, we must somehow unravel – if not sever – the thread tying us to our European heritage. Our topography, climate, and local history are recruited by Ghibellines to establish the imaginative distance from a heritage neither Ghibellines nor Guelphs are quite willing to renounce.

I argued several years ago in 'Here Is Us: The Topocentrism of Canadian Literary Criticism'[11] that the focus on topography and climate in the search for Canadian cultural identity could be called 'topocentrism,' that is, the belief that human cultures are in some not clearly specific sense the product of the physical environment. It is a necessary axiom for Canadian Guelphs adapting nineteenth-century cultural theories to Canadian realities since they cannot – as Canadian Ghibellines can – appeal to empire, race, language, or historical continuity to legitimate Canadian distinctiveness. But as Burckhardtian Tories, Canadian Guelphs cannot renounce history, even though they must renounce empire – whether British or American. Lacking an historical breach with the British and a geographical, racial, linguistic, or historical separation from the Americans, Canadian Guelphs have chosen a mysticism of place, *faut de mieux*.

It was not clear to me when I wrote 'Here Is Us' how deep-seated topocentrism is in European cultural theory. The state of Israel, for example, is legitimated almost entirely on a topocentric postulate of some spiritual union between the Jewish people and the soil of ancient Palestine.[12] Canadian topocentrism – interestingly enough – is the inverse of Zionist topocentrism. Instead of holding that the soil of England, France, Scotland, Germany, Italy, or wherever is sanctified ground to which we are forever mystically linked, we argue that *our* spiritual constitution is to some degree formulated by the soil and climate of our immediate environment.

When we turn to the issue of canon-formation, we find that early Ghibelline forms of topocentric cultural commentary expected to find a reprise of European literary history in Canada. If the literature of Europe began with myth, advanced to epic, and culminated in tragedy as the nineteenth century supposed, then Canadian literature should ground itself in myth before attempting the more 'advanced' form of epic.[13] Such a model canonized pioneer works such as Susanna Moodie's *Roughing It in the Bush* or Catharine Parr Traill's *The Canadian Crusoes*. 'Mythopoeic' works such as Sheila Watson's *The Double Hook* and Robert Kroetsch's *The Words of My Roaring* or *The Studhorse Man* fill the mythic spot in such a model. Of course, it is commonly understood that the Canadian reprise of literary history will be simultaneous rather than serial. Hence 'epic' works such as E.J. Pratt's *Brébeuf and His Brethren*, Hugh MacLennan's *The Watch That Ends the Night*, or Rudy Wiebe's *The Temptations of Big Bear* and *The Scorched-Wood People* will be found alongside the more 'primitive,' 'mythic' works.

An interesting twist to the formation of the Canadian canon in fiction is a consequence of the unsuitability of the bourgeois realistic novel to the task of forging an indigenous culture. Symbolic, allegorical, and mythopoeic or romance forms of prose fiction are much more suitable to the task.[14] As a result realistic novelists like Hugh MacLennan, Morley Callaghan, and Mordecai Richler are the exception rather than the rule among canonized Canadian novelists. Sheila Watson, Robertson Davies, Robert Kroetsch, Leonard Cohen, and Margaret Atwood all permit fantasy, magic, mysticism, or the uncanny in their fiction.

Margaret Laurence stands almost alone in her generation as a canonized novelist working within the conventions of bourgeois realistic fiction, a tradition that T.D. MacLulich nonetheless regards as central to the Canadian novel.[15] Laurence's fiction belongs to a canonical line that begins with Catharine Parr Traill and is continued by Frederick Philip Grove, Sinclair Ross, and W.O. Mitchell. This line has an Eastern correlate in the fiction of Morley Callaghan, Hugh MacLennan, Ernest Buckler, and Alice Munro. All but one of these 'realists' are Ghibelline in that they are all concerned to articulate the difficulties of maintaining a European cultural heritage in an alien soil. Margaret Laurence is the one exception. Laurence's fiction is rather more concerned with escaping – or at least reformulating – a European heritage which weighs on the Canadian imagination like a dead hand.[16] But if Laurence is Guelph, so is Robert Kroetsch, whose novels and critical prose reveal so clearly his project to forge a *Canadian* imagination by re-enacting European history rather than by maintaining continuity with it.

The Canadian canon has not been generated by an application of either Guelph or Ghibelline criteria – even though most disputes about canon are fought by appeals to such criteria. But works that fail to internalize the cultural stresses we have been discussing – like Morley Callaghan's novels – have a very difficult time legitimating themselves as genuinely Canadian. On the other hand, otherwise peripheral novels such as Mordecai Richler's *The Apprenticeship of Duddy Kravitz* and Leonard Cohen's *Beautiful Losers* have achieved canonical status because they do internalize them.[17]

An all-too-brief glance at such internalizations in three canonized authors roughly contemporaneous with one another might test the usefulness of the foregoing observations. We find an almost pathological instance of such an internalization in the 'Afterword' to Margaret Atwood's *The Journals of Susanna Moodie*. She imagines Susanna Moodie rising from the grave on hearing 'the twentieth century above her, bulldozing away her past, but she refused to be ploughed under completely. She makes her final appearance in the present, as an old woman on a Toronto bus who reveals the city as an unexplored, threatening wilderness. Susanna Moodie has finally turned herself inside out, and has become the spirit of the land she once hated.'[18] This characteristically pointed Atwoodian vision expresses very clearly both a Ghibelline nostalgia for a civilized state once possessed, but now lost, and a macabre representation of the topocentric notion of a mystical union with the soil. Moodie is a Canadian Persephone defiantly rising from the grave, not into Demeter's garden world, but into a labyrinthine city as cold and alien as the wilderness it has replaced. And notice the Burckhardtian flavour in her fear of the twentieth century 'bulldozing away her past.'[19]

Atwood's vision of Moodie as a vulnerable corpse half-buried in an hostile land is just one version of the Burckhardtian motif of isolation from a parent culture. A.R.M. Lower's portrayal of Canada itself as an unwanted child abandoned by its British and American parents is another: 'Canada was an accident: unwanted, certainly, and soon forgotten by one parent, the land from which the Loyalists came; unwanted, too, and often neglected by the other parent, the mother country. The parents had separated in anger; Canada was their unwanted, bastard child. Her people have continued to have a psychology appropriate to their parentage.'[20] Both Atwood and Lower reflect the tension between Arnoldian paternalism and Burckhardtian continuity. The Americans renounce their history, but we are either abandoned by our spiritual heritage or have our memories bulldozed by the neighbouring juggernaut.

Robert Kroetsch's handling of this theme is the inverse of Atwood's and Lower's Burckhardtian *angst*. Picking *As for Me and My House, The*

Double Hook, and *The Mountain and the Valley* as the three classic modern novels in the Canadian tradition, Kroetsch explains:

One hears in each of those three titles a kind of opposition, a basic contrary that is implicitly sexual in its inclination towards interpenetration: the need of violence. In each there is a pastoral world that is violated out of its original innocence ... The grammar of violence in these three novels I would define with the phrase 'ceremonies of disbelief.' In all three novels there are ceremonies of order, Christian in derivation, though touching on other systems of conviction (systems of family, systems of community). But conviction is indeed what the system becomes. And the convicts, in each novel, are tempted appallingly by silence.[21]

Kroetsch's belief that old convictions make convicts of their adherents is clearly anti-Arnoldian and anti-Burckhardtian. Instead of tradition, and heritage, he invokes a Nietzschean conflict which – in the structuralist rhetoric of the period of his essay – he calls a 'grammar of violence.' Whereas Atwood's Moodie resists a wilderness and an 'American' city alike, Kroetsch reads his three canonical novels as representing violations of a pastoral world. Neither clearly Ghibelline nor Guelph, Kroetsch seems more Jacobin, a Nietzschean celebrator of conflict and violence.

It is difficult to imagine fictive worlds more starkly opposed than those of Atwood and Kroetsch. Atwood's heroine rises reluctantly from her grave, hoping to save her memories by facing an urban labyrinth as threatening as the wilderness she tried to tame. Kroetsch's novels portray satyrlike males violating a pastoral world that apparently had lain awaiting them for millennia. Kroetsch's satyrs are constrained from the full enjoyment of their rapine by the chains of 'conviction' – of Christianity, family, and language. But these restraints are external and instrumental, not internal and moral.

For my money Kroetsch's most profound articulation of these themes is to be found in *Badlands*, a fabular tale in which the Eastern palaeontologist, Dawe, is set against a motley crew of Westerners: the farmer, McBride; the young miner, Tune; the native woman, Anna; the Chinese cook, Grizzly; and the drifter, Web. Dawe's efforts to *appropriate* the land by discovering a fossil is successful. But the discovery of 'Daweosaurus' costs Dawe his wife, his daughter, and eventually his life, as well as the life of young Tune.[22] All of this is starkly opposed to the Burckhardtian notion of 'spiritual continuity.' Yet the novel presents itself as an effort by Dawe's daughter, Anna, to recover her father by telling – and re-enacting – his story, his history. But the 'history' is always exposed as fiction in Kroetsch's work.[23]

My third novelist, Margaret Laurence, also picks *As for Me and My House* as a work formative of her imagination. She has said that among Canadian novels 'it seemed the only completely genuine one I had ever read about my own people, my own place, my own time.'[24] Laurence's praise of Ross's novel is based on unmistakably topocentric and Guelph principles – simply that it is a novel about Manitoba and Manitobans in the twentieth century.

The Diviners derives much of its considerable power from an internalization of the stresses arising from the clash of Arnoldian and Burckhardtian cultural theories in its heroine. The two lovers in the novel, Morag Gunn and Jules Tonnerre, are profoundly isolated from their parent cultures. Morag is an orphaned descendant of the Scottish Selkirk settlers, raised in poverty and on a heroic, fictionalized 'history' involving her great-grandfather, Piper Gunn, and his wife – also Morag – told to her by her stepfather, Christie Logan. Jules is a Métis who can speak neither French nor Cree, raised on neglect and a similarly heroic 'history' involving *his* eponymous grandfather.

According to Morag's memory of Christie's tales, the Red River settlers were landed at the wrong place, a thousand miles from their supplies: 'Well, then, there they were. So Piper Gunn, he takes up his morsels of belongings, his kettle and his plaid and his axe, and he says to his woman Morag, *Here we are and by the holy Jesus here we will remain.* And then didn't his woman strap onto her back the few blankets and suchlike they had, and her thick with their unborn firstborn, and follow.'[25] According to Christie, the Gunns had to fight Indians and half-breeds. 'Slew them in there dozens, girl. In their scores,' he tells Morag. Morag asks him, 'Were they bad, the breeds and them?' 'No,' he says at last. 'They weren't bad. They were – just there' (86). The contrast between the virtually abandoned Selkirk settlers contesting possession of a hostile land with Indian and Métis as poor and desperate as themselves, and the Traills imperially taking possession of an unpeopled wilderness is very stark. To underline the contrast, Laurence invokes Traill a few pages later and imagines her writing morally uplifting advice for *The Canadian Settler's Guide* in response to 'when we were at one time surrounded by forest fires which threatened the crops, fences, stock, stable, cabin, furniture and, of course, children' (97).[26]

Unlike the Ghibelline Moodies and Traills, the Gunns bring almost nothing with them from the old country – neither significant possessions nor notions of social superiority, like those expressed in the introduction to the 1854 edition of *Roughing It in the Bush*: 'In most cases emigration is a matter of necessity, not of choice; and this is especially true of the emigration of persons of respectable connections, or of any station or position in the world ... Nor is it until adversity has pressed sorely upon the proud and wounded spirit of the well-educated sons and daughters of old but impoverished families, that they gird up the loins of the mind, and arm themselves with fortitude to meet and dare the heart-breaking conflict.'[27] The Gunns have only what they can carry, and the Tonnerres have even less – just the skills of hunters and fighters, and a misplaced faith in the 'Prophet' (Louis Riel).

As a Gunn, Morag had no spiritual continuity with the Old World. Her stepfather's clan, the Logans, are listed in the 'old book,' but the Gunns are not, and in any case Morag renounces that imagined past: 'The Gunns have no crest, no motto, no war cry, at least according to what it says in the old book Christie still hauls out from time to time. Just as well. It's all a load of old manure' (162). At university she also renounces her personal past, lying about her shamefully poor background to her professor, Dr Brooke Skelton, whom she soon marries. In a parody of the Moodies' emigration, they move 'back' to Toronto, a city she thinks of as paradise (201).

But Morag is finally unable to renounce her *personal* past, and in reclaiming her Manitoba roots, she also reclaims the *collective* past of Manitoba history. As with Kroetsch, the 'history' that maintains a Burckhardtian spiritual continuity is pointedly *quasi*-fictional. Christie's tales become her own novels, and Lazarus's tales become Jules's songs. (They are collected at the end of the novel.) Just after the publication of her first novel, *Spear of Innocence*, Morag meets Jules, now a singer of Métis legend in Toronto. In a Guelph application of Burckhardtian principles, she cannot have Jules and Manitoba without renouncing Brooke and Ontario. Soon she is alone travelling west, having indeed renounced her husband and Ontario – the realm of Catharine Parr Traill and Susanna Moodie. Her 'spiritual heritage' is symbolized by Jules's child already forming in her womb and by the prairie bluffs she sees from the train: 'A gathering of trees, not the great hardwoods of Down East, or forests of the North, but thin tough-fibred trees that could survive on open grassland, that could live against the wind and the winter here. That was a kind of tree worth having; that was a determined kind of tree, all right' (282).

Because *The Diviners* is a memory novel, Morag's whole life, and the cultural tensions that formulated it, are tenuously resolved in the person of the ageing Morag, and her daughter, Pique. At the end of the novel, Pique is going to live for a while with her Métis uncle at Galloping Mountain; Jules is dying in an Ontario hospital; and Morag – also in Ontario – continues to write her imagined heritage, looking, as she says, ahead into the past and back into the future. Kroetsch's *Badlands*, confronting the same cultural and historical tensions, concludes with Anna Dawe (the palaeontologist's daughter and framing narrator) and Anna Yellowbird (his young Indian concubine on the expedition) throwing Dawe's field-notes (symbolic of his effort to appropriate the land) into a mountain lake. The dreamers in Laurence's novel are allowed to inhabit the country they have invented. Kroetsch does not permit his characters any such luxury. The dreams of Dawe, Web, Tune, and even farmer McBride are vulgarly dismissed by Anna Yellowbird as futile, 'like pissing in the ocean' (270).

The Diviners fits into the heart of the Canadian canon because it does not reject the Ghibelline sentiments of Traill and Moodie, but internalizes them as the spiritual heritage that a Western Canadian must absorb and transcend. Thus, there is a strong Tory strain of continuity in Laurence's novel despite its great stress on the complete isolation of Morag and Jules from their European past. The novel rejects the American and Whig strain of meliorist optimism, but it retains the Arnoldian theme of self-improvement and remains optimistic on this score. Atwood's *Journals of Susanna Moodie* is much darker and more elegiac, but remains within Arnoldian and Burckhardtian themes of self-improvement and cultural continuity. Kroetsch's *Badlands*, although pessimistic, is not elegiac. It flouts Burckhardtian notions of continuity, as well as Arnoldian notions of cultural appropriation and acculturation, and also Traill's theme of self-improvement. Dawe is the only character committed to Arnoldian values, and he is probably the least attractive character in the novel. Anna, his daughter, says of him: 'it was no fortune at all to be his wife, his daughter. But a son, born of his flesh and blood and blind obsession, might at least have grown up to kill him' (109). His desperate search for dinosaur bones, and his daughter, Anna's, obsessive search for *his* history, mock the Burckhardtian principle of continuity. For these – and other reasons[28] – *Badlands* has not achieved a canonical status comparable to the other two works, despite its concern with *echt* Canadian motifs of place, history, race, and fiction – and its technical perfection.

DERMOT McCARTHY

Early Canadian
Literary Histories
and the Function
of a Canon

The stability of the Canadian literary canon is a fiction needed by both its proponents and its challengers. This stability legitimizes the former by providing them with the authority of tradition, and the latter by providing them with a tradition they can proceed to 'delegitimize' by revealing its authority to be bogus.

Recently, contemporary criticism in Canada and abroad has increasingly put into question the concept of canonicity and the phenomenon of the literary canon as a cultural force. In the Canadian situation, however, no challenge to the contemporary canon can be complete, or achieve a level of subversion sufficient to bring about any serious structural damage, which does not address the canon both theoretically, as a principle of structuration, and concretely, in relation to its full historical development as a structure.

Any critique of the contemporary Canadian literary canon which does not address these issues risks envelopment in the very structure it seeks to challenge or dismantle, and will inevitably become a prisoner of the histories it ignores. Many contemporary challenges to the canon do not represent a dismantling of the forces that have constructed it, so much as a reconfiguring of it in terms of other powers. Canonicity as structure and instrument remains, but with different authorities now vying to empower it.

The contemporary Canadian literary canon as 'institution' is a product of the university as a cultural institution. But where are the anti-canonic challenges coming from? They are issuing from within the same cultural institution that constructed it – from the same departments, in the same journals, through the same university presses, and often for the same 'institutional' reasons, viz., for appointment, promotion or advancement, or tenure – reasons which reflect as much on the structure of the university as institution, or on the individual career that must conform to that structure, as on the theoretical or ideological issues of canonicity itself. This suggests, at the very least, that the contemporary anti-canonic impulse may actually be a feature of the canon-structure or canon-function; and this presents the troubling paradox that such challenges are precisely what canonicity – if not any one canon – needs in order to be perpetuated. To use a biological metaphor, it may be nothing more than a technique evolved by this organism to adapt to changes in its environment, a way of shedding a skin or an increasingly useless appendage in the process of growing a better defence or tool for survival.

It is not enough merely to establish the 'fictive' status of a literary canon by disestablishing its 'institutional' authority. Nor is it sufficient merely to identify the ideological agenda that the canon serves to implement. It is the fundamental 'organizing' power of the canon as structure and its insinuations into cultural life as what must be considered, ultimately, a political force which must be uncovered. For this, analysis must take both the long view backward and the close view inward.

What follows in this essay is no more than a cursory beginning to a discussion of the writing of Canadian literary history as a cultural practice rather than as a narrowly literary discourse. It takes as its premise that the writing of literary history is itself part of a total cultural project and that, as a method of structuration, the literary canon it produces serves as well as reflects the goals and principles of that project. This premise therefore entails a view of the contemporary Canadian canon which sees it as a culmination of this larger project, and not merely of the last twenty-five years of academic criticism. Just as the university as cultural institution in Canada cannot be understood in terms only of the last twenty-five years, so the significance of the literary canon which has issued from it cannot be understood in so narrow a framework. And just as the university itself cannot be understood in isolation from the social and historical forces which have determined it, so the literary canon cannot be understood solely in relation to the institution which most recently has controlled it. Both 'institutions' must be examined as products of a larger cultural project. The *Literary History of Canada* (1965) does not represent an act of literary autogeny. The origins of the most powerful version of Canadian literary history of the past quarter century, the displaced Protestant teleology of Frye's 'Conclusion' to the *Literary History*, are to be found in the nineteenth-century anthologies, just as the perspective on Canadian literature that most influenced Frye, A.J.M. Smith's in his introduction to the 1943 *Book of Canadian Poetry*, achieves its structure as a result of the difficult contortions Smith must make in order to maintain a continuity with a literary history he also wants to redirect. Any challenge to the contemporary literary canon must begin with the history of that canon; but also, in order for that challenge to bring about something different in the way of a structure of literary discourse, it must attempt to see what the writing of that history has put in place, and why.

From its beginnings in the nineteenth century, the writing of Canadian literary history has been organized around the extra-literary concept of the 'nation' and has structured itself through the use of various metaphor-systems of organic growth or natural process. In the twentieth century, even after what Claudio Guillen describes as the New Critics' reaction against the use of 'external means of support' to discuss literature, and the development of various kinds of structuralism to rediscover 'an independent focus ... in poetics or poetry itself,' the writing of Canadian literary history has remained fastened to its founding obsession of national self-definition and self-promotion.[1] The writing of this literary history is complicated, moreover, by the internalization of these extra-literary concepts through a fusion of topo- and logocentric premises which results in the national literature being interpreted as the 'voice' of the 'people,' and in the canonical privileging of only those works or oeuvres which express the 'spirit of place' or 'spirit of the people' – these being, for all intents and purposes, one and the same.

What Leon Surette has called the 'topocentric' orientation of Canadian criticism, an orientation that has dominated Canadian literary history from its outset, should be seen as an inevitable corollary to the problematic of a criticism and literary history committed to serving a nationalistic program, and specifically, the definition/differentiation of the 'nation.'[2] For, if our origins do not make us different, and if we lack an historical action/event which the collectivity can accept as having made us different, then all we are left with to 'ground' our sense of difference is the uniqueness of place itself. Geography must serve in the place of history; space must overdetermine time. Or, in Frye's most famous formulation of this determinism, the question of Canadian identity is not phrased in terms of 'Who am I?' but rather as

'Where is here?'³ The early anthologies and literary histories of Dewart, Lighthall, Baker, Logan and French, Stevenson, MacMechan, and Pierce seek not only to define 'here,' but to give to that place the power of inspiriting presence by (con)fusing aesthetic form and national coherence.

In his introduction to *Selections from Canadian Poets* (1864), E.H. Dewart announces his conservative/recuperative intentions as an anthologist with an extremely significant – if also unfortunate – metaphor: he aims 'to rescue from oblivion some of the floating pieces of Canadian authorship worthy of preservation in a more permanent form.'⁴ Dewart's sense of the literary culture as a flotsam of unharvested fragments in need of gathering, ordering, and presenting is important, as is the notion of the anthology as a 'permanent form.' The anthology is clearly regarded as an instrument of literary history and canon-formation. However, when Dewart describes the contemporary political and social situation as 'the tendency to sectionalism and disintegration' (*SCP*, x), it is also clear that the literary history and canon are conceived as instruments of national unity. The gathering of the scattered texts into a 'permanent form,' the selection and organization of a literary canon, and the ideological program of nation-building and identity-definition, all cohere isomorphically from the beginning in Canadian literary history.

Dewart organizes his material into three sections: 'Sacred and Reflective,' 'Descriptive and National,' and 'Miscellaneous Pieces.' The combination of topics in the second heading illustrates the tendency at the outset to define the national identity in topocentric terms. The spiritual theme is apparently paramount, and literature is the record of the spiritual 'progress' (*SCP*, ix) of a people. Moreover, in the same way that a work of literature may contribute to the formation of an individual reader's character, so 'a national literature is an essential element in the formation of a national character. It is not merely the record of a country's mental progress: it is the expression of its intellectual life, the bond of national unity, and the guide of national energy' (*SCP*, ix). The latter quotation reflects the fusion of historicizing and moralizing behind Dewart's selection of poets and poems, as well as the significant association of spirituality with 'progress.' The national literature presumably cannot contribute to the formation of the national character until it is first presented to the audience as such. The 'nation,' like the 'people' and the 'national literature,' is the construction of the anthologist–literary historian.

Dewart's critique of colonialism initiates a central feature of nationalist literary discourse. Colonialism retards the development of the nation by allowing foreign images of cultural identity to fill up the mirror of art, which should reflect the native reality. It allows these foreign images to intrude between that reality and the reflective institutions of cultural (re)production. Each new anthology or literary history thus claims to be a new mirror of the nation, its novelty defined in terms of the diminishing presence of foreign cultural models, forms, or images, and the burgeoning fullness of native self-presentation.

Poetry, for Dewart, is the great synthesizer of mind and matter, spirit and form (scp, xi), and when he argues further that it 'may be regarded as occupying in the world of mind, a place and a purpose analogous to scenes of beauty or grandeur in the material world' (scp, xii), he is not only attempting a defence of the aesthetic life against an uncomprehending philistine community, but also trying to bring about an ideological cohesion based on the 'complementary' relations of the aesthetic and the practical, a complementarity that ultimately becomes a central concept in Canadian literary histories, the concept of a univocal spiritual-material progress.[5] Poetry brings about the unanimity, the spiritual cohesion and coherence, of the worlds of matter and spirit, of fact and value, of the useful and the beautiful. The poetry anthology seeks to do this in terms of and for the 'national' entity, the 'people.' Thus, if 'the Poet's work is a lofty and sacred work' (scp, xiii), so too is the anthologist's. For the anthology aspires to give 'permanent form' to this sense of a nation as a coherent unity made up of complementary rather than contradictory elements. Dewart's language brings together the material and the spiritual when the 'treasures of the universe' (scp, xii) are confirmed as 'the works of the Creator' (scp, xiii). Poetry presents this interpenetration of material and spiritual worlds. Moreover, the 'nation' itself is subsumed in this totalization, as spiritual entity and political, cultural, and historical reality. Thus poetry serves an essential role in making this coherence a functioning cultural cohesion.

Dewart then shows that the anthologist himself serves a function as 'harmonizer' – and in the process lays down the foundation for what becomes a canonical critical binarism – when he identifies Charles Sangster and Alexander McLachlan as the two pre-eminent Canadian poets. He emphasizes how 'unlike' they are, and how 'any comparison between them is inappropriate' (scp, xvii–xviii). In his summary of each poet's qualities, Sangster emerges as the poet of 'elaborate elegance and wealth of descriptive power,' with 'something of Miltonic stateliness and originality of style' (scp, xviii) – a prefiguring of Smith's 'cosmopolite'; while McLachlan is clearly Smith's contrary – but Dewart's complementary – figure of the 'native' singer, praised as 'the sweetest and most intensely human of all our Canadian bards' and commended for his 'gushes of noble and manly feeling' (SCP, xviii). What is of note here is that what Dewart, in the nineteenth century, is at pains to establish as a coherent and cohesive tradition of *complementaries*, Smith, in the twentieth, will be happier presenting as a tradition of *contradictory* impulses.

The confusing but functional historicizing/moralizing impulse continues in W.D. Lighthall's *Songs of the Great Dominion* (1889).[6] Lighthall makes revisionist claims for his selection, saying that Dewart's representation of Canadian poetry 'has become antiquated' and 'no longer represents what is being done' (SGD, xxxv). He seconds Dewart's evaluation of Sangster, however, calling him 'the first important national poet,' but also describes him as the 'nature-loving Sangster' (SGD, xxv). This linking of 'national' and 'nature-loving' marks the further consolidation of the topocentric fusion of place, identity, authenticity, and authority in the process of Canadian canon-formation. In Lighthall's hierarchy, Sangster is joined by Roberts and Crawford, and McLachlan is demoted. Roberts is the 'foremost name in Canadian song at the present day' who 'struck the supreme note of Canadian nationality in his "Canada" and "Ode for the Canadian Confederacy"' (SGD, xxiv). With Lighthall, the topocentric definition of Canadian nationalism overwrites Dewart's more universalist notions.

Lighthall has an important advantage over his predecessor; he can look back to a concrete historical moment which he presents as 'epoch'-making, a turning-point towards national maturity. In his view, the most important development in Canadian poetry since Dewart's selection has been 'the tone of exultation and confidence which the singers have assumed since Confederation, for up to that epoch the verse was apologetic and depressed' (SGD, xxxv). Time was beginning to produce a history to complement the definition of national identity as the experience of place.

This is also evident in J.G. Bourinot's consolidation of Canadian history into a quasi-systematic pattern with three phases: 'the era of French-Canadian occupation which ... had its heroic and picturesque features'; the 'era of political and constitutional struggle for a larger measure of public liberty which ended in the establishment of responsible government ... '; and the 'era which dates from the confederation of the provinces.'[7] This social-political systematization is soon reflected in the literary histories. Bourinot's quaintly 'heroic and picturesque,' but politically illiberal, French-Canadian phase, followed by the politically – that is, more seriously – heroic Anglo-Saxon phases of nation-building, is paralleled in literary historical terms when pre-Confederation literature that cannot be seen to reflect the collective struggle for national self-determination is relegated to the canonic margins, as 'informative' but 'imitative' or 'incidental,' while that which describes transcontinental travel and exploration, or regional detail with the specificity that suggests mastery, is privileged as a kind of literary equivalent to physical and political control over the environment; the writers of the Confederation generation then come to occupy canonic centrality because of the coincidence of their literary 'maturity' with that of the political will and character of the 'people.' The style makes the nation when it comes to critical discussions of the Confederation-era poets in early Canadian literary histories.

The problematic of Canadian identity when confronted by the American pattern of national formation is at the heart of Roy Palmer Baker's *A History of English-Canadian Literature to the Confederation* (1920). The book is aimed at the American reader but is intended to counter the mutual misunderstanding of the two nations that developed during the war years. In the course of this bridge-building, Baker insinuates his argument that Canada *is* a nation. It is a difficult argument to make to an American reader, for American national identity is based on a sense of difference that is also superiority. Baker must argue that a national identity based on continued membership in the 'Britannic Allegiance' is not a contradiction. His history is related to the cultural nationalism of Lighthall, but the argument is broadened, paradoxically, almost to a transnational extent when he declares his aim to 'show the intellectual continuity of the English-speaking peoples and the fact that, in spite of their differences, they are unescapably one.'[8] In the turn to English as the transnational (yet for him, still national) denominator, Baker prefigures the internationalism of literary modernism, a de-nationalizing perspective which results in significant revisionary arguments in Canadian literary criticism, beginning with Smith and Kennedy in the 1920s and 1930s, and achieving formal canonic expression in Smith's introduction to his *Book of Canadian Poetry* in 1943.

In Baker's view, the Loyalist rejection of the American Revolution was not sufficient to generate a Canadian literature. It is the repulsion of American invasion during the War of 1812 which becomes his turning-point. It provided Canadian writers with a quasi-national success to counter the defeatism that haunted the culture through the Loyalist mentality (Baker, 71), and Canadian literary history has its real beginnings for him in the Romantic-nationalistic movement following the war. He reads the work of Moodie and Traill in this context. *Roughing It in the Bush* is 'a national classic' (Baker, 121), and Moodie's prose and verse 'together ... show the growing sense of national unity and the emergence of a new attitude towards Nature and the ordinary concerns of life' (Baker, 122). Baker considers John Richardson 'the father of Canadian fiction' (Baker, 4) and discusses him as well in relation to the nationalistic-Romantic movement.[9] Richardson and Rosanna Leprohon 'represent in a striking manner the evolution of the national spirit' (Baker, 139). For Baker, the tradition of the Canadian novel clearly owes its beginnings to the nationalistic spirit, and his canonic novelists are Romantic-nationalist storytellers.

He has the same view of the history of Canadian poetry. With Dewart and Lighthall, Baker considers Sangster 'the most significant poet of the Pre-Confederation Period' (Baker, 159). 'It is Sangster's distinction that he felt the pulse of the national spirit which was beginning to beat, however faintly, throughout Ontario' (Baker, 161), though his 'place in Canadian literature rests on his descriptive and religious poetry' (Baker, 163). *Hesperus and Other Poems and Lyrics* (1860) 'makes secure his position as the first interpreter of Nature' (Baker, 163). Baker's epithet echoes Lighthall's praise. Dewart's anthology had canonized Sangster and McLachlan; Lighthall had extended this to include Sangster, Roberts, and Crawford. Baker maintains Sangster's position, and in his organization of the development of Canadian poetry into two 'schools,' the 'School of Goldsmith' and the 'School of Byron,' Baker, like Dewart, prefigures Smith's polarization of Canadian poetic history (Baker, 166–7).

In his conclusion, Baker pulls out all the stops in his effort to use the literary history of Canada as a means of linking American and Canadian cultures. However, in rejecting cultural continuity with the mother country, while maintaining the obvious political connections, Baker creates a Janus-faced Canadian national identity, one face looking south to the future and the other looking east across the ocean to the past.

By writing a history of Canadian literature to the Confederation, Baker 'institutionalizes' that political event as a historical marker which separates the national prehistory from that which he describes as 'the emergence of Canadian nationality.' In Lighthall's anthology and in Baker's literary history, Confederation comes to be the event that starts Canada's historical clock running. This historical time is further spatialized as ground covered in Logan and French's *Highways of Canadian Literature* (1924, 1928), a literary history in which the nationalist impulse becomes further embedded in an academic discourse. Logan[10] intends his 'synoptic' approach – Frye also uses the term to describe his critical approach[11] – to identify the 'social and spiritual origins' of the literature, distinguish certain 'epochs' and 'movements,' bring out the relations and influences among the writers, and show 'how, gradually, they expressed in literature the slowly emerging consciousness of a national spirit and a national destiny in the Dominion.'[12] Thus the function of the literary history and the canon is to show how the literary development mimes the social, political, and cultural progress of the nation, and further, how that progress is both material and spiritual, as well as coherent and cohesive.

J.D. Logan's self-conscious systematizing of Canadian literary history should be understood as the continuation of the premises of nineteenth-century Romantic literary history into the twentieth century. The writing of these early Canadian literary histories coincides with the myth of the consolidation of the national spirit and indeed plays a role in that myth-making. The tension in various versions of Canadian literary history between teleological visions based on models of cultural continuity and those based on models of discontinuity reflects the conflict in Romantic literary histories between the 'national' and the 'universal.'[13] In Baker's and Logan's literary histories, the tension in the concept of a national literature with universal significance is controlled by the metaphor-system of growth from a colonial, derivative culture to a mature national identity in which 'maturity' is not just national but a particular geographical, political, and cultural version of a universal ideal. Later, Smith's privileged 'cosmopolitan' tradition in Canadian poetry also can be seen to participate in the evolution of a 'mature' Canadian literature at the same time as the topocentric orientation of that identity gives it a nationalistic distinctiveness among other world cultures. Smith's 'cosmopolitan' ideal attempts a synthesis of national distinctiveness with international 'merit' and represents the fusion of the traditional criterion of universality with the modernist standard of 'internationalism.'

In Guillen's view, 'the central role of the idea of structure in our time may be ascribed ... to the search for an "order" or a "sense" in a fast-changing, time-filled, historical world left to its own devices – bereft of any external or eternal source of meaning.'[14] Literary historians have responded to this situation with four procedures: the discovery of 'deep structures' in history; the isolation of critical events or moments in history; the abstraction of final causes or essential concepts, like progress, redemption, or revolution; and the recognition of 'enduring constructions and meaningful relations.'[15] Logan's 'synoptic' literary history, like Baker's, attempts all four. The 'deep structure' of Canadian literary history is the coincidence of the national imagination with the nationalist spirit. Eventually, the history of that imaginative life coheres around such decisive events as the achievement of responsible government, Confederation, and participation in World War I. The imaginative life is metaphorized as growth, flowering, flow, and progress from fragmentation to coherence, sectionalism to unity, reflections of the mother country to images of authentic selfhood, a coherence, unity, and selfhood which redeem the 'prehistory' of the nation as the long search for the promised land of nationhood and modernity. Finally, the topocentric orientation of these literary histories identifies as 'enduring constructions and meaningful relations' the central concern with the particulars of place and nature. Indeed, only literature which illustrates this concern is granted centrality in the canonizing structures themselves. Logan even privileges 'Canadian' Nature over other Natures to prove the superiority of Canadian literary achievement over another national literature (HCL, 369).

When Logan praises the way that the organization of Lighthall's anthology brings out 'the essential nature, will, and ideals of the Canadian spirit, of the Canadian people' (HCL, 384), he illustrates not only the point that 'to limit, subdivide, and distinguish is to make order and system possible,'[16] but also the tension between the 'syntagmatic' and 'paradigmatic' that Lionel Gossman ascribes to all historical narrative: 'In historical writing, the signs of language become signifiers in a secondary system elaborated by the historian. What already has meaning at the level of language becomes an empty form again until, being brought into relation with an historically definable *signifié*, or concept, it constitutes a new sign at a different level of meaning. Historical discourse thus has the character of a language constructed out of material that is itself already language.'[17] In Canadian literary history, the 'secondary system' of discourse is that of cultural nationalism. A work like *Wacousta*, for example, or a group of poems by Lampman or Duncan Campbell Scott, cease to be what they are for a reader in the act of reading and become signs in that historical discourse. Gossman refers to 'the tell-tale scar separating the two parts of the page' in a history – the gap between the text and the footnotes – and says that this constantly draws attention to the 'discontinuity between past "reality" and the historical narrative' itself.[18] In any literary history, every movement from the historian's own language into a quotation from a 'primary' or 'illustrative' text similarly reminds the reader of the discursive fabrication taking place.

Gossman outlines the trend in Western historiography towards an increasing concern with and demand for unity and coherence in historical narratives. In his view, with neoclassical historiography, 'history ... is turned into destiny, and time made into the medium in which a timeless order unfolds.'[19] Nineteenth-century Romantic literary history continues this process by configuring destiny as the life of the nation. Early Canadian anthologists and literary historians participate in this in their obsession with presenting a national literature as the voice or embodiment of the national spirit. Even Frye, with his vision of the 'peaceable kingdom,' would seem to fit into this process of history's translation into destiny.[20] Gossman's point that in historical narrative, time and space themselves are merely signifiers within the system of the discourse is also relevant. The topocentric privileging of place in Canadian literary history, while it may function as a compensatory orientation within the discourse itself – a compensation for the 'lack' of a temporally defined history composed of 'monumental' events – is a privileging of signifiers which, in Gossman's view, have no external reference but only significance within the discourse of Canadian literary history – because that discourse, over time, has established that orientation and has privileged the works which present it, in the process of defining its own validity.

Any literary history, or criticism, for that matter, which does not address its subject, explicitly or obliquely, from the topocentric orientation will be relegated to the margins of that discourse in comparison to those that do. As Barbara Herrnstein Smith has argued, repeating a version of Charles Altieri's point that 'functions establish criteria,'[21] 'the privileging of a particular set of functions for ... works of literature may be (and often is) itself justified on the grounds that the performance of such functions serves some higher individual, social, or transcendent good, such as the psychic health of the reader, the brotherhood of mankind, the glorification of God, the project of human emancipation, or the survival of western civilization.'[22] In Canadian literary history, the privileged set of functions is the imaging of the nation and the articulation of the spirit of the people, functions which embed the transcendent notion of the nation in the apparently concrete particulars of the 'local,' 'regional,' and 'realistic.' It is the health of the 'national' psyche, the brotherhood of the 'nation,' the glorification of the 'national spirit,' the emancipation of the 'colony,' the survival of a distinctive cultural and political entity, 'Canada,' which together compose the 'social and transcendent good' served by these functions. The privileging of this set of functions has driven the process of canon-formation in Canadian literary history and has resulted in a version of Wellek's and Warren's 'logical circle': the nationalistic function of the literary histories produces a canon of works that illustrates the national identity, and that canon leads to the continuation of the literary history as the literary reflection of the national identity.[23] Such apparently aesthetic classifications as the 'local,' 'regional,' and 'realistic' are pre-evaluative. They produce a canon which creates its own 'value' as it promotes itself.[24] Description becomes prescription.

Any canon is thus self-perpetuating; or, as Herrnstein Smith puts it, both teleological and tautological.[25] This is Eliot's sense of the tradition as 'an ideal order' which is 'complete before the new work arrives' and which is only 'altered' by the new work in a way that results in a 'conformity between the old and the new.'[26] It is also Frye's sense of the 'total form' or 'total pattern' of literature.[27] It is also reflected in Atwood's approach to editing *The New Oxford Book of Canadian Verse in English* (1982), not only as 'a personal memorial' to A.J.M. Smith, but 'with the same sense of cultural mission that Smith himself pursued.'[28] Atwood's attitude to her predecessor, boldly expressed through the metaphors of 'haunting' and 'propitiation,' is her own powerful version of Eliot's 'historical sense,' or 'a perception, not only of the pastness of the past, but of its presence.'[29] It also clearly illustrates Guillen's point that 'literary traditions are oriented to the present and to synchrony. They are only vaguely, or sentimentally, historical.'[30] Atwood's additions to Smith's canon are her additions to 'an ideal order'; and her respect for that order results in selections that will add to its 'completeness' by extending rather than fracturing it.[31] The mystification in Eliot's notion of tradition – continued in Frye's 'totalizing' imagery – is that the canon is always 'complete' if never finished: 'complete' before the 'supervention of novelty,'[32] and afterwards. This is how the canon works as a teleological apparatus.

Dewart, Lighthall, and Baker illustrate that Canadian literary histories and anthologies, and the canons they have produced, are notably concerned with *telos* – defined as the national identity – from the outset. With Logan this is found in his 'synoptic' method's concern with the 'Whole' (HCL, 15), which results in the writing of a literary history which not only proves the existence of that 'Whole' but which shows the evolution of that completeness as an unbroken spiritual and historical continuity. Logan does this by first providing pre-Confederation culture with spiritual, intellectual, and social continuity and coherence, and then providing political coherence through the *telos* of Confederation (*HCL*, 20). The growth of Canadian literature is thus synchronized with the spiritual and political development of the nation. The effect on the process of canon-formation is that authors are privileged not only according to *where* they were born, but also according to *when* they were writing. Logan organizes Canadian literature into three categories: 'Incidental Literature,' 'Nativistic Literature,' and 'Native and National Literature' (*HCL*, 21). The first describes anything written, at any time, by a foreign transient. The second refers to works by permanent residents and native-born writers. The last category refers to post-Confederation writing by 'native-born Canadians.' With obvious exceptions in the first, the three categories reflect a chronological order, but more importantly, an evaluative hierarchy. In this respect, the terminological distinction between the second and third categories is interesting. 'Nativistic' is clearly inferior to 'native' – nativistic works are 'retroactively ... part of the genuine literature of Canada' (*HCL*, 55) – and yet, with the exception of the works of 'permanent resident *emigrés*,' there is no distinction except in terms of the native-born writer's political identity. When the latter is 'pre-national,' the writing is 'nativistic'; when post-Confederation and thus 'national,' it is 'native.' That is, the concept of 'native,' for Logan, is politically, or nationalistically, derived. (A continuity of this line of thought might help to explain the tragic confusion about 'native rights' in our contemporary political and social culture.)

Logan constructs a national history based on a scheme of temporal succession which has the force of what Edward Said describes as a 'spatial togetherness.'[33] Like Baker, Logan identifies proto-nationalistic patterns: 'particularly after the war of 1812 and during the rebellion of 1837, there appeared in the Canada's some *genuinely* aesthetic verse and prose ... (*HCL*, 23, emphasis added). 'Genuine,' from the Latin *genuinus*, originally meant 'innate' but came to mean 'authentic,' in the sense of 'really proceeding from its reputed source or author.' For writing to be 'genuinely aesthetic,' it would seem, it must be implicated in the drive towards national identity. It is this nationalistic 'spirit' which is the legitimizing authority, for Logan. Here again is the fusion of logocentric and topocentric premises which organizes Canadian literary history. The canonic writer is the 'voice' of the people/place; the canonic work 'speaks' to the people, for the people, because it has the spirit of the people/place within it, 'innate.' It is precisely – and often literally – in these terms that early, and later, Canadian literary histories select their canonic writers and works, and in particular, discuss the importance of the Confederation-era poets.

Logan, for example, describes Roberts as 'the "Voice" of the Canadian Confederacy' (HCL, 114); moreover, in his volume *In Divers Tones* (1887), Roberts 'changed from an Artist to a Prophet, from an Artificer in verse to a Voice – the Voice of one crying in the wilderness and trying to make straight the paths of the Canadian people' (HCL, 114) – to the peaceable kingdom, presumably.[34] But while Roberts is the 'Inaugurator of the First Renaissance in Canadian Literature' (HCL, 115), it is Lampman who is 'the greatest poet that Canada has produced, greatest as a nature-poet, and as an interpreter of the essential mind and heart of the Canadian people and country' (HCL, 128). The way Logan expresses this canonic judgment of Lampman is the quintessential expression of the topocentric-logocentric orientation of Canadian literary history and canon-formation. Lampman is such a canonic giant because 'he is a subtle interpreter of the Canadian national spirit by way of a new and philosophical interpretation of Nature in Canada.' It is this which makes him *par excellence* the poet of the Canadian Nation and Nationality' (HCL, 128).

Logan's language outlines a tandem political and spiritual process, each drawing the other out into historical manifestation. 'Innate' and 'natural' sentiment becomes 'genuine' 'national sentiment,' which supports political and social 'unification,' intellectual and commercial 'expansion,' and political 'consolidation'; all of which in turn produce an 'inevitable' 'change in aesthetic and artistic conscience,' which then results in literature which is 'suddenly' 'different [that is, "better"] in substance, form, and technical artistry or craftsmanship' (HCL, 24–5). The teleological vision synchronizes the 'national' life. Logan's pre-Confederation/post-Confederation periodization – and in this he is representative of this tradition in Canadian literary history – is 'a criticism of becoming. It attempts to make time intelligible or meaningful by creating an order, a parallel level, that is more or less removed from temporality itself.'[35]

With the exception of W.E. Collin's *The White Savannahs* (1936), which does not aspire to large-scale canonic argument, other versions of Canadian literary history before Smith's *Book of Canadian Poetry* (1943) do not deviate from the pattern established by these early anthologists and historians. Archibald MacMechan, in *Head-Waters of Canadian Literature* (1924), and Lorne Pierce, in *An Outline of Canadian Literature (French and English)* (1927), both write in the tradition of nineteenth-century Romantic literary history. Where MacMechan strikes out on

his own is in his ranking of the poetic canon above that of fiction –
'The novelists do not speak for Canada as the poets do' – and in his
adamant portrayal of the founding linguistic traditions as two hostile
solitudes.[36] Pierce, however, begins to identify a new function for
Canadian literary history and canon-formation – national unity. In his
view, 'the true sources of our national greatness' will not be understood
until French and English authors 'share equally in any attempt to trace
the evolution of our national spirit.'[37]

The title of Lionel Stevenson's *Appraisals of Canadian Literature* (1926)
makes it clear that he is out to form a canon: 'the line of exclusion ...
must be drawn somewhere.'[38] In language which recalls Logan's use
of 'innate,' Stevenson's canon is to be formed of 'literature that is
inherently of some distinctive Canadian quality' (ACL, vii). The function of the canon is still nationalistic, but now it must serve Canadian
interests in competition against other national literatures. As a consequence, Stevenson initiates a universalist manoeuvre which prefigures
Smith's later privileging of 'cosmopolitanism' and 'eclectic detachment.' He takes the already established tradition of the literary canon
as 'mirror and brush,' so to speak, of the national identity and expresses
it in terms which recall the plot of an equally traditional 'Universal
History' – the theory that 'there is a single central subject or theme in
the unfolding of the plot of history.'[39] Canadian literary history, from
the first anthologies, has been obsessed with the 'single central subject
or theme' of national identity and has presented that identity as
'unfolding' in the 'plot' of the national history; indeed, the growth of
that identity *is* the plot of the national history. Stevenson combines
this national plot with a universal process/progress when he defines
his 'distinctive Canadian quality' as 'an instinctive pantheism,' or the
recognition of 'a spiritual meaning in nature and its identity with the
soul of man' (ACL, 12). Accordingly, Archibald Lampman, D.C. Scott,
Marjorie Pickthall, Robert Norwood, F.G. Scott, and Wilson MacDonald
are his first-order poets.

Stevenson's universalist/nationalist strategy, however, does not pro-
pel the Canadian canon into the same literary time and space as Smith's
later internationalism. Stevenson is concerned with consolidating a
Romantic canon *against* what he clearly perceives to be a growing
modernist threat, whereas Smith is concerned with establishing a Canadian modernist movement at the centre of the same canon.[40] Smith's
Book of Canadian Poetry (1943) can be said to inaugurate the second
stage of Canadian literary history, and like that stage, it represents
both a continuity and break with this extended Romantic-nationalist
tradition. During the 1930s, a growing pressure was exerted on the

canon by the influx of modernist artistic values as well as by the impact of revolutionary social and cultural events upon the traditional sense of the mimetic relation of literature to history. The dominant topocentric orientation remains, however, with the logocentric concept of the national 'voice' being hidden – if also divided – in the privileging of place under the labels of 'regionalism' and 'realism.' An apparent historical revisionism seems to describe the efforts of A.G. Bailey and E.K. Brown to demystify the Romantic relation between history and culture contained in the early histories, but they, like Smith, cannot escape the weight of the combined topocentric perspective and nationalist impulse. But that is another chapter in the story, or 'emplotment,' of Canadian literary history.

It is not possible to state with equanimity that the Canadian tradition, like the American, has achieved a 'stable canon'; nor is it clear whether the present collection of essays is a sign of Canadian canon-formation entering its 'revisionist' stage, or whether Canadian literary history has perversely jumped from an unstable, unconsolidated canon to a condition of perpetual self-interrogation. Perhaps there will never be a Canadian canon but only a tradition of canonic anxiety.

Early Canadian literary histories establish the function of the literary history, anthology, and literary canon in Canada. Because of the perceived cultural force and the self-perpetuating nature of this function, even a major revisionist attempt like Smith's to move away from the exclusively nationalist role of literature as a cultural institution is unable to build any essentially different edifice. Similarly, Frye's version of Canadian literary history, self-admittedly indebted to Smith's (re-)pioneering effort, maintains the nationalist impulse even as it aspires beyond it. Not until the writing of Canadian literary history and the concept of the canon escape their nationalistic premises, and the topocentric/logocentric orientations which structure them, will that history and any canon it produces achieve a broader range of socio-cultural function, as in Altieri's proposal for a canon-as-repertoire of moral, ethical, political, philosophical, and aesthetic choices, or in some other ideologically 'contrastive' formulation.[41] Until that escape, Canadian literary history is doomed to remain a prisoner of its founding monomania, endlessly repeating the same story to itself, moving the same or similar canonic units like chess pieces in an irresolvable stalemate, and its historians will remain locked like Lampman's 'prodigious' prisoners in the 'iron tower' of the nineteenth century in 'The City of the End of Things,' or like the academic canonizers who hang from the ceilings in the 'university college' of the twentieth.

The Canon between the Wars: Field-notes of a Feminist Literary Archaeologist

National literary canons are deceptively fluid entities. Apparently fixed at each moment in history, they nevertheless assume different shapes in response to new fashions and shifts in social value – much like the French children's cartoon character Barbapapa. The contours of a canon are governed not by the inherent qualities of certain texts, but by the values attributed to them by those in power according to their current agendas and the particular configuration of national, aesthetic, and sexual politics that best serves their interests.[1] To cite Terry Eagleton: 'the so-called "literary canon," the unquestioned "great tradition" of the "national literature," has to be recognized as a *construct* fashioned by particular people for particular reasons at a certain time ... "Value" is a transitive term: it means whatever is valued by certain people in specific situations, according to particular criteria and in the light of given purposes.'[2] When Terry Lovell reminds us that 'with a few notable exceptions ... it is authors rather than books that survive,'[3] she suggests that the construction of the canonical author entwines critical judgments with biographical facts, not the least of which is gender. Jane Tompkins has shown how the American canon, cast in the mould shaped by valorizers of Hawthorne, established critical criteria that marginalized his female contemporaries who had been deemed more significant by the culture for whom they wrote.[4] Similarly, one formative dimension in the construction of the Canadian canon has been the valorization of national themes (e.g., *man* against the land) which implicitly exclude the work of many women writers active before the current era.[5] In addition to the still prevalent modernist critical embargo on 'feminine' concerns and the subsequent demotion of social and domestic issues as 'sentimental' (and not explicitly 'Canadian'), historical and biographical factors conspire against the reputations of Canadian women writers. Simply by virtue of their sex, women have lacked the opportunity to acquire the professional credentials (possessed by professors, clergymen, judges, elected officials, civil administrators, publishers, etc.) that both dignify a nascent national literature and foster the personal connections within the power structure that fortify literary value. Hence women writers of the past, who were barred from the academic and editorial institutions that shape the canon, have been vulnerable to both lionization and quick devalorization on grounds that are implicitly or explicitly gender-related.

During the post-Victorian era, from approximately 1918 to the 1940s, the canon of English-language Canadian literature was particularly arbitrary and malleable, governed less by cultural consensus than by the whims and agendas of certain individuals in positions of power. The literary heroes and perceived traditions of a small country grasping for identity at the slippery edge of two gigantic English-speaking domains, while struggling to reconcile its Romantic inheritance with the encroaching wave of modernism, were not constructed by the reading public at large so much as by backstage decisions of publishers, editors, and English professors. These men formed a loose 'invisible college'[6] distinctly masculine in gender and taste that determined who and what got into print and into anthologies, and which works received prizes and plaudits. During this period of canonical transition, the position of women writers reached a particularly low ebb, as demonstrated by the surprisingly faint profiles of Isabella Crawford and Sara Jeannette Duncan,[7] canonized today as two major writers from before the First World War.

In the United States, according to Paul Lauter, the 1920s saw the growth of the 'academic institutionalization of reading choices.' As the study of local literature gained respectability as an academic discipline, the locus of canon-making shifted from 'individuals, families, literary clubs and certain magazines' to the post-secondary classroom. The conferring of literary value shifted accordingly from the domain of a largely female reading audience to the control of an almost exclusively male professoriate and their influential friends, whose choices inevitably reflected their own class, gender, and racial orientations.[8] In Canada, a modified version of this process began with four book-length (mostly professor-authored) surveys of Canadian literature published during the 1920s and culminated in (poet-professor) A.J.M. Smith's influential anthologies a few decades later.[9] Deeper insight into some of the ideas and activities of Canada's canonical 'gatekeepers'[10] can be acquired in serendipitous forays into this country's scattered archival collections, where, despite the vagaries of preservation and indexing, the researcher occasionally makes significant, unexpected discoveries.[11]

Each of the episodes discussed below illustrates a particular phase of attempted or achieved canon-formation in early modern Canadian literary history; collectively they demonstrate the haphazardness of that process. They also disprove the current comforting myth, as recently voiced by Marguerite Anderson, that 'from the very beginning, women writers have played a leading – if not principal – role in the development of Canadian literature, in English Canada as well as in Québec.'[12] The following examples indicate that both nationalists (represented by John Garvin and Lorne Pierce) and modernists (represented by E.J. Pratt) disregarded women writers because they were attempting to define a Canadian literature characterized by 'virile' attributes; the Romantics (represented by Pelham Edgar and Andrew MacPhail) constructed a literary feminity that supported the assumption of the others that women were incapable of strong, concrete writing. Together, these otherwise very different men shared a self-conscious awareness of their role as cultural arbiters and shapers of their country's literary destiny. Their arrogance and short-sightedness arise from the social values of their time: reassessing the past through the smug lenses of historical hindsight, we can at least concede that they meant better than they achieved.

The 1920s were a decade of enthusiasm for Canadian literary enterprises probably unmatched until the centennial ardour of the late 1960s. Writers declared their professionalism with the founding of the Canadian Authors' Association, and readers were treated to the publication of four new full-length surveys: Archibald MacMechan's *Head-Waters of Canadian Literature* (1924), J.D. Logan and Donald G. French's *Highways of Canadian Literature* (1924), Lionel Stevenson's *Appraisals of Canadian Literature* (1926), and Lorne Pierce's *Outline of Canadian Literature* (1927). In addition, two more ambitious projects were blueprinted: Lorne Pierce's Makers of Canadian Literature series and John Garvin's proposed Master-Works of Canadian Authors.

Margery Fee has expertly documented the chequered history of the Makers of Canadian Literature series, questioning the wisdom of launching a projected thirty-five-volume set of semi-scholarly studies with Albert Durrant Watson's book on Robert Norwood, and also of according humorist Peter McArthur the same degree of attention as William Kirby, John Richardson, and Stephen Leacock. Altogether, only thirteen volumes ever appeared, ten on English-language authors. These included – in addition to the five already named – volumes on Thomas Haliburton, Charles G.D. Roberts, W.H. Drummond, Arthur Stringer, and Isabella Crawford (the lone woman so honoured).[13] While this selection may seem rather lopsided, a list of the titles that never saw print fills some gaps: volumes were planned on George Frederick Cameron, W.W. Campbell, Bliss Carman, Ralph Connor, James De Mille, Norman Duncan, Charles Heavysege, Joseph Howe, Pauline Johnson, Archibald Lampman, Charles Mair, Gilbert Parker, Marjorie Pickthall, Robert Service, the Strickland sisters, and D.C. Scott. Pierce's major divergences from the current canon of pre-modern literature are the inclusion of his friend Albert Durrant Watson (physician and spiritualist poet) and 'Dean Harris' (the Catholic historian, Rev. William Richard Harris), and the virtual exclusion of women. Frances Brooke, Anna Jameson, Rosanna Leprohon, Jean McIlwraith (two of whose titles were to be among Garvin's initial choices), Sarah Anne Curzon, Susie Frances Harrison, Ethelwyn Wetherald, Sara Jeannette Duncan, L.M. Montgomery, and Nellie McClung are a few whose contributions to the making of Canadian literature should have been self-evident in the early 1920s. Less surprising is the small number of women selected to join the coterie of writers and professors producing the books: 'Katherine Hale' (Amelia Garvin) wrote the published Crawford volume; Grace Blackburn's on Arthur Stringer and Ethel T. Raymond's on Pauline Johnson remain in manuscript, and Margaret Lawrence agreed to write about Albert Durrant Watson.

Garvin's Master-Works of Canadian Authors series,[14] also conceived during the early 1920s, was aimed at a different audience. While Pierce's modestly designed blue cloth-bound volumes priced at $1.50 apiece reflect his practical knowledge of the book trade, Garvin, who had turned from a successful career in public school administration to the more lucrative insurance business, aimed his product at the luxury market. In his 1923 announcement, the volumes would be $6 each if bound in buckram and $10 for full Morocco; in 1927, when the list had been reduced to fifteen titles from twenty-five, the set would cost $105 in its cheapest format and $135 for the carriage trade. As a result, Garvin's venture failed more spectacularly than did Pierce's and of some thirty-five titles mentioned in various letters and prospectuses, only three ever appeared: Paul Kane's *Wanderings of an Artist* ..., George Monro Grant's *Ocean to Ocean*, and Charles Mair's

Tecumseh .... With regard to canon-formation, the most interesting features of Garvin's changing list are his serious attention to romance novels subsequently deemed utterly forgettable, his increasing focus on the literature of exploration, travel, and settlement, and the consistency with which he, like Pierce, reduced the contribution of women to a bare token.

Garvin initially designated as Canadian master-works De Mille's *The Dodge Club Abroad* and *Helena's Household* (along with *A Strange Manuscript*), *The Span O' Life* by William McLennan and Jean McIlwraith, McIlwraith's *The Curious Career of Roderick Random*, W.D. Lighthall's *The False Chevalier* and *The Master of Life*, and, when he could not get copyright clearance for Roberts's poems, two of his historical romances. Within a year, however, his list had altered significantly and was headed instead by the exploration accounts of Radisson, Alexander Henry, and Alexander Mackenzie and included Moodie's *Roughing It in the Bush* and Anna Jameson's *Winter Studies and Summer Rambles*. In its final fifteen-volume incarnation, seven of the titles are non-fiction. Fiction, represented by *Wacousta*, *The Golden Dog*, *The Clockmaker*, *Helena's Household*, and half a volume of E.W. Thomson's Old Man Savarin stories, is dominated by a taste for historical romance; poetry is reduced to selections by Thomson, Howe, Heavysege, and Mair. The obvious inference is that Garvin was tailoring his canon of 'Master-Works' to meet the pragmatic and conservative taste of the businessmen he had targeted as his market. Expendable (or unavailable) were the higher-brow poets, while women, as a literary group, were almost utterly ignored. In addition to McIlwraith, Jameson, and Moodie, the female authors deemed worthy of consideration during the initial phases of the project were Crawford, Pauline Johnson, and Agnes Laut (*Lords of the North*); by the end, only Moodie and Jameson remained. Only three women were ever invited to join the elite list of authors, professors, and parliamentarians chosen to write the introductions. Agnes Laut agreed to do the Radisson volume, while Mazo de la Roche, who was initially lined up for Jameson, was later replaced by 'Katherine Hale' (Amelia Garvin), who was also assigned Pauline Johnson.

The ease with which the ambitious projects of Pierce and Garvin overlooked the contributions of Canada's female authors was obscured by the temporary canonization of two women poets who were adopted as Romantic icons by the anti-modernist movement. During the 1920s and 1930s, when Louise Morey Bowman, Constance Lindsay Skinner, and Dorothy Livesay were the major female figures among the poets interested in introducing imagist and modernist practice to Canadian poetry, the darlings of the country's conservative establishment were Marjorie Pickthall and, after the latter's untimely death, Audrey Alexandra Brown. Their histories illustrate the degree to which canonization was bestowed upon persons (or personae) rather than works, and the method of the canonizers, who sought to fulfil their retrogressive cultural agenda by constructing idealized representations of a young, naïve, spiritualized, and desexualized female poet who would save Canadian literature from the crudities of the modern era.

Pickthall, whose career began as the century turned, was for a time the focus of what E.K. Brown later termed a 'cult'[15] of popular and academic cultural Romantics who shared Lorne Pierce's admiration for a poet who – in his view – 'dwelt all her days in the realm of the spirit.'[16] In Diana Relke's summation, 'what Marjorie Pickthall did best for the men who advanced her career, promoted her image, and published her books – powerful men such as Archibald MacMechan, Andrew MacPhail, and Lorne Pierce – was to postpone a little longer the day when they would have to face the fact that the Golden Age of Victorian Romantic poetry in Canada was over.'[17] Upon Pickthall's death at the age of thirty-nine, in April 1922, the past could have been laid to rest. The following month, in his address to the Royal Society entitled 'Poetry and Progress,' Duncan Campbell Scott gently bade farewell to the era represented by Pickthall and Lampman, and invoked T.S. Eliot's interpretation and appropriation of John Donne as poetic mentor for the post–Great War period. Scott and Roberts, the two surviving major poets of the late nineteenth century, had cheerfully begun to accommodate new sensibilities into their own practice. Yet just as the next generation of A.J.M. Smith, F.R. Scott, and A.M. Klein was beginning to make its presence felt at McGill, the old guard represented by Pelham Edgar (professor of English literature at Victoria College) and Andrew MacPhail (professor of medicine at McGill and former editor of the *University Magazine*) made a final effort to preserve its values by exalting Audrey Alexandra Brown.

Pickthall at least had the tragic good fortune to die while at the height of her reputation, but Brown was to suffer the cruelty of utter rejection, and today, sequestered in a Vancouver Island nursing home, she refuses to communicate with enquiring academics. While in her mid-twenties (she was born in 1904), Audrey Alexandra Brown was cast as Pickthall's successor by an older generation of literary and political authority figures that included, in addition to MacPhail (b. 1864) and Edgar (b. 1871), parliamentary librarian Martin Burrell (b. 1858), and former prime minister Sir Robert Borden (b. 1854).[18]

During the later 1920s and through the 1930s, this informally educated and physically disabled young woman, dwelling far from the centres of Canadian culture (in Nanaimo, then Victoria), was celebrated as a natural 'untutored' 'genius'[19] who would restore Canadian poetry to its proper Romantic mode. Her work, which reminded Pelham Edgar of 'the old days of Marjorie Pickthall,' would be well received by a Depression audience, which he described as 'a public starved of beauty.' Edgar's recognition that 'of course the modernists will have nothing to do with her' only enhanced Brown's appeal.[20]

Edgar's project exploited Brown's youth, innocence, gender, and lack of higher education, and therefore implicitly doomed her from the start. While she submitted to the advice of her elder male mentors, the diffident tone of her correspondence with her publisher relays her fear that she was incapable of the poetic development necessary for the mission projected onto her.[21] In 1944 the Royal Society of Canada awarded Brown the Lorne Pierce Medal, bestowed annually since 1926 to acknowledge 'achievement of special significance and conspicuous merit in imaginative or critical literature written in either French or English.' Nominated by octogenarian Duncan Campbell Scott,[22] Brown was the youngest and only the second female recipient of this honour,[23] yet after 1948 no publisher would accept her books. Although her verse continued to appear in British Columbia newspapers, by 1960 she had disappeared from all anthologies[24] and had been expelled from the canon.

The forces that promoted Brown were not unrelated to those that denied Irene Baird the Governor General's Award for fiction in 1939 for *Waste Heritage*, her documentary novel about the recent occupation of the Vancouver post office by the unemployed. As with Brown, Baird's vulnerability to the whims of the literary power network, whose operations were governed at least as much by personal acquaintance as by aesthetic judgment, was exacerbated by her isolation on the West Coast. At this time the Governor General's awards were under the jurisdiction of the national executive of the Canadian Authors' Association, whose procedure was less than systematic. According to the historian of the CAA, wartime judging consisted of 'farming out the selected books among friends, employees, and relatives, anyone who had time to read and comment wisely.'[25] A 1940 letter from W.A. Deacon (past president of the Toronto branch) to national secretary Charles Clay describes how the contest between Baird's book and Franklin McDowell's historical novel, *The Champlain Road*, was won by McDowell (also a member of the Toronto branch) because of the preference of E.J. Pratt (current Toronto branch president) for 'massive-ness and sweep and historical perspective' – like Pratt's own epic poems. Deacon, no great advocate of social realism, argued that Baird's book, as 'a fragment of social history ... not only lacks epic conclusive-ness but hasn't any real end,' and miscalled the future when he pre-dicted that 'twenty years from now nobody will read Waste Heritage ... but they will read The Champlain Road as they now read The Golden Dog.'[26] Although McDowell's book had been written at Deacon's sug-gestion,[27] it seems not to have occurred to Deacon that he should have absented himself from judging this contest. Instead, his letter documents the power of personal connections: Deacon had not yet met Baird and wanted to support 'my friend McDowell, who is one of the finest men I know and a great asset to the literary movement.' His object in writing to Clay was to persuade him to make the judgment in McDowell's favour unanimous to avoid an appearance of personal advocacy on his own part. Yet Deacon recognized (quoting his wife) that 'this woman can write' and suggested to Clay (who initially pre-ferred Baird) that the appropriate resolution was to support Baird's application for a Guggenheim Fellowship, which, unlike the Governor General's awards at that time, would bring her money.[28] However, Baird did not receive the Guggenheim, and the net result was that she was left with nothing.

This episode points to a little-known role played by poet-professor Pratt in the shaping of Canadian poetry between the wars, when Hugh Eayrs at Macmillan paid him as a consultant (the rate seems to have been $10 per book).[29] Though this work lacked sufficient significance in Pratt's life to be mentioned in David Pitt's recent biography, Pratt's recommendations were formatively influential upon the publishing careers of many less established poets. In a discussion of canonicity, it is important to be aware that at Macmillan, preliminary decisions that would ultimately affect later stages of the process (i.e., whether or not to publish a poet, and which of her poems to include in her book) were being determined by a poet on his own way up the canonical ladder. The examples of Pratt's backstage power that I accidentally discovered while researching the files of women authors in the Macmillan papers at McMaster University suggest that the subject deserves fuller investi-gation: he was consulted in 1934 and 1936 regarding the poetry of Irene Moody, and in 1937 he recommended cuts to Louise Morey Bowman's *Characters in Cadence* that were announced to the poet in an astonishingly firm letter from Hugh Eayrs. Eayrs also followed Pratt's advice regarding the selection of poems for *Frozen Fire* by Floris

McLaren, whom Pratt commended for her 'virile' work.[30] Hence Pratt's known taste aroused the ire of Doris Ferne when advised by Eayrs that her book had been refused on Pratt's recommendation. 'I know Dr. Pratt is kind,' she wrote back, 'but he does like *virile* [her emphasis] material and I do not think he would be a good judge of my work ... He likes me very much personally I know, but he does not care for work that is light and delicate, and after all everyone does not want red meat.'[31]

The omission of Dorothy Livesay, the most prominent avant-garde Canadian woman poet of the 1930s, from the landmark 1936 modernist anthology, *New Provinces*, further confirms the fact that the decades between the wars were not propitious for the reputations of women authors in Canada.[32] Yet during the first half of the twentieth century, a strong community of female writers established themselves as competent professionals. Before the 1920s, L.M. Montgomery and Nellie McClung were as popular and wrote as well as their male counterpart, Charles W. Gordon ('Ralph Connor'), but lacked the canonical valorization bestowed by the latter's profession as man of the cloth. By the 1930s, women comprised the majority of the members of the CAA (whose mandate was to advance the interests of professional authors in Canada), a fact that may account for the viciousness of F.R. Scott's attack on the 'poetesses' of the association in his well-known satirical poem 'The Canadian Authors Meet.' The gendered subtext to Canadian literary politics surfaces in Kathryn Colquhoun's 1940 description of the treatment accorded Madge Macbeth, first woman national president of the CAA, around the time she was elected to a second term (she would be the only president to serve three terms);

[Macbeth] had a pretty mean reception here [Toronto] when she came from Ottawa to make a speech at the Annual CAA dinner. Pratt was in the chair and he, and Prof. De Lury, spoke so long, that she didn't get a chance to say a word. A lot of people thought that it was a put up job, as Pratt had charge of things as chairman. Then, when she was elected National President, none of the Executive, Pratt, Deacon or Edgar, attended the Convention ... She is a very charming woman, and is a far better speaker than any of these men. Perhaps that is the reason they have given her the 'cold shoulder.'[33]

Graphic illustration indeed of the modernist battle between the sexes for possession of the literary turf, described by Sandra Gilbert and Susan Gubar in *No Man's Land!* They draw only on British and American examples for their account of the devaluation of women writers and women's writing that accompanied the male modernist attempt to construct a literary history devoid of women, based on 'an implicitly masculine aesthetic of hard, abstract, learned verse that is opposed to the aesthetic of soft, effusive, personal verse supposedly written by women and Romantics.' Yet it would be quite appropriate to insert a few Canadian names into their conclusion that 'to poet-critics from Lawrence, Eliot, Pound, and Williams to Ransom and Blackmur, a literary landscape populated by women, whether they were scribblers, mentors, or great artists, may have seemed like a no man's land, a wasted and wasting country.'[34]

From the refusal of our cultural canonizers to pay serious attention to Jessie Sime, Florence Randal Livesay, Madge Macbeth, Jessie Louise Beattie, and Isabel Ecclestone Mackay (to name only a few), we can infer that the assumption underlying the reception of women authors in Canada during the critical canon-forming decades between the wars was that women's writing was expected to conform to a Romantic/ sentimental/domestic model. Those who followed suit and did not practise modernism were then easily dismissed and have disappeared from sight, while those who engaged with modernist methods were seldom taken as seriously as their male counterparts and have been consistently under-represented in the canon.

The failure of the current academy to remedy this situation is graphically illustrated by one of the few anthologies devoted to the period under discussion, George Parker's *The Evolution of Canadian Literature in English, 1914–1945* (1974). On the cover is a late painting by Emily Carr – an appropriate selection, especially as *Klee Wyck* (a collection of very anthologizable sketches) won the Governor General's Award for non-fiction in 1941. Within the book appears the work of three women, Dorothy Livesay, Mazo de la Roche, and Anne Marriott – but nothing by Carr. Here the role of the woman artist/author has been deemed decorative rather than substantive in an anthology where the representation of women has been reduced to three writers in a field of eighteen. In a recent interview, Phyllis Webb described the modernist legacy that shaped her own entry into literature:

I never questioned the patriarchal order when I was at the beginning of my writing life. I was surrounded by all these super-brilliant men and they allowed me in. It didn't feel sexist at the time. But now when I look back on the way that the history of Canadian literature has been written, it's been documented mainly by Frank Scott and A.J.M. Smith themselves and they have created their own little history.[35]

To restore the reputations of Phyllis Webb's predecessors and revalue their work, it is necessary to un-write the Smith/Scott history of Canadian literature. But it will take more than Rosemary Sullivan's recent anthologies, *Stories by Canadian Women* (1984) and *Poetry by Canadian Women* (1989), to undo the marginalization of women in the prevailing canon of Canadian writers from the first half of this century.

Leonard Cohen, Phyllis Webb, and the End(s) of Modernism

Polemical Introduction[1]

The process of canon-formation in Canadian literature has largely taken place over the last twenty-five years: during, that is, the period of tremendous expansion both in the publication of Canadian writing and in the complementary practices of criticism and institutional teaching. This period is also, in the wider field of literary history, one of transition and interplay between modernism and postmodernism.

I use these terms with some hesitation: postmodernism especially is now bandied about so widely, and in such loose and imprecise ways, that its value as a distinction within critical discourse may well be questioned. At a later stage in this paper, I outline briefly the commonly understood senses of these terms; but almost every writer on modernism and postmodernism now seems to be devoted as much to blurring the distinction as to sharpening it. The 'post,' we are told, does not really indicate temporal sequence; the two movements are implicated in each other. When I use them in this essay, then, they should be understood as having a Derridean mark of erasure hovering over them: I find them useful, even unavoidable, as rhetorical categories, but I do not ultimately believe in their existence.

Given these qualifications, then, what has been the effect on 'the Canadian canon' of its being formed during the period in which these two movements were in transition and interplay? Since canon-formation is an intrinsically conservative process, the dominant effect has been to enshrine modernism (or, more precisely, the *late* modernism of the 1960s and 1970s) as the canonical mainstream of contemporary Canadian literature. This can more clearly be seen in the canonization (one might even say deification) of Margaret Atwood and Robertson Davies. As the critical process filters down from the exalted heights of academic journals like *Essays on Canadian Writing* to the more mundane levels of the books page in *Maclean's*, one might at times be forgiven for thinking that Atwood and Davies are the only two authors in Canada – though Alice Munro, Mavis Gallant, and the memory of Margaret Laurence are also occasionally mentioned. The fiction of this canon is basically realist, though the realism is often very sophisticated in its handling of narrative technique, and it may veer towards the fantastic; the poetry is metaphorical, dominated by the short lyric; and the criticism is thematic and expository.

At the same time, there is a kind of postmodernist alternative canon, promoted in more esoteric journals such as *Open Letter*, which has made much more limited inroads into the popular view of Canadian literature. The fiction of this canon features either metafictional self-reflexiveness, or else the overt abandonment of plot; the poetry is metonymic, moving towards the open form and the long or continuing poem; and the criticism is formal and theoretical. (It is thus frequently subject to charges of academic elitism.) Major figures here would be bpNichol, Robert Kroetsch, and George Bowering. Much feminist writing, such as that of Daphne Marlatt and Lola Lemire Tostevin, seems more closely allied to the postmodernist canon: but a key aspect of feminist theory has been to question the very idea of canon-formation itself.

This paper is focused on the work of two poets, Leonard Cohen and Phyllis Webb, who occupy equivocal positions in relation to this emerging canon and anti-canon. Cohen seems to be securely placed in the modernist canon: of the forty-four major anthologies surveyed by Margery Fee,[2] he appears in twenty-five. His position in literary history, as a major writer of the 1960s, is unchallenged. He is also, like Atwood and Davies, a figure well known to the popular (non-academic) audience, both in Canada and in Europe. Yet his 'modernist' work is continually contaminated (if that is not too loaded a word) by the gestures of postmodernism.

Webb also appears to come out of a strongly modernist tradition, but her work, especially in recent years, has drawn much more attention and support from critics in the postmodernist tradition. She has never achieved quite so secure a place as Cohen's in the mainstream: she appears, for instance, in only eighteen of Fee's anthologies. In

1974 Frank Davey wrote that she 'stands at the juncture between the modernist and post-modernist sensibilities.'[3] My argument in this essay is that both Webb and Cohen stand at this juncture; but that Cohen may ultimately be seen as a modernist in the trappings of postmodernism, while Webb is a postmodernist in the trappings of modernism. It is for this reason, I would argue, that Cohen has been more easily assimilable into the dominant canon.

Another way of phrasing Davey's point is to say that Cohen and Webb stand at the end(s) of modernism. 'End' is here to be understood both as 'aim' or 'purpose,' and as 'final point in a temporal sequence' – and it is always potentially plural. The 'end' (purpose) of modernism may be to fulfil itself, its own aesthetic; or it may be to provide the opening out of its own mode into that of postmodernism. So modernism may or may not 'end' (finish): it may be seen as being superseded by a subsequent movement, or it may be seen to be living on (in) its own post-.

Leonard Cohen and Phyllis Webb

The poetic careers of Leonard Cohen and Phyllis Webb may not at first glance appear very similar. Cohen has always been a poet much in the public eye, ever since, quite literally, he invited an NFB film crew into his bathroom; Webb has led an altogether quieter, more reclusive life. The popular image of Cohen would place him on a concert stage in front of a sold-out audience of adoring fans; Webb would be envisaged sitting alone on the shore of Salt Spring Island.

Beyond these differences in the images they have come to project (or to have projected on them), there is a strange parallelism in the broad outlines of their two careers. Both began writing and publishing poetry in Montreal in the early 1950s and were associated with the small magazines of that time, such as *CIV/n*. Webb's first appearance in book form was as part of *Trio* in 1954, and her first solo volume, *Even Your Right Eye*, appeared in 1956 – the same year as Leonard Cohen's *Let Us Compare Mythologies*. At that time, both were seen as young writers of great promise, but their work was known mainly within the narrow circles of the Canadian literary audience, especially in Montreal.

For both Webb and Cohen, the first half of the 1960s was a period of intense creativity, during which they produced the finest work of their early careers; but, while Webb's work continued to reach only a specialized readership, Cohen made a decisive breakthrough to a wider audience. In 1962 Webb published *The Sea Is Also a Garden*; in 1965 she turned from extended philosophical meditation to the clarity and compression of *Naked Poems*, a beautiful book, but published only in a limited edition. Cohen's *The Spice-Box of Earth* (1961), on the other hand, not only established his reputation as a sensuous and romantic lyricist, but also became the best-selling single volume of Canadian poetry. Darker and more sinister, *Flowers for Hitler* (1964) added to his reputation for flamboyant gestures and outrageous excess. During this period, Cohen also published two novels: *The Favourite Game* in 1963 and *Beautiful Losers* in 1966.

After 1966 both Cohen and Webb entered periods of crisis in their writing, though in Cohen's case this is complicated by his shift of emphasis to the medium of popular song. From his first album, *Songs of Leonard Cohen* (1968), onwards, Cohen has maintained a steady output of recordings and concert appearances: so it cannot really be said that he ever lapsed into silence in quite the way that Phyllis Webb did. But the *written* texts which Cohen published (or, more significantly, did not publish) during the decade of the 1970s are all marked by radical uncertainty and self-questioning. This crisis was first signalled in 1969, when Cohen turned down the Governor General's Award given to his *Selected Poems*, saying that while he himself appreciated the honour, the poems forbade it. The poems continued to demonstrate a similar recalcitrance: in 1972 *The Energy of Slaves* launched a direct attack on the poet's own image and standing:

> I have no talent left
> I can't write a poem anymore
> You can call me Len or Lennie now
> like you always wanted[4]

Death of a Lady's Man (1978) is more indirect in its strategy, using a supplementary layer of commentary to undercut and question the rhetorical efficacy of the poet's language and authority.

Webb's silence during this period was more complete. Between *Naked Poems* in 1965 and *Wilson's Bowl* in 1980, only a handful of poems appeared in print: two new pieces in the 1971 *Selected Poems*, and occasional poems in magazines and anthologies such as *Mountain Moving Day*. Webb was at work on a projected series of poems on the Russian anarchist Kropotkin, but this 'legendary' collection never coalesced, surviving only as fragments in *Wilson's Bowl*. For Webb, as for

Cohen, the 1970s was a period of withdrawal, doubt, self-questioning, and minimal publication.

In the 1980s both poets have cautiously re-emerged. Neither has quite regained the confidence or productivity of the early 1960s, but both appear to have broken through the barriers of the previous decade. Webb's reappearance in *Wilson's Bowl* was followed by the justly deserved Governor General's Award for *The Vision Tree* in 1982, by *Water and Light* in 1984, and by *Hanging Fire* in 1990. Cohen's *Book of Mercy* (1984) is a volume of prose poems and prayers in which the vocation of the poet is once again proclaimed rather than doubted; he has gone on to produce two of his finest records, *Various Positions* (1985) and *I'm Your Man* (1988). The latter was a huge popular and critical success (especially in Norway!) and returned him to the forefront of public attention.

In their poetic careers, then, Leonard Cohen and Phyllis Webb offer one possible paradigm for the history of Canadian poetry over the last four decades. Both have their roots in the earlier traditions of Canadian modernism through their contacts in 1950s Montreal: Webb through her friendship with F.R. Scott; Cohen through his close associations with Louis Dudek and Irving Layton. Both took part in the burgeoning of Canadian poetry and publishing during the early 1960s, in the retrenchment of the 1970s, and in the cautious pragmatism of the 1980s.

For both Cohen and Webb (as, indeed, for all successful writers), this history has also presented a problem: they have had to confront the accumulations of their own public images as well as their relationships to new styles and younger generations. The image of the romantic Leonard Cohen, brooding over his tortured soul with a succession of blonde young women on his arm, or the image of the reclusive Phyllis Webb, contemplating silence on her lonely island, may be reductive and clichéd, doing little justice to the subtlety and complexity of their poems, but there is a sense in which such images are now, whether the writers like it or not, *part of their work*. In an age in which so much peripheral attention is devoted to authors – in interviews, magazine articles, television features, academic criticism, publicity campaigns, writers' festivals, etc. – it is harder than ever for a reader to maintain a separation of the writer and the work. The writer becomes as fictional as the text; the writer's public image, whether deliberately created or not, *is* a text, and must be read as such.

In this broader sense, 'text' includes not only the officially published work (poems, novels, essays) and its semi-official margins (interviews, concert appearances, book covers), but also the inscription of the poet's *voice*. The limitations of Cohen's vocal range (which he both observes and exploits in his recordings) are as much a part of his signature as Webb's intensely expressive, beautifully modulated reading voice is of hers. The voice, however, is not a privileged access to the 'presence' of the author: it is that presence dramatized, projected, *staged*.

Cohen's career as a popular singer has of course made him acutely aware of voice, and of the degree to which his public image is part of his work; he has participated in the shaping of that image with wit, irony, and detachment. Even the rejection of the Governor General's Award, however sincere it may have been, contributed strongly to the canonization of Leonard Cohen in his anti-poet stance. Everything from the plain dark suits he constantly wears to the incongruous banana he holds on the cover of *I'm Your Man* plays with or against the associations of the 'Black Romantic' image: the edge of self-parody allows him to distance himself from the absurdity of the pose while at the same time indulging in it anyway. But Webb's image of aloofness and isolation, if less consciously chosen and manipulated on her part, is no less unavoidable. Refusal to play the publicity game becomes another move in the game.

Even before he began releasing records, Cohen's work was directed to a public audience; the poetry readings of the early 1960s, such as those preserved in the NFB documentary *Ladies and Gentlemen, Mr. Leonard Cohen*, show his considerable skill as a stand-up comedian. In entering the world of popular music and concert touring, Cohen was putting himself on the line, offering his own presence and persona as the focus of his work. The enormous stresses which this produced may be seen in *Bird on the Wire*, a documentary by Tony Palmer, filmed during Cohen's 1972 tour of Europe. The constant pressure of touring – the physical demands of the travel, the need to give interviews at every stop, the demands of fans who can switch in a moment from adoration to hostility, the singer's sense of responsibility to the musicians in his band, to the managers, to the promoters – all of this culminates, in the film, in the moment when Cohen walks off a Jerusalem stage, unable to go on singing. The film closes with a memorable image of Cohen sitting on the floor of the tour bus, huddled close into himself, seeking a privacy which has long since vanished.

Yet in many ways Cohen is very good at playing the role of popular musician. In journalistic interviews, he is constantly able to come out with gnomic statements which simultaneously conform to, and mock, the popular idea of 'the poetic.' For example, in an interview with Pia

Southam in a Vancouver magazine called *V*, published in December 1988, he responded to the question 'How has your attitude to love changed over the years?' by saying,

In those days, when I wrote about love I was touched by those images very much; but I didn't know what the real bondage of love was. I hadn't been wiped out by love. I hadn't taken the wound. I'd seen it, but I had never surrendered. I was moving awfully briskly from flower to flower. I saw the dangers, the pain, the beauty; I saw the essential quality, but I never surrendered until I was a lot older. A song like 'I'm Your Man' is on the other side of that surrender. It's only after having taken the wound that you can write the kind of song which is beyond funny. It's kind of desperate humour. It's only when you're no longer much of a prize that you can offer yourself so generously to somebody else.[5]

This is the kind of copy that journalists dream of. But what is the critic to make of it? Is this a throw-away comment to a casual interviewer, a piece of pretentious condescension, or is this a poem? Is it part of the Leonard Cohen canon?

Given the attractions of writing personality profiles, and of telling us once again about who Suzanne was or wasn't, it is not surprising that there is comparatively little serious critical writing about Leonard Cohen. The 1970s saw two books, by Michael Ondaatje in 1970 and by myself in 1978, as well as important articles by Sandra Djwa, Douglas Barbour, and Linda Hutcheon; but the last few years (with the exception of a fine article on *Death of a Lady's Man* by Ken Norris) have been largely devoid of new considerations. It is surely time for a reassessment of the early work, and especially of *Beautiful Losers*, in the wider historical perspective. And the whole body of Cohen's songs is still scandalously unattended to.

Although Phyllis Webb's public profile has never been as high as Leonard Cohen's, her very reclusiveness has itself become a part of her image. In many ways, this has had a more seriously distorting effect on the reading of her work than Cohen's notoriety has had on his. For, though Webb's poetry is often private and solitary, it has always had also a dimension of public care and political concern. The great weakness of Webb criticism has been to present her as inward-turning and solipsistic, to the exclusion of that political world on which Jacobo Timerman turns his astonished eye in 'Prison Report.'[6] As recently as 1987, George Woodcock could still write that 'for Phyllis Webb, growing maturity as a poet has meant growing withdrawal – a narrowing of contacts with the world paralleling a narrowing of the circle of the creative self,' and that she 'has also practised austerities and simplifications in her life and has sought the reclusion that all good artists, like all saints, find necessary at some time in their careers.'[7] This not only demonstrates a limited appreciation of Webb's work for CBC radio (collected in *Talking*) and her active engagement in the work of Amnesty International; it also represents a drastically reductive reading of her poetry.

Yet this image of Webb as a 'saint' has persisted in the criticism of her work. Nowhere is it more evident than in the bizarre article which John Bentley Mays published in *Open Letter* in 1973. While Mays accuses John Hulcoop (not without some justification) of romanticizing Webb as 'a devotee of the "Priestess of Motion," '[8] he himself is busy transforming her into *his* Romantic image of the suffering, damned artist in the lineage of Sade, Artaud, or Plath. At the end of this line stands, evidently, John Bentley Mays: Webb's poetry is only the excuse for a somewhat tedious self-examination of how the author's naïve 1960s idealism withered in the 1970s.

Implicit in both Woodcock and Mays is the accusation that Webb's work confines itself to an ivory tower of political naïvety (rather than the painfully transparent and fragile 'glass castle' which is Webb's actual image). This accusation was picked up by Frank Davey in his entry on Webb in *From There To Here* (1974), which describes her poetry as 'vain, private, and inconclusive' (262). While Davey is in most cases a very astute critic, this is one comment which says a good deal more about Frank Davey than it does about Phyllis Webb: and what it says is that Davey in 1974, arguing for the advent of a postmodernist literature in Canada, saw Webb at that time as the epitome and culmination (the end) of the modernist tradition to which he was opposed.

In his introduction to *From There to Here*, Davey lists Webb among the 'older modernist poets' (22) whose work is being replaced by the young writers of the electronic age. But in his entry on Webb, Davey recognizes that the case is not quite so simple. It is there he writes that 'Phyllis Webb's poetry stands at the juncture between the modernist and post-modernist sensibilities' (264). Davey's book was one of the earliest statements in Canadian criticism of what have come to be recognized as the broad outlines of the modernist/postmodernist distinction. He describes the characteristics of modernist poetry as 'rigorously disciplined rhetoric, mythic and historical reference, rigidly sculptural structure, and totally impersonal and unemotional tone' (19). The poem is seen as an aesthetic object whose internal formal organization is more important than its external reference; modernism's ideals were those of control, of organic unity, or ironic distance, and of impersonality. On the other hand, postmodernism is radically open-ended, resisting the closure of modernist form. It denies that a writer can ever be fully in control of her work; but rather than deploring this fragmentation, as modernism would do, it celebrates and exploits it. Whereas modernism used its 'mythic and historical reference' as touchstones of order and stability in which to attempt to ground the flux of the chaotic present, postmodernism uses myth and history as elements of intertextuality which extend the free play of reference, which take the text even further into the open-ended field of dissemination. The impersonality of modernism (the judicious self-effacement of T.S. Eliot, for instance) still implied that there was a unitary self, present but hidden, in the figure of the elided artist; postmodernism foregrounds the presence of the writer (the injudicious self-promotion of George Bowering, for instance) but scatters any sense of unity in that self by making it part of the textual play.

The early lyrics of Leonard Cohen can be seen as exercises in modernism, displaying a high degree of formal unity and elaborate rhetoric. Often using regular stanzas and rhyme-schemes, they are presented as polished artefacts, the 'well-wrought urns' approved by the modernist New Critics. Steeped in religious and mythological imagery, they create their own enclosed world, whose values are aesthetic and self-referential. The figure of the poet is presented, reverentially, as a kind of priest or saint, moving in the sacred world of art. The title of Cohen's first book, *Let Us Compare Mythologies*, is in itself a summary of modernist practice: mythology is assumed to contain a general truth, a grounding of experience, which can be discovered by the comparative process of juxtaposition or collage. 'Let us compare mythologies' is one of the major formal impulses of modernism, from the *Cantos* of Ezra Pound to the structural anthropology of Claude Lévi-Strauss.

This modernist stress on the beautiful object persists through *The Spice-Box of Earth* and Cohen's first novel, *The Favourite Game*; but then he attempted a violent reaction against it. *Flowers for Hitler* is, in its strange and excessive way, the first Canadian gesture towards postmodernism. Rejecting the modernist ideal of the well-made, formally complete poem, Cohen presented poems which were deliberately ugly, unfinished, and jarring in tone, accompanied on the page by revisions, deletions, and crude little drawings. Romantic evocations of mythology were replaced by a nightmare vision of a history slipping into oblivion: 'I believe with a perfect faith in all the history / I remember, but it's

getting harder and harder / to remember much history.'⁹ A note on the
back cover proclaimed that 'this book moves me from the world of the
golden-boy poet into the dung pile of the front-line writer' – or, it
might be argued, from the well-wrought urns of modernism to the
harsh discontinuities of postmodernism. It *might* be argued – for it is
equally possible to see the pose of the 'front-line writer' as simply the
reverse side of the coin of the 'golden-boy poet,' and to argue that in
Flowers for Hitler Cohen is still pursuing a modernist rhetoric in its
negative form.

The paradoxical nature of Cohen's approach to postmodernism is
even more apparent in *Beautiful Losers*. Again we have the trappings
of the postmodern: a novel which breaks every rule of traditional form;
a wild mixture of tones, topics, and styles; a narrative voice which is
radically dispersed and fragmented, putting into question the very
possibility of the unitary subject. When F. proclaims, 'Connect nothing.
Place things side by side on your arborite table, if you must, but connect
nothing!'¹⁰ he could be laying out a prescription for the postmodernist
novel. Robert Kroetsch, for instance, has argued that the dominant
trope of modernism is metaphor, with its vertical layering of images,
while that of postmodernism is metonymy, with its horizontal exten-
sions – side by side, connecting nothing. *Beautiful Losers* is the arche-
typal postmodernist novel.

And yet – the opposite is also there to be argued. In my 1978 study
of *Beautiful Losers*, I wrote that 'in fact the book is highly organized,
held tightly together by a network of images and connections. Douglas
Barbour has pointed to the paradox of a book which proclaims "Connect nothing" and then insistently offers connections which must be
made; a book which "prepares to abandon all systems" in a systematic
manner.'¹¹ In that study I concentrated in a systematic manner on the
imagery of the 'stem' emerging from the broken 'system': an image
which Cohen is still pursuing more than twenty years later when he
sings, in 'First We Take Manhattan,' 'They sentenced me to twenty
years of boredom / For trying to change the system from within' (*I'm
Your Man*). It is the kind of paradox which one encounters repeatedly
in Leonard Cohen: the systematic breaking up of systems; the artful
proclamation of the anti-art pose. Cohen is trying to become a postmodernist, one might say, but he is going about it in a very modernist
manner.

In the same way, Cohen's career as a pop singer has taken him
to the heart of the electronic media which Frank Davey saw as the
harbingers of postmodernism. Cohen's songs have taken him away

from the comparatively narrow and elitist readership of published poetry and towards a mass audience, in Canada and especially in Europe, of a kind that no other Canadian writer has enjoyed. But again one might argue that Cohen has approached this postmodernist medium in a modernist way. Most of the song lyrics return to the tightly controlled and polished forms of his early poetry: regular rhyming stanzas, shining epigrammatic images. The songs again project the Romantic figure of Leonard Cohen as priest or saint; even the gestures of self-parody – 'I was born like this, I had no choice / I was born with the gift of a golden voice' ('Tower of Song,' from *I'm Your Man*) – serve mainly to reinforce the image that they pre-emptively mock. In live performance, the texts of Cohen's songs remain relatively stable: unlike Bob Dylan, who is constantly shifting both words and music in performance, Cohen makes very few changes. Even the anecdotes he tells to introduce the songs are repeated year after year. The vulnerability of early concert appearances (such as those documented in *Bird on the Wire*) has been replaced by a confident mastery on stage; Leonard Cohen has become a modernist singer.

The degree to which Cohen, for all his (very important) gestures towards postmodernism, has remained fundamentally a modernist writer may also be evident in the very limited *influence* he has had on subsequent Canadian writers. It may be that Cohen's style is too individual, not to say idiosyncratic, to be successfully copied; any attempt would end up as parody or pastiche. Even so, he remains an isolated figure, and his work in the 1970s and 1980s has pursued its course quite separately from the main currents of Canadian poetry during these decades. However one defines these currents – the documentary long poems of Ondaatje and Atwood; the feminism of Marlatt and Mouré; the 'continuing poems' of Nichol and Kroetsch – nothing could be farther removed from them than Leonard Cohen's *Book of Mercy*.

Phyllis Webb, on the other hand, has been highly influential on all these currents. One way of assessing the variety of this influence, and also of appreciating at a glance the tension between modernism and postmodernism in her work, is to look at the back-cover blurbs for her 1980 volume, *Wilson's Bowl*. The writers who here pay tribute to Webb range from Northrop Frye, whose role as the mentor of the 1950s 'mythopoeic' poets places him at the centre of Canadian modernism, to bpNichol, the very epitome of postmodern experimentation and open form. In between are two poets – D.G. Jones and Margaret Atwood – who are more difficult to characterize. They both deal with the fragmentation and uncertainty of the postmodern age but are also drawn towards the tightly controlled, elliptical, and ironic forms of modernist poetry.

Even in the short form of the complimentary blurb, each of these writers approaches Webb's work in terms of his or her recognizable presuppositions. Frye, for all his theoretical doubts about evaluation, is magisterial, authoritative, and highly evaluative. 'This is a very rich and rewarding book,' he tells us: 'a landmark in Canadian poetry.' He points to the theme of 'failure' but sees it, not as the inescapable condition of postmodernist writing, but rather, in modernist terms, as a problem to be dealt with. 'The book finds its way through "failure," ' he proclaims, 'and emerges with some beautifully lucid poems at the end.' What he values, then, is not the question but the answer, not the failure but the lucidity.

Similarly, D.G. Jones, who in his own work often conveys a sense of tight-lipped desperation, sees Webb's poetry as *countering* the post-modern condition: 'In a world that promises ever less in the way of real community or even communication, Webb reminds us of our communion with the dead.' Webb is here evoked as a prophetic figure, in the modernist tradition of Eliot's Tiresias or the Odysseus of Pound's first Canto. Atwood too sees Webb in terms of the mythological pattern of death and rebirth: 'She walks into the sea and returns.' This last comment is surely more typical of Atwood's own surfacing protagonists than it is of Webb's Lilo Berliner, who walks into the sea and does not return. But my point is that both Jones and Atwood choose to praise Webb in modernist terms: for them, Webb's poetry rescues order out of disorder, and it does so by means of a modernist appeal to mythology as a stabilizing and order-giving force. Thus for Jones, Webb is allowed, after her communion with the dead, 'to celebrate spring'; for Atwood, she conducts a 'courageous struggle with an angel who blesses reluctantly but does bless.'

Nichol's blurb is quite different; it appeals rather to the values of the postmodernist alternative canon. It makes no mention at all of content or thematic pattern, but concentrates on the form of the poems. Webb is described as 'a writer whose care to get things right informs every word and every line of her poems, who moves fluidly between a diversity of forms and modes'; and Nichol numbers himself as one of 'those of us who have learned from & followed her work.' This is a finely balanced comment. The 'care to get things right' emphasizes Webb's craft, but at the same time Nichol praises the fluidity of her movement between a diversity of forms and modes, that is, the open-

ended and postmodernist aspect of her work. As a poet influenced by
Webb, Nichol responds both to the care and to the fluidity; as one who
has 'learned from & followed her work,' he sees her (in the same way
as he saw Sheila Watson) as a modernist whose writing nevertheless
provides an opening into postmodernism.

Working along similar lines, Robert Kroetsch has argued that Webb's
Naked Poems mark the true beginning of the postmodernist long poem
in Canada. In his essay 'For Play and Entrance: The Contemporary
Canadian Long Poem,' Kroetsch writes:

> Trace: behind many of the long poems of the 1970s in Canada is the shadow
> (Jungian?) of another poem, a short long poem.
> 1965: Phyllis Webb, *Naked Poems.*[12]

Kroetsch's explanation, both of the nature of that influence and of his
paradoxical phrase 'a short long poem,' is cast explicitly in terms of
postmodernism (the resistance to lyric closure) and of Derridean poststructuralism (trace, *différance*):

> A kind of hesitation even to write the long poem ... Webb, insisting on that
> hesitation. On that delay. On nakedness and lyric and yet on a way out,
> perhaps a way out of the ending of the lyric too, with its ferocious principles
> of closure, a being compelled out of lyric by lyric:
> The poet, the lover, compelled towards an ending (conclusion, death,
> orgasm: coming) that must, out of love, be (difference) deferred.[13]

What Kroetsch sees here in Webb's work is the way in which even its
most traditional and modernist elements (her mastery of the lyric form,
for instance) were breaking down into postmodern indeterminacy.
Naked Poems begins with the lyric impulse, in its starkest, most minimal
form ('naked'), but the very conditions of that minimal lyric force it
towards the extended sequence, and towards its final, open-ended
question, 'Oh?' 'Compelled *out of* lyric *by* lyric,' the sequence enacts
the way in which the postmodern emerges from the end(s) of modernism. The 'post' of postmodernism does not indicate mere temporal
sequence; rather, it is what Derrida would call a deconstruction, or
even what Leonard Cohen (ironically) would call a changing of the
system *from within.*

It is that openness, I would argue, which explains why Webb's poetry
has continued to influence other writers (Nichol, Marlatt, Thesen,
Wah ...) in ways that Cohen's has not. Cohen's work, brilliant as it is,

remains at some level closed. Such gestures as *The Energy of Slaves* and *Death of a Lady's Man* are desperate, but not entirely successful, attempts to break out of that closure. It is in this sense that I argued earlier that Cohen is a modernist in the trappings of postmodernism, while Webb is a postmodernist in the trappings of modernism.

Both Cohen and Webb reach to the end(s) of modernism. Cohen, one might argue, is stuck there: like F. in *Beautiful Losers*, he could say of himself, 'I was the Moses of our little exodus. I would never cross. My mountain might be very high but it rises from the desert.'[14] For Webb, the ends are definitely plural. Her work shows that there is no single end or purpose to modernism; by the very intensity of the questioning which her long silence subjected it to, modernism in her poetry breaks through to its complementary pair, its waiting Other.

In the works of both writers, modernism and postmodernism play against and with each other in ways which present, in exemplary form, the issues Canadian poetry has faced in the last three decades. This movement is not yet finished; the compression of contemporary literary history is such that our canonical figures are still alive, still changing, still writing. The emerging canon has been slow to recognize the full challenges of postmodernism: Leonard Cohen, for all his outrageousness, has been easier to assimilate than Phyllis Webb. But the canon *is* an emerging one, and any account of it now has to be provisional. It would certainly be my hope that the breaking down of the modernist/postmodernist distinction, so evident in recent criticism, will also be reflected in the evolution of canon-formation: and in this process, the examples of such writers as Leonard Cohen and Phyllis Webb may well be more useful than those of more easily categorized figures.

DENIS SALTER

The Idea of
a National Theatre

I

A national theatre, like a national literature, can never be ideologically neutral. It emerges from a specific set of moral, aesthetic, and political values, some explicit, but most implicit, effective precisely because they are so hard to discern. All these values have been instrumental in the formation of styles of performance, audience expectations, the repertoire, and more general beliefs about the function of theatre in an emergent culture. Agitation for a distinctively *Canadian* kind of national theatre begins as early as the nineteenth century and, despite increasing scepticism, remains unabated even now. The most important essays on the topic tend to assume, with only a few misgivings, that the theatre should commit itself to the never-ending task of building a sense of national destiny.

This notion quickly became a form of cultural and political orthodoxy. To question it, even for a moment, to propose a different set of values, can in fact seem subversive, perversely un-Canadian. What are those orthodox values? Why and how were they developed? What kind of national theatre have they attempted to give us? and what (reductive) mythology of nationalism have they succeeded in advancing? In the process, which plays and productions have been canonized? and which haven't? These and related issues are the ones I mean to treat here, through an examination of play texts, theatre history, and dramatic criticism, together with the many periodical essays on the status of theatre in Canada, particularly in the main nationalistic phases leading up to World War II.

The word *national* is always difficult to define; its meaning tends to change significantly from one period to another, so that generalizations are apt to be misleading. But, whichever the period, it tends to be a term of exclusivity, privileging a dominant set of values and frequently bordering on the xenophobic. Accordingly, cultural values would be generated, disseminated, and preserved on behalf of specific, self-protective, and self-validating communities which would seek to arbitrate standards of taste and excellence while insisting on the importance of theatre in the development of a civilized society. Throughout both the nineteenth and the twentieth centuries there is a recurrent, disturbing theme: the theatre should be used as an instrument of cultural assimilation. In this way, Canada would manage to become a homogeneous, unique, and readily identifiable nation-state, as distinctive, in its own way, as Britain, France, and the United States, the imperializing cultures to which it instinctively liked to compare itself.

In 1823, for example, an article on the religious, moral, and pedagogical importance of English theatre in Montreal unwittingly anticipated Lord Durham by arguing that French Canadians should be encouraged to see good quality English plays: 'the effects would doubtless be salutary, by tending to impart those feelings so much in unison with British hearts.' Since, according to popular stereotype, French Canadians were known to like imitating English fashions and manners (a sign of their colonialized position?), the writer also suggested 'that considerable attention should be bestowed on procuring scenery appropriate and striking,' together with stirring musical accompaniment. These compelling special effects would help them not only to understand the play but also to improve their English. Although the writer was far too discreet to recommend that French Canadians actually relinquish their own language and culture, this assumption is implicit in every shopworn point that is made about the civilizing influence of what is called a 'well regulated Theatre.'[1] These kinds of ideas might be exceptional, yet they turn up repeatedly and partly explain, of course, why Quebec even now must continue to struggle against the appropriation of its cultural difference and the denial of its status as a distinct society.[2]

Such attitudes are not, in fact, restricted to Quebec and its problematic relationship with the rest of Canada. As recently as 1945, Alice Rowe-Sleeman argued that a Canadian national theatre, like the various national theatres which Canadian soldiers had seen overseas during the war, would contribute to the consolidation of national unity by insisting on 'a standard of speech accepted by all Canadians.' At the same time, it would be based 'on a common fund of ideas and ideals, and a means of communicating them,' an observation which was meant to regulate not only repertoire but the style of performance.[3] This was a simple, if potentially despotic, restatement of the nineteenth-century conception of the sovereign nation-state, powerful, dominating, committed to self-serving myths about its right to colonize its own people in the name of a civilized art form. Like the 1823 essay on English theatre in Montreal, Rowe-Sleeman wanted to centralize authority in a reductive set of values which would not be tolerant of a range of political, linguistic, and artistic possibilities. Her essay was a response to the postwar mood of nationalistic rejuvenation, a kind of euphoria which seemed to have learned nothing from the war itself about the violent destructiveness which results when nationalism turns, as it so often will, into mere jingoism.

Even the academic mind was not immune to these tendencies. Embarrassed by Canada's apparent lack of theatrical achievement, Arthur L. Phelps argued in a seminal essay published in 1939 in the *University of Toronto Quarterly* that 'Canadian drama must be in our words, made out of the stuff of our own people,' and in a fervent declaration of the need for cultural independence, he urged us in no uncertain terms to sever the 'European connection,' to embrace our manifest cultural and political destiny in the New World.[4] However deeply felt Phelps's faith in the theatre as a mirror of nature, as a form of representation which will help us to know ourselves, this part of his essay now seems unnecessarily doctrinaire – an appeal to a type of post-colonial liberation which was in fact based on nineteenth-century assumptions about nationalistic supremacy which the war itself would do so much to challenge.

Indeed, no matter how earnestly it invokes the pluralistic values of liberal democracy, the idea of a national theatre is potentially self-defeating and potentially dangerous. Like an anthology of masterpieces, it can attempt to establish a masterful agenda sanctioning the values by which certain members of society wish to present themselves. Apparent consensus can easily mask the process by which other members of society have been excluded and disempowered. The essential question – whose nation is being represented on stage? – will often remain unanswered or indeed is too troubling even to be posed in the first place. If Phelps's proposals had been enacted, for example, immigrant Europeans living in Canada would have been forced to look to art forms other than the theatre for the kinds of self-reflective themes and images which would help them to assert their own rightful position in Canadian society. And, paradoxically, by advocating the consolidation of our collective status as North Americans, first and foremost, Phelps's proposals would in fact have encouraged – rather than resisted – our absorption within U.S. culture, a consequence which would have seriously undermined his own nationalistic aspirations.

And yet, as George Woodcock and others have argued, nationhood in itself does not necessarily lead to aggressive and self-aggrandizing forms of behaviour. There are various types of nationalism: jingoism, chauvinism, and patriotism are the extreme forms, employed not merely to protect one's own legitimate interests, but also to rationalize one's 'right' to subdue other nations. At the same time, however, there is another kind of nationalism in which a given group of people are joined together by a common heritage of linguistic, cultural, political, social, and perhaps religious values – an ideological complex which to function completely must always subject its premises and methods to rigorous re-examination. Individuals acquire their sense of both personal and public identity from their relationship to this kind of nationalism, which is a product of their assent and cannot exist otherwise.[5]

The theatre, responding to this kind of nationalism, does not merely reflect existing values, for to do so would make it vulnerable to appropriation by dominant groups. Instead, it engages in the interrogation and continuous re-creation of values, resisting appropriation and marginalization, at all costs, and taking seriously its responsibility to be broadly inclusive rather than narrowly exclusive in both its principles and methods. In Canada the theatre has *sometimes* been idealized as a form of knowledge which can assist in the development not of one but of many forms of nationalism – different ideologies, communities, identities, all of them accommodated rather than assimilated. Ann Saddlemyer, for example, in her essay 'Thoughts on National Drama and the Founding of Theatres,' argues that Canadian drama has always been characterized 'by arriving, exploring, questioning, and, above all, by celebrating the discovery of *place*,' an idea which manages the difficult task of reconciling centralizing nationalistic authority and so-called regional differences without effacing the latter.[6] But this, I think, is a relatively unusual critical position and reflects mostly on current theatrical practice which has in some ways attempted, as Richard Paul Knowles argues elsewhere in this volume, to undermine the institutional and dramaturgic structures which have helped to silence or muffle the 'voices (off).'[7] In earlier periods, however, the theatre, by allowing itself to be annexed to the agenda of nationalism, had only succeeded in sacrificing its autonomy. This deliberately limited the range and type of representational forms by which Canadian society could in fact seek the public re-enactment of its own identity on stage.

II

During the important period from the latter part of the nineteenth century until the beginning of World War I, critics tended to ask one essential question: where is cultural authority located and on behalf of which specific communities is it being exercised? Canadian nationalists were alarmed when they examined the theatre. With few exceptions, most of it was imported from Britain or the United States; they looked in vain to theatre for a reflection of something even nominally Canadian. There were of course some Canadian performers, including Charlotte Morrison, Harold Nelson, Julia Arthur, and Margaret Anglin, who struggled to remain in Canada, or who made their careers abroad but returned home now and again with touring productions. But the plays originated from other cultures, and to large extent, no one really minded. 'There were too many Canadians who were physically loyal to the new land,' Robertson Davies has explained, 'but who remained exiles in matters of the spirit. You might as well have asked for an indigenous form of government, or an indigenous religion, as ask for Canadian art.'[8] People eventually did ask, often and insistently, for recognizably *Canadian* plays, actors, and directors: Hector Charlesworth, for example, disgusted by the low calibre of U.S. touring shows, argued as early as 1897 that 'perhaps the only future for the [Canadian] theatre lies in Government subsidies, as in France,'[9] a proposal repeated decade after decade by those concerned with elitist cultural values rather than mass commercial appeal. Similarly, B.K. Sandwell can be found advocating Canadian cultural and economic independence as early as 1911, a theme to which he returned many times throughout his career, though invariably qualified by his wariness of what he in 1933 described as 'self-conscious patriotism.'[10]

Charlesworth and Sandwell, among others, recognized that Canadian theatre would never in fact succeed as a mere business enterprise. What it needed was government intervention to generate its principles, develop its structure, subsidize its budget, and cultivate the tastes of its audience. Ostensibly, its values would be determined collectively, but in practice they would evolve from notions about theatre as a form of high culture which were mostly borrowed from the English model of a national theatre. Indeed, many of the early advocates of a Canadian national theatre had an unresolved perspective which made the whole project fundamentally problematic. On the one hand, they wanted to protect Canada from u.s. cultural penetration, and they wanted to cut off cultural ties with England. On the other hand, a vestigial anglophilia, combined with a predisposition towards European culture, made them willing members of the British Empire, with its (incipient) vision of a commonwealth of semi-autonomous nations. Contrary to their own professed intentions, they in fact managed to compromise Canada's cultural independence, giving it a vaguely English cultural orientation which was in fact vulnerable to u.s. monopoly interests. They therefore helped to found the essential cultural/economic model which influences the structure of Canadian theatre to this day.

In England, ideas about how a national theatre ought to be constituted developed in reaction to the kind of unofficial national theatre which Henry Irving had formed at the Lyceum Theatre in London from 1878 to 1902. A brilliant actor and director, Irving almost single-handedly refined existing theatrical practice, achieved an enviable standard of performance, partially restored the texts of Shakespeare, and made the theatre into the kind of respectable art form which Victorian critics and audiences found irresistible. Apart from Shakespeare, he was mostly interested in dated romantic melodramas and had little but contempt or indifference towards the new drama of ideas as practised by Ibsen and Shaw. Somewhat old-fashioned in his business practices, he was wary of anything approximating state interference and relied exclusively on box-office receipts to generate his revenue. Although he recruited a kind of loose company of competent actors, with few exceptions he and his lifelong partner Ellen Terry starred in all the main productions, in the glorious tradition of the nineteenth century. Dedicated to long runs and to increasingly lavish production values, Irving became the acknowledged leader of his profession, and in 1895, in honour not merely of his personal achievement but of profoundly changing attitudes towards the social and artistic importance of the theatre, he was the first actor ever to receive a knighthood. As 'Sir Henry' he imparted a high moral tone of gentlemanly seriousness to the English theatre, a legacy which has been kept alive in the twentieth century by actor-managers like Lord Olivier and Sir John Gielgud.[11] Irving took his complete Lyceum productions to Canada on six separate tours from 1884 to 1904, cultivating a widespread taste for scenic beauty and heightened acting, and laying down the conservative artistic standards by which critics like Charlesworth and Sandwell tended to measure both touring and indigenous productions throughout their influential careers.[12]

Despite their admiration for Irving's achievement, Charlesworth and Sandwell were also interested in a well-publicized discussion, taking place in England, about whether or not it would be possible to establish an official national theatre which would borrow from Irving's example but make improvements to it at the same time. Inspired by the example of the Comédie-Française and other continental European theatres, an impressive number of actors, directors, critics, and authors – including William Archer, Matthew Arnold, Frank Benson, Augustus Harris, Henry Arthur Jones, Bram Stoker, William Poel, John Martin-Harvey, and, most importantly, Harley Granville Barker – argued over a period of many years that, unlike the Lyceum, a national theatre should not be vulnerable to the commercial pressures of the market-place, but should in fact receive generous state subsidies to ensure its financial independence. This would give it the opportunity to create a challenging repertoire produced according to unparalleled standards of excellence. The repertoire would emphasize Shakespeare but would also include less well known but nevertheless important English drama, from all periods, together with the translated classics of European dramatic literature. This national theatre would not merely be a museum of masterpieces, but would also commission and stage new plays dealing with contemporary life in a whole variety of styles and forms. Set up as a permanent company of accomplished actors, emphasizing ensemble performances rather than merely star-turns, it might also manage to establish an affiliated theatre school, based on both traditional and innovative principles, from which it would recruit its new actors.[13]

These proposals, motivated by an almost Puritanical zeal for artistic excellence, emerged from a set of frankly elitist attitudes which assumed that all members of society, irrespective of class and education, would benefit from exposure to the theatre. If nothing else, it would help to cultivate their tastes, allowing them to discriminate between what was good and what was bad. Understandably, these proposals tended to be vague in defining exactly what was meant by their evaluative categories, but they were so idealistically articulated that few people seem to have minded or taken the time to examine them carefully.[14] This projected national theatre was not simply intended for people living in Britain, but was also meant to spread cultural enlightenment throughout the colonies. 'Let us do things as befits this great Empire which we mouth so much about,' an impassioned parliamentarian declared during one of the many heated debates on the subject. 'Do not let us have our [National Dramatic] House compared to some House in Germany like Stuttgart or Wiesbaden. Let it be a British House of which the United Kingdom may be proud, and ... let it be a House that will speak to Canada, South Africa, and the Antipodes.'[15] As dutiful members of the Empire, Canadians did in fact listen: whenever they turned their thoughts to the founding of their own national drama and their own national theatre, they repeatedly looked to the British example – for ideas, precedents, and practical advice.

In England those advocating a national theatre wrote books and articles and gave speeches, in which they tested out ideas, outlined plans, and encouraged an awareness of the pedagogical, aesthetic, and moral functions of theatre in the so-called advancement of civilization. Many of these people also visited Canada and therefore had an immediate influence upon the growing sense of what a Canadian national theatre might accomplish. Bram Stoker, as Irving's business and acting manager, was well known to Canadians and liked to praise the example of the Lyceum along with more up-to-date notions of how that example should be refined. John Martin-Harvey was also warmly received in Canada, first as a longtime member of Irving's Lyceum company, and then as an independent actor-manager who made seven tours across the country from 1914 to 1932 with his own productions of nineteenth-century pot-boilers, Shakespeare, and a few modern plays. Frank Benson toured Canada with his Shakespearean repertoire and, surprisingly, was granted an honorary doctorate by McGill University in 1913. This was an unusual form of legitimation at a time when actors could still be treated as mere rogues and vagabonds. Benson, however, by taking a form of high culture to the far-flung colonies, was certainly a special case. Benson and Martin-Harvey made public addresses (some of which were published) to Canadian Clubs and similar patriotic organizations in which they were given to comparing the state of theatre in both England and Canada, and not always to the detriment of the latter. Harley Granville Barker visited Canada in 1915 to speak at the opening ceremonies of the short-lived Canadian National Theatre, which was being run by the Drama League in Ottawa at the Victoria Memorial Museum; he returned in 1936 as a distinguished adjudicator at the still fledgling Dominion Drama Festival. His adjudications were eagerly reported in newspapers across Canada, and he published a seminal article, 'The Canadian Theatre,' in which he discreetly likened Canada's nascent theatre to Elizabethan England's.[16]

Martin-Harvey and Granville Barker made an especially strong impression on Canadian thinking about how the English model of a national theatre could in fact be adapted to the Canadian context. Over a long period, their arguments were developed by academics like Arthur L. Phelps and W.S. Milne; by playwrights like John Hoare, Fred Jacob, John Coulter, and Herman Voaden; by critics, of course, like Charlesworth and Sandwell; and, most importantly, by Vincent Massey. As a generous private benefactor, founder of Hart House Theatre at the University of Toronto, play anthology editor, Dominion Drama Festival supporter and executive member, governor general, and head of the Massey Commission, Massey has left an indelible impression upon Canadian cultural history. All these men, given their historical situation, could only assume that culture and nationalism were inseparable issues. Like the English advocates of a national theatre, they, too, wanted to establish a theatre which would serve as a physical embodiment of national pride – a symbol of Canada's status not as a provincial culture merely appended to England but as a leading culture within the English-speaking world. At the same time, they thought the theatre would help to unite the disparate regions of the country into the semblance of one nation, united forever. They were preoccupied, as we now say, with the discourse of cultural and political authority, as they attempted to transpose it to a readily identifiable Canadian context; but, as noted earlier, by adapting and somewhat refining an essentially imported model, they were unwittingly helping to weaken Canada's attempts to achieve cultural sovereignty. They were also managing to embed a set of reactionary cultural values which a number of Canadians found suspect, though a serious challenge to those values has only been mounted recently.[17]

They had a tendency to think of theatre as an instrument for the dissemination of high culture, which often meant a repertoire of Shakespeare. Martin-Harvey explained that in the English national theatre, Shakespeare would be presented at least once a week, and clearly he thought that Canada ought to do likewise.[18] Meanwhile, Shakespeare was the most important dramatic model for many of our playwrights, including Charles Mair and Wilfred Campbell.[19] As an arbiter of taste, Shakespeare could not be faulted. He was part of a long and enviable acting tradition, he expressed so-called universal, trans-historical values, and he could be readily accommodated to both high and low forms of theatrical culture. Moreover, as an unimpeachable symbol of

Old World cultural superiority, he belonged to the Elizabethan age, the period of expanding imperial power to which Granville Barker had so generously likened Canada. Shakespeare, then, by a not unreasonable stretch of the imagination, could be regarded as a Canadian playwright. Martin-Harvey, touring Shakespeare across Canada, saw himself as a man with the 'humanizing and spiritualizing' responsibilities of an early missionary, and he was not being the least bit disingenuous when he said that he had come to fulfil 'the crying need of Canada for the best that the world of British drama can give.'[20] Like his mentor, Irving, Martin-Harvey was knighted for his services to the theatre, and as 'Sir John' he brought a refined, quasi-aristocratic manner to what is essentially a coarse art. Together, he and Irving contributed to a recurrent theme in Canadian ideas about the founding of a national theatre: the theatre is basically a conservative, civilizing art form; it is not a place for innovation and iconoclasm.[21]

This bias towards English culture, combined with a faith in Shakespeare as a canonical writer, proved detrimental to the development of an indigenous Canadian theatre, no matter how broadly defined. Since no Canadian could ever emulate, let alone match, Shakespeare's achievement, generation after generation has had difficulty overcoming the 'anxiety of influence,' a condition which was only made worse by the establishment, in 1953, of the Stratford Shakespearean Festival. But not only classical texts caused this kind of insecurity. When proponents of a Canadian national theatre were not holding Shakespeare up as a model of excellence, they were concentrating their attention on the plays and playwrights of the European avant-garde: Granville Barker and John Galsworthy in England, Gerhart Hauptmann and Hermann Sudermann in Germany, August Strindberg and Henrik Ibsen in Scandinavia, and Eugene Brieux together with Emile Zola in France. These were admittedly difficult works which some critics such as Charlesworth nevertheless believed should be performed in Canada in place of formulaic road shows coming out of the United States.[22] On the face of it, nothing seemed inappropriate about these ideas. If implemented, they would allow Canadians to experience an enlarged (meaning, a more civilized) repertoire of not only classical plays, such as Shakespeare's, but also the sort of new plays which were quickly getting a reputation as modern masterpieces. In this way, cultural prestige seemed to be guaranteed. But here, too, there was a controlling paradox at work: by deciding to annex themselves to so-called world culture, Canadians would in fact be ignoring the cultivation of their own repertoire, an act of self-effacement at odds with the professed ideals of cultural nationalism.

To get contemporary European plays into Canadian theatres, John Hoare recommended, in an important 1911 article, that we should create the kind of experimental repertory theatres found in England – most notably, Miss A.E. Horniman's Gaiety Theatre in Manchester – where resident companies, properly subsidized and strongly committed to the cultural life of their particular communities, presented short runs of a varied repertoire. Hoare, like many Canadians, was here much influenced by Granville Barker, who had written an article on the ideals of the repertory system in the January 1911 issue of the *Fortnightly Review*, from which Hoare quotes at considerable length. Typically, Hoare did not recommend that Canadians independently set about the task of establishing their own version of a repertory theatre. Instead, he suggested that Horniman's company should be brought to Canada for a six-week run in Toronto and Montreal, and that a working committee be formed to consult not only with Horniman and (of course) Granville Barker, but with any number of similar repertory theatres on the Continent: 'bring the residuum to Canada, adapt it to the needs of the country, and on that foundation let us work out our own ideals for the ultimate achievement of a Canadian national theatre.'[23] His vision was effectively political: a national theatre, he argued, would 'help to strengthen the unity of the nation'; anticipating regional conflicts and disparities even then, he was opposed to a single national theatre building in, say, Ottawa, and recommended instead that a number of theatres be built across the country. They would be expected to exchange productions on occasion, so that, collectively, they would form a diversified though nonetheless 'unified structure representative of the Canadian national theatre.'[24]

An unusually far-sighted commentator, Hoare was in fact outlining the very kind of regional theatre system which grew up in Canada over fifty years later, during the 1960s and 1970s, partly in response to the sense of national pride awakened by the Centennial celebrations in 1967. At the same time, however, Hoare's proposed set of interconnected repertory theatres also anticipated some of the structural weaknesses of that system, particularly its difficulties in establishing something as inclusive as a national repertoire. Impatient with American-style theatre, and mostly concerned with figuring out how to adapt European practices to a Canadian context, Hoare mentioned Canadian plays and playwrights only as a kind of uncommitted afterthought.

His eagerness to valorize an imported repertoire, however avant-garde, was confirmed by his somewhat defensive remark that 'art and drama must of their very essence be international, of all times and of all peoples.'[25] Thus, like Martin-Harvey's devotion to Shakespeare, Hoare's seemingly innocent proposals for a European-derived repertory network had a paradoxical effect: they actually legitimated an international, rather than a national, repertoire and in this way subverted the very premise on which the European repertory ideal was based: direct, possibly even controversial, engagement with the social, cultural, and political needs of specific communities.

Similar criticisms can be made of Vincent Massey's urbane reflections, over many years, on the practical structures which were needed to create what Massey, at one level, seems to have thought desirable – a national repertoire of Canadian-made plays on Canadian topics in a Canadian idiom and presented in a recognizably Canadian style. Massey deserves our attention for many reasons, partly because his odd mixture of conservatively radical thinking is so representative. A cultural mandarin at heart, Massey heaped contempt on Broadway-style productions and suggested, like Hoare, that the future of the Canadian theatre was in the kind of repertory system established at the Gaiety Theatre in Manchester and at the Abbey Theatre in Dublin. Opposed in principle to long runs, the star-system, and theatre demeaned by the profit motive, Massey wanted Canada to set up a series of regionally based theatres which would produce not just foreign plays but also new Canadian plays. It was his fervently expressed hope that there would eventually be a substantial body of proven plays (Canadian classics, in other words) to which artistic directors would automatically turn when planning their upcoming seasons. Above all, Massey took a practical view towards the art of the theatre. He insisted that to learn their craft properly, playwrights had to work cheek by jowl with a director and a company of actors, and not in makeshift venues like community halls but in properly equipped purpose-built theatre buildings. Anton Chekhov had worked at the Moscow Art Theatre, Stanley Houghton at the Gaiety Theatre, and Eugene O'Neill with the Provincetown Players; in Canada, Carroll Aikins had not only written the Indian tragedy *The God of Gods* but was the artistic director of the Home Theatre near Naramata, BC. These were the kinds of collaborative arrangements which Massey had in mind, for they seemed to promise greatness.[26]

These ideas, expressed as early as 1922, were in some ways forward-thinking and, like Hoare's 1911 article, anticipate things done today to extend the Canadian repertoire. The playwright-in-residence programs, sponsored by the Canada Council, are a version of Massey's belief that play-writing is not just a literary art but a technical skill which can be mastered through a combination of talent and hard work. But, again like Hoare, Massey was in effect doing little more than importing a European idea as a ready-made solution to Canada's problems, despite the existence of crucial differences which he overlooked. In England, for example, the repertory theatre system partly originated as a challenge to the hegemonic cultural authority of London through an emphasis on the accurate representation of regional attitudes, stories, and accents. It was meant as a radical alternative to conventional theatres, not as a substitute for them. In Canada, however, there was effectively nothing else (apart from imported touring productions and a widely spread amateur theatre) to which the repertory system could be an alternative. Thus, the whole idea ran the risk, at least in theory, of becoming what we now call 'mainstream,' that is, conventional theatres supporting the status quo. And indeed, this is exactly what happened when the repertory idea eventually got turned into our current system of regional theatres. Robbed, through a combination of historical, geographic, economic, and cultural forces, of the possibility of being even somewhat radical in intention and execution, they have become, to a great extent, nothing more than state-subsidized versions of the kinds of commercial, u.s.-style theatre which they were in fact designed to replace. Their commitment to the ethos of nationalism – conservative, radical, or otherwise – has been mostly confused, marginal, or non-existent.[27] Massey, as a certain kind of cultural nationalist, could not of course have foreseen these particular developments, although one can argue that they came about partly because the original model he proposed was clearly inappropriate for Canada and derived from his perhaps overly zealous admiration for English cultural achievements. Massey's continuing embarrassment over Canada's status as a mere colonial power frequently betrayed his better judgment.

Among his many contributions to the development of Canadian theatre, Massey edited an important two-volume collection, *Canadian Plays from Hart House Theatre*, which, despite his eclectic aspirations ('In mood and in treatment, they cover a wide field') in fact reflects a rather narrow range of styles and themes, and has to rely on Merrill Denison's early attempts at a Canadian approach to dramatic realism for three out of eleven plays.[28] Uncertain as to what mature Canadian drama would eventually be like, Massey nevertheless had some ideas based on a subtle if evasive understanding of the ideological problems inherent in any attempt to advance the cause of cultural nationalism. Inspired, as he himself admitted, by both Bernard Shaw and Henry Arthur Jones, Massey believed in the drama as a persuasive moral force. By this, he did not mean didacticism, Grundyism, or propaganda, but rather the willingness to face difficult questions straight on without 'prejudice and cant.' He said that he wanted Canadian playwrights to be honestly engaged by their society. Thus he was particularly bothered by caricatures such as the Jack Canuck figure who tended to appear in Canadian novels. At the same time, he was clearly made uncomfortable by overt forms of Canadian nationalism, no matter how honestly they were espoused. Canadian plays, he argued, should not merely be self-conscious displays of 'local colour,' must avoid anything as reductive as 'a Canadian point of view,' and should not seek to be homogeneous in subject matter and theme. Instead, they should represent the diversity of the country, while of course avoiding the temptation to sentimentalize or falsify the full complexity of Canadian life.

What did Massey really want Canadian drama to accomplish? Here, alas, he tended to lapse into the kind of pleasantly vacuous generalities favoured by people who have to make too many speeches. He believed, it would seem, in something rather abstract and ineffable, what he called 'a characteristic feeling, manner or style' which would emerge (but why? and how?) from an 'automatic and inherent' form of Canadianism. Nationalism, then, was all right, as long as it was not merely an exercise in patriotism,[29] and as long as it stimulated 'the creation of beauty in every form.'[30] Citing John Millington Synge, Massey decided that he wanted a Canadian drama that would be not only full of 'joy' but also sharply critical of Canadian society – though in a detached, well-meaning kind of way – just as Synge in *The Playboy of the Western World* had been so sharply critical of Irish life that he managed to set off 'riots in Dublin until the Irish public learned to tolerate a realistic treatment of their eccentricities.'[31] Taken to its logical conclusions, this last statement makes it seem as if Massey did not mind if the theatre were readily ignored by people who were not prepared to change their political agenda; at least the theatre could take satisfaction in the less provocative responsibility of providing an accurate reflection of existing social realities.

Massey's references to the example of Synge and Ireland are much less daring than they might seem and betray his distrust of the theatre as an instrument for active social intervention. He in fact gives the impression of someone so ill-at-ease with the mandate of Canadian nationalism that he feels compelled to sublimate it into something indefinably spiritual, or to displace it into the preoccupations of another nationalistic culture, like Ireland. Moreover, despite his professed interest in Synge, his moral earnestness (perhaps a vestige of his early Methodism) together with an air of aristocratic privilege, evident in every aspect of his argument, seem very much removed from Dublin theatre riots, Irish peasantry, and nationalism as a legitimate expression of cultural and political sovereignty. Would he really have approved if a Canadian had written a play as controversial as *The Playboy of the Western World*? He wanted, whether he would admit it or not, a much more refined kind of Canadian drama which would do credit to our reputation abroad as a civilized middle-power of some influence which could be trusted for its common sense, generosity of spirit, and willingness, if required, to toe the line. Massey wanted, in fact, to depoliticize the Canadian theatre in order to aestheticize it into an innocuous form of cultural prestige: as an 'Imperial Canadian,' as his biographer Claude Bissell aptly describes him, this was the only attitude he knew how to adopt.[32]

III

In all the many essays on the subject, it was repeatedly asserted that a Canadian national theatre, like the railroad and other government-sponsored initiatives, would be made to serve the cause of national unity. Surprisingly, in many periods, there were few dissenting voices asking if the ideology of nationalism, or at least of this kind of programmatic nationalism, should be rigorously contested as an instance of political and artistic tyranny. In this climate, new plays sometimes had difficulty existing as autonomous works of art and could be quickly co-opted and judged by their degree of Canadianism, a category of value (not unlike the worst excesses of thematic criticism) which could be manipulated to supplant generic, dramaturgic, stylistic, and similar evaluative criteria. Playwrights, such as Charles Mair and Wilfred Campbell, could be persuaded to let their art serve the nationalistic mandate, depending, of course, on the definition of nationalism (and its cognate forms, such as British or sometimes even u.s. imperialism) which prevailed in any given period.[33] Similarly, actors, directors, and designers might also be willing to subscribe to the notion that performance should make its contribution to the evolution of a single – or, at least, a unified – sense of identity. But how was this inclusive objective to be accomplished, given the perennial problem of a small population spread out across a huge land mass, much of it uninhabitable?

Our first (and, indeed, only) real national theatre, the Dominion Drama Festival, came into existence in 1932, at the suggestion of the governor general, Lord Bessborough. Newly arrived in Canada from England, Bessborough had found himself more than a little disappointed by Canadian culture, though he was much impressed by the amateur theatre movement. He argued that there ought to be an annual festival of productions originating from across the whole country so that the amateur movement not only would acquire a sense of collective purpose and a common showcase, but also, through a regular opportunity to interact and exchange ideas, learn how to judge different standards of work. Rigorous but fair adjudications by imported theatre professionals, highlighted by the awarding of prizes, would guard against complacency and would help to improve audiences' powers of discrimination.[34] Bessborough, like many of the advocates of a Canadian national theatre, immediately linked theatre and nationalism; with the kind of rhetorical flourish which Massey favoured, he wrote on the souvenir program of the first Final Festival held in Ottawa in April 1933: 'The spirit of a nation, if it is to find full expression, must include a National Drama.'[35]

But, as it turned out, Bessborough and many of the key executive members and advisers of the DDF (including Vincent Massey, who was an influential figure for many years) were fundamentally ambivalent in their attitudes towards the founding of a repertoire of Canadian plays. Bessborough, an admirer of the conservative nineteenth-century tradition of Irving and Martin-Harvey, seems to have not been all that interested in new plays. For him, the theatre mostly meant Shakespeare and other standard-bearing classical works.[36] Accordingly, throughout its influential history, the DDF, at least until its reorganization as Theatre Canada in 1970, tended to privilege an international repertoire, with a strong emphasis on the modern masterpieces of the late nineteenth and early twentieth centuries. New Canadian plays got comparatively less attention. Sometimes there could be stiff opposition within the various DDF groups to staging them at all, the result of a demoralizing anti-Canadian prejudice; moreover, the imported adjudicators might not understand why they could be important, at least to Canadians. This lack of understanding – or masked conflict between different cultural expectations – could carry over to production styles. Malcolm

Morley, for example, an enthusiastic but somewhat old-fashioned adjudicator, objected to Toronto being called 'Trunt' and defended himself by declaring: 'It is the standardization of pronunciation that is needed in Canada and this is one of the duties of the Drama, professional or amateur.'[37]

Not surprisingly, these kinds of critical assumptions tended to produce a narrow sense of what the word *Canadian* might mean when attempting to label a play. Frequently, it referred to a stylistically unadventurous, thematically straightforward, and politically conservative work which dealt with formulaic, certifiably Canadian topics like backwoods life (Merrill Denison's *Brothers in Arms*), prairie winter storms (Gwen Pharis Ringwood's *Still Stands the House*), the hardships of the Depression (W. Eric Harris's *Twenty-Five Cents*), or urban poverty (Mazo de la Roche's *Low Life*). Merrill Denison was an old standby for competing groups who felt obliged to do something Canadian, but who were not up to the risk of creating new work. The controversy that had originally broken out during the 1920s at Hart House Theatre over Denison's deliberately unromantic, quasi-realistic depiction of rural life was either conveniently forgotten or no longer relevant.[38] Herman Voaden, however, was thought too avant-garde (even though his work was clearly derivative), particularly for groups determined to win prizes, and the adjudicators – Malcolm Morley, again – found his self-conscious experiments in 'symphonic expressionism' far too difficult to evaluate using the mechanical point system devised by the DDF executive.[39]

Since the adjudicators got star-billing as foreign experts, there was an understandable reluctance to question their judgments; but this patriarchal structure, reinforced by the white-tie-and-tails protocol of both the regional and final festivals, merely enhanced our neo-colonial anxieties, doing a good deal to suppress our committed engagement with our own culture, here and now. Incredibly, it was not until 1965, over thirty years after its founding, and just five years before its reorganization as a non-competitive festival, that a Canadian-born adjudicator with Canadian stage, TV, and radio experience – Guy Beaulne – was invited to adjudicate the Final Festival competition in Brockville. Like the ideas for a national theatre put forward by Hoare in 1911 and by Massey in 1922, the DDF remained effectively motivated and structured by a pre–World War I, Eurocentric vision of the theatre. This made it hard, even during the revolutionary upheavals of the 1960s, for the emerging, pluralistic, modern values of Canadian society to be adequately (re)presented on our so-called national stage. That central question – whose nation are we in fact seeing? – was often ignored, argued out of existence, or forced to go underground, until the DDF, in its new guise as Theatre Canada, finally self-destructed in 1978.

Despite the positions that might be taken by individual adjudicators, such as Allan Wade, Barrett Clark, and André Van Gyseghem, the DDF was institutionally opposed to plays with a left-wing political agenda. They were clearly at odds with its own hierarchical structure and genteel airs, but also with its earnest attempts to disseminate the self-evident virtues of high culture. In November 1936 the DDF executive had discussed the troublesome issue of 'Propaganda Plays.' This was done partly in response to Granville Barker's decision at the Final Festival in Ottawa the previous April to award prizes to the London Little Theatre for its production of W. Eric Harris's original play *Twenty-Five Cents*, a sentimental but honest examination of the suffering brought about by the Depression, as well as to the Progressive Arts Club of Vancouver for its production of Clifford Odets's *Waiting for Lefty*, an intensively realistic critique of U.S. capitalism. The DDF executive decided that such plays would be tolerated ('there would be no disposition to refuse any play on the ground that it presented advanced or unconventional thought') but, at the same time, it confirmed its responsibility to aesthetic value rather than mere ideological agitation ('there would be reluctance to accept plays which appeared to be proposed rather on account of their tendency to shock than for their artistic or dramatic merit').[40]

This equivocal position was seriously tested the next year when the Theatre of Action, based in Toronto and part of the loosely organized workers' theatre movement, entered Irwin Shaw's expressionistic anti-war play *Bury the Dead* in the 1937 regional festival held in Toronto. The adjudicator, George de Warfaz, praised both the play and the production, but the Hart House Theatre audience, 'all soup and fish ... very elitist,' as Toby Ryan has called them,[41] was not so sure how to react. The production then went on to the Final Festival competition in Ottawa, adjudicated by Michel Saint-Denis, who responded much less enthusiastically than de Warfaz. Saint-Denis, because of his European temperament, training, and experience, was apt to favour what he once called 'a high degree of civilized culture.'[42] In their final remarks, both Saint-Denis and the governor general, Lord Tweedsmuir, suggested that competing groups ought to think more about ways to make audiences laugh in order to relieve the miseries of the Depression; not surprisingly, prizes went to plays like John Coulter's

Irish comedy *The House in the Quiet Glen*. In a speech a few months later in Toronto, Saint-Denis 'warned of the danger inherent in all productions setting forth propaganda in which "the cause" was sometimes allowed to triumph over the theatre rather than being equal to and enhancing it.'[43] Hugh Eayrs, chairman of the committee organizing the Toronto regional festival, had supported the production of *Bury the Dead* in the face of some quite stiff opposition. Two years later, in 1939, when the organizing committee in London, Ontario, decided not to invite the Theatre of Action to the Final Festival with its production of the (again controversial) play *Life and Death of an American*, Eayrs felt, as a matter of principle, that he had to resign in protest. The DDF had effectively suppressed the voice of social reform; art, not politics, was to be the order of the day.[44]

IV

When Granville Barker, Wilfred Campbell, and others compared Canada and Elizabethan England, they were trying to be forward-looking and optimistic.[45] But the analogy only disclosed their preoccupation with the theatre as an effective instrument of trans-historical cultural imperialism. Granville Barker was in essence suggesting that Canada ought to do little more than become a latter-day version of Elizabethan society, appropriating Shakespeare as its house-dramatist to ensure its status as a cultural power-broker on the international scene. Canada's claim to uniqueness, together with at least the possibility of putting forward a quite different set of political and cultural concerns, was being cancelled out by its subtle absorption within an expansionary metaphor which it could never manage to realize, even though, as a dutiful colony, it would give itself an inferiority complex trying to do so.

At the same time, the debate about a Canadian national theatre was to a great extent being influenced not only by Irving and Martin-Harvey but also by the discussion, conducted by Matthew Arnold and others, about how England's national theatre should be organized to ensure that cultural enlightenment would be brought, like civilization itself, to the uneducated masses, thereby deflecting the assertion of philistine values in English society.[46] But in Canada, the confluence of Elizabethan-style attitudes towards imperialism with Victorian-derived notions of how the stage ought to be legitimated as a form of high culture effectively placed Canadian theatre inside a kind of time capsule from which it has only recently begun to emerge. This influence, supported by recurrent outbursts of anti-American sentiment as well as Canada's sense that it really should try to become a unified nineteenth-century kind of nation-state, helped to consolidate a number of popular ideas about the purpose and structure of theatre in Canadian society. In brief, the theatre was meant to embody a supposedly all-encompassing, normative, and homogeneous set of moral/artistic values which would be protected from scrutiny, as was true of the DDF, by their alignment with authority figures like the governor general, our enduring symbol of British monarchy.

By investing so much of ourselves in these outdated ideas, we in fact succeeded in alienating ourselves from a polyvalent conception of nationalism as we tended to suppress marginalized constituencies whose artistic and political values transgressed the dominant paradigm. We also made it difficult – and, indeed, in some periods, impossible – to conceive of theatre as something that can exist entirely separate from the agenda of nationalism, or that might question the system of traditional values on which nationalism is inevitably based.[47] Similarly, the preoccupation with realistic plays (and the cognate form, especially in the nineteenth century, of the history play) favoured empirically based, low mimetic types of referentiality and merely reinforced the assumption that a play has a combined moral-artistic responsibility to be distinctively Canadian. At the same time, the relentlessly linear perspective built into the Elizabethan expansionary metaphor simply contributed to a bad case of cultural displacement. Thus, it was naïvely assumed that *the* classic Canadian play, which would allay all our fears about our neo-colonial insufficiency, would be written and staged one day ... once we had in fact grown up to be just as important as other cultures. Put this way, the problematic issues inherent in the very notion of *the* classic play could be endlessly deferred.[48] So, too, could the very idea of 'Canada' itself, no matter which theatrical (dis)guises it decided to adopt.

Voices (off): Deconstructing the Modern English-Canadian Dramatic Canon

The canon of English-Canadian drama has only recently begun to take shape. Before the 1980s few Canadian scripts received a second production; little scholarly work was devoted to Canadian drama and theatre; and the publishing and teaching of Canadian plays were quixotic and unpredictable. During the 1980s, however, the canon began to solidify, with the appearance in 1984–5 of three national anthologies; the 1989 publication of *The Oxford Companion to Canadian Theatre*; the appearance in 1985 of a Canadian entry in the Longman Literature in English series with a chapter on drama; the publication in 1987 of an introduction to English-Canadian theatre by the editors of the *Oxford Companion*, and of a compilation by one of those editors of critical commentary on the anthologized plays; and the blossoming throughout the 1980s of courses and programs in universities across the country.[1]

These enterprises are rooted, of course, in the often unconscious and usually unstated empiricist assumption that a stable, universalist dramatic canon and theatrical 'mainstream' can and should be established. The editors of the three anthologies refer in their volumes to collections of 'major' works by 'established' dramatists[2] and to a 'national repertoire' that 'define[s] the field,' achieves 'legitimacy,' and establishes 'a real Canadian theatre.'[3] One states his intention 'to present as definitively as possible the highlights of modern Canadian drama in English.'[4] Reviews of the anthologies celebrate them as 'collections of unprecedented comprehensiveness and usefulness,'[5] particularly for the 'expanding educational market ... where the ever elusive search for the definitive "Canadian Classic" continues.'[6]

The establishment of the canon is seen by many as a sign of Canadian drama's coming 'of age,'[7] its reaching a turning point in what the vocabulary of prefaces and introductions reveals to be a Darwinian belief in an 'evolving tradition.'[8] In the context of this discourse, work outside the current mainstream is accommodated, if at all, as 'avant-garde,' a military metaphor that accepts as potentially valuable plays that 'develop out of' current forms and aspire eventually to take their places in the established canon. Plays that fail to qualify as part of the mainstream or of the avant-garde are either dismissed as failing to reach standards to which they may not aspire, or classified as 'alternative' theatre, a label that serves to affirm the centre rather than the possibility of re-centring.

I

The theatre is an institutional practice on almost every level, and it functions as an institution in Canada, as elsewhere, to produce and circulate a specific set of values. As an art form engaged in mounting 'productions' for paying audiences, professional theatre promotes and partakes in the commodification of culture, and therefore privileges 'affirmative culture,'[9] art that reinforces currently dominant forms and values. These are the same forms and values privileged by public and private sources of funding for theatre, by publishers and anthologists, and by educational and cultural institutions. These values, combined with those of Canadian cultural nationalism, work to marginalize the more subversive values, forms, and structures embodied in and employed by more actively and openly political, feminist, 'ethnic,' or regional playwrights and theatre companies. Perhaps more insidiously, 'acceptable' or assimilatable representatives of these kinds of work, in these days of self-conscious liberal pluralism, are themselves subverted by appropriation. They are recontextualized and contained within the boundaries of the institution, neutralized and muffled within the lethal embrace of the canon.

It is ironic that the Canadian dramatic canon is being constructed at a time when the concept of a literary canon has been under attack on several theoretical fronts. Most would now accept Terry Eagleton's argument that the so-called 'literary canon,' the unquestioned 'great tradition' of the 'national literature,' has to be recognized as a *construct*, fashioned by particular people for particular reasons at a certain time.[10] Chris Brookes, however, in his history of Newfoundland's Mummers Troupe, describes the 'cultural superstition that permeates [Canadian] society from the school system to the Stratford Festival: ... that the best art has 'universal artistic value.' The classics, for example, are considered to have this pristine quality. They have it, apparently, in spite of the weather, in spite of the size, class, or racial composition of their audience, the price of tickets, or even a revolution in progress outside the auditorium. Universal art is the counterpart of political tyranny: if you don't like the show then there's something wrong with *you*.'[11]

Brookes is attacking what Marcuse calls 'essentialist humanism,' the silent assumption underlying literary and dramatic canons that art exists somewhere in the realm of transcendental humanity, outside and above its immediate social and cultural context.[12] According to the cultural materialist analysis, the universalist canon deflects attention from social issues to individual psychology, and thereby pre-empts any impetus for social change. Alan Sinfield argues that 'the twin manoeuvres of bourgeois ideology construct two dichotomies: universal versus historical and individual versus social. In each case the first term is privileged and so meaning is sucked into the universal/ individual polarity, draining it away from the historical and the social – which is where meaning is made by people together in determinate conditions and where it might be contested.'[13]

Feminist analyses concur. Rejecting the project of including plays by women in the dominant canon *and* the concept of a feminist canon, for example, Jill Dolan disputes claims to universality and argues that 'any canon is by definition exclusionary';[14] and feminist film critic Janet Staiger argues that 'claims for universality are disguises for achieving uniformity, for suppressing ... optional value systems ... It is a politics of power.'[15] Cultural materialists and feminists in recent years have also extended their arguments to acknowledge and support 'ex-centric' forms of expression developed out of a wide range of so-called 'ethnic' experiences and cultures.[16]

In Canada these theoretical positions are supplemented, especially in the realm of theatre with its precise local audiences, by the arguments of regionalists, many of whom resist the thematic, stylistic, and ideological tyranny of a 'branch-plant' theatrical structure and a centralized publishing industry. The conceptual modes of analysis of Canada's history and culture that have shaped the establishment and financing of theatre, as of other economic and cultural activities, depend on a dichotomy between central Canada and the regions, that, like the individual/social and universal/historical dichotomies, privileges the former term. As Stanley E. McMullin argues, 'the heartland/hinterland model ... assumes that the heartland perpetuates a state of underdevelopment in the hinterland regions, which includes control over cultural "industries."'[17] The models coincide in the assumption that the privileged term represents the realm of 'real art,' intrinsically superior to the temporally, politically, sexually, or regionally 'ex-centric.'

The educational system, of course, by selecting certain works and labelling them universally valuable, perpetuates currently privileged systems of value. Barbara Herrnstein Smith argues that, 'by providing [students] with "necessary backgrounds," teaching them "appropriate skills," "cultivating their interests," and, generally, "developing their tastes," the academy produces generation after generation of subjects for whom the objects and texts thus labelled do indeed perform the functions thus privileged, thereby insuring the continuity of mutually defining canonical works, canonical functions, and canonical audiences.'[18]

Finally, if all else fails, the sheer economics of artistic production militate against inclusion in the canon of anything experimental, much less subversive. As Kathleen Flaherty says, 'government agencies decide what to fund; corporations decide which projects to back; audience members decide which events to buy tickets for. How much exploration can the taxpayer, the patron, the paying public be expected to support?'[19]

Within strict limits, in fact, they are willing to support a good deal, providing that the product sells and can be readily assimilated. Max Horkheimer and Theodor Adorno, in their analysis of 'the culture industry,' describe the economic pressures exerted by what journalists might call 'arts and entertainment': 'It is still possible to make one's way in entertainment, if one ... proves appropriately pliable ... Once his particular brand of deviation from the norm has been noted by the industry, he belongs to it as does the land-reformer to capitalism. Realistic dissidence is the trademark of anyone who has a new idea in business ... In the culture industry, too, the liberal tendency to give full scope to its able men survives ...' 'Not to conform,' they continue, 'means to be rendered powerless, economically and therefore spiritually – to be "self-employed." When the outsider is excluded from the concern, he can only too easily be accused of incompetence.'[20]

Inclusion in the canon, however, can be equally problematic if acceptance, together with the concomitant recontextualization, becomes assimilation. Dolan, for example, analyses at length how Marsha Norman's potentially powerful feminist statement in 'night, Mother was 'bent' to fit the canon. Dolan shows how production of the play on Broadway and its critical reception effectively neutralized the disruptive potential of the script.[21] If the commercial conditions of Broadway play production seem far removed from the purity of the Canadian experience, it is interesting that three years before the appearance of Dolan's essay Ann Wilson had made the same point about the Toronto production of Caryl Churchill's Cloud Nine.[22]

A comparable process of assimilation can take place in the publishing of scripts, especially in anthologies. In an excellent analysis of the publication of American poetry anthologies, Alan C. Golding illustrates the ways in which, 'when a teaching anthology ... canonizes ... outsiders ... it renders their work culturally and intellectually harmless.' The self-conscious pluralism of so-called 'comprehensive' anthologies, he suggests, by systematizing and classifying the work, neutralizes it.[23]

II

It is worth examining the English-Canadian dramatic canon – how and why it has taken the shape it has, what it includes, what it excludes, and to what extent it assimilates the 'ex-centric' – in order to determine the degree to which it conforms to the patterns outlined above. For the purposes of this paper, I will assume that the modern English-Canadian canon is more or less accurately represented by the three national anthologies, and that it derives in part from the theatrical repertoire, in part from the publishers' lists, and in part from the group of plays that have received significant scholarly attention. There is no doubt that the anthologies have shaped curricula from the moment they appeared and have heavily influenced subsequent scholarship. Although at least one of the anthologists disclaims any canon-making aspirations,[24] the inevitable impression that the volumes give is the one made explicit by the editor of the Talonbooks collection: 'The intention of Modern Canadian Plays is to present as definitively as possible the highlights of modern Canadian drama in English.' Not surprisingly, Wasserman claims that these highlights are of transcendent value: 'I have tried to avoid all extrinsic criteria (regional representation, generic variety etc.) and have included only those plays that have had a major impact on the Canadian theatre so far, and that promise to remain significant for a long time to come.'[25]

The anthologies include a total of thirty-one plays by twenty-two writers. One play – John Herbert's *Fortune and Men's Eyes* – is in all three collections, while three others – David Freeman's *Creeps*, David French's *Leaving Home*, and John Coulter's *Riel* – appear in two. Playwrights Herbert, French, Sharon Pollock, and James Reaney are represented in all three, while Freeman, Coulter, Michael Cook, George Ryga, George F. Walker, and Gwen Pharis Ringwood have work in two. The following playwrights are represented in only one of the collections: Herman Voaden, Robertson Davies,[26] Gratien Gélinas (the only Québécois included in any of the anthologies, which do not claim to represent French-language drama), William Fruet, Carol Bolt, Rick Salutin (with Theatre Passe Muraille), Aviva Ravel, John Gray (with Eric Peterson), David Fennario, Erika Ritter, Margaret Hollingsworth, and Allan Stratton. This list corresponds in its 'highlights' to W.J. Keith's selection of playwrights for discussion in *Canadian Literature in English*: he singles out from the modern period the work of Ringwood, Coulter, Davies, Reaney, Ryga, Cook, and French – an astonishingly conservative and literary list. L.W. Conolly, by compiling reviews and critical accounts of the collected plays, reinforces the editors' judgments, and he adds material on four uncollected plays, implicitly arguing for their canonical status: another play by French (*Leaving Home*); another by Reaney (*Sticks and Stones*); John Murrell's poetic historical play, *Waiting for the Parade*; and Theatre Passe Muraille's most naturalistic script, *The Farm Show*, the only pure collective creation in the bunch.

At first glance this would seem to be an eclectic and comprehensive selection. However, it is worth examining the plays included and some of the factors that lie behind their selection. The most obvious characteristic of the 'canonical' plays is their conservatism. As one reviewer of the three anthologies notes, 'the tone of caution is all-pervasive: docu-dramas, collective writings, and experimental pieces find little place in any of these editions. All of the plays collected are "main stream" efforts: all are cautiously chosen, and controversial works are avoided; ... all are recognized pieces, or are written by "recognized" playwrights.'[27] It might be added that sixteen of the twenty-two playwrights are white males – or seventeen of the twenty-three if Conolly's addition of John Murrell is included; all three anthology editors, together with all of the authors and editors cited in note 1, are also white males; almost all of these men are of Anglo-Saxon or Anglo-Irish extraction; and most of the plays received their first professional production in Central Canada or in one of the 'branch-plant' regional theatres. *Fortune and Men's Eyes,* the one play to appear in all three anthologies, premiered in New York.

The entire history of Canadian theatre, of course, is dominated by the conservative, colonial, and hierarchical. Benson and Conolly, in *English-Canadian Theatre,* describe the nineteenth century's 'calculated exploitation of Canada by commercial theatre interests in the United States and Great Britain' and conclude that 'theatrically speaking, Canada was an occupied country for most of the nineteenth century and nearly half of the twentieth.'[28] Law, order, and a predetermined concept of culture preceded settlement throughout Canadian history; similarly, theatrical *structures* in Canada have always preceded – or in the case of Canada's native peoples, superseded[29] – theatrical *activity.* When concerted efforts have been undertaken to cultivate a Canadian Theatre, the structures established by government – the 'regional theatre' model, the CBC, the Dominion Drama Festival – have been centralized, hierarchical, and nationalistic, all of which are traditional attributes of the forces behind the construction of national canons.[30]

It is not surprising that the regional theatre system failed to produce 'a real Canadian theatre,' in Wasserman's phrase, who laments that in the late 1960s Canadian theatre was 'entrenched and conservative,' and that 'with few exceptions the regionals served up homogenized theatre: safe, commercial seasons of British and American hits plus a smattering of world classics.'[31] Consequently, the rebellious 'alternate' theatre movement, which in spite of George Luscombe and other evidence to the contrary most critics date, significantly, to Canada's 1967 centennial year, was militantly nationalistic. Critics and journalists for the next two decades interpreted extraordinarily divergent activity in small theatres across Canada as the groundwork for a Canadian national repertoire that would take its place beside the repertoires of other 'mature' nations. Wasserman does so using some revealing rhetoric: '1967 was ... the year that English Canadian drama began to achieve legitimacy ... Right across the country, audiences and critics, buoyed by a new national self consciousness and pride, were taking note of this latest cultural phenomenon – plays written by Canadian playwrights, performed by Canadian actors in Canadian theatres. And they were good!'[32]

Not surprisingly, there seems to be nationalist bias in the selection of the canon, and a recurring emphasis in reviews and criticism, in

Conolly's collection and elsewhere, on how plays help to define a uniquely Canadian national character. The plays selected for the anthologies privilege Canadian settings and characters (only George F. Walker's *Zastrozzi* has no explicit Canadian connection), while the large number of plays set in exotic or fanciful places or times have been largely ignored. The preponderance of Canadian history plays in the anthologies, moreover, reflects a critical focus on the construction of Canadian myths that is best exemplified by the argument and title of Don Rubin's article 'Celebrating the Nation: History and the Canadian Theatre.'[33] This focus distorts not only the overview of Canadian drama and theatre, but also the discussion of individual works: critics interested in the construction of national myths, for example, have tended to ignore the essentially *de*constructive function of the many metatheatrical plays on Canadian historical subjects.

Related to the concern for Canadian identity is the high percentage of realistic and naturalistic plays in the canon. Attempts to answer Northrop Frye's question 'Where is here?' in dramatic terms have naturally resulted in such realistic portrayals of people and place as *The Farm Show*, French's Mercer trilogy, or the 'social realist' plays of Herbert and Freeman. The success of the project can be ascertained by the ecstatic 'That's us!' that was used to describe the opening-night audience's reaction to *Leaving Home*,[34] or the sometimes wrong-headed praise for the 'slice-of-life' realism of Herbert, French, or Freeman.[35] But realistic and naturalistic forms have come under increasing scrutiny in recent years from several critical quarters. The most sustained and systematic analyses come from materialist feminists, many of whom argue, as Dolan does, that

realism is prescriptive in that it reifies the dominant culture's inscription of traditional power relations between genders and classes. Its form masks the ideology of the author, whose position is mystified by the seemingly transparent text. Catherine Belsey suggests that in conventional readings of realist texts, the reader is identified as the subject position from which the text is made intelligible ... 'Certain ranges of meaning ... are "obvious" within the currently dominant ideology, and certain subject positions are equally "obviously" the positions from which those meanings are apparent.'[36]

Feminist film critics discuss the 'male gaze' as defining the subject position behind the lens and in the audience in classical realist films,[37] and it is similarly the white middle-class male gaze that defines the subject stance in most theatrical realism, reducing other groups depicted to objects of that scrutiny, or psychological 'case studies,' while requiring that all audiences 'learn' to see as white middle-class men.[38]

Canadian realist drama frequently focuses on the so-called under-privileged – the handicapped, prisoners, native groups, or the poor – but it usually does so in such a way as to place its audiences in the position of voyeurs or of self-congratulatory liberal 'concerned spectators.' The audience in these plays witnesses a crisis – the central structural principle of realist drama – that is interpretable as deviation from a social norm that is restored at the play's resolution. Raymond Williams's comments are applicable here, as he points out the 'contra-diction between the social radicalness of much naturalistic theatre ... and the formal methods of such drama. The discourse of the play may be urging change, criticism, rebellion; but the dramatic forms ... inevitably enforce upon us a sense of the unalterable solidity of this social world.'[39] The comments could have been made in reference to French, Freeman, Herbert, Fennario's *Balconville*, the early plays of Sharon Pollock, or much of the work of George Ryga.

Not all naturalistic drama serves the voyeuristic impulses of the Canadian theatre's predominantly middle-class audiences. Contempo-rary plays such as Ritter's *Automatic Pilot*, or even such historical dramas as Pollock's *Walsh*, rely on the identification of that same audience with angst-ridden professionals who struggle to accommodate themselves to social situations that are by implication unchangeable. Richard Ohmann, in his analysis of the shaping of the canon of American fiction during 1960–75, provides insights relevant to this group of plays, and to any understanding of canon-formation in the last half of the twentieth century in North America. He defines a 'professional-managerial' class, the background and interests of which help to determine what is considered to be canonical, and describes a process of neo-catharsis that pre-empts subversion by exploiting the concept of individual responsibility. He points to characters 'represented as analogous to "us" rather than as "cases" to be examined and understood from a clinical distance,' and his analysis explains a good deal about what has come to be part of the Canadian dramatic canon:

Every public voice seemed to be saying ... 'History is over, though progress continues. There is no more poverty. Everyone is middle class. The State is a friendly power, capable of ... solving its problems ... through legislation that itself is the product of your ideas and values ... You are therefore, the favoured people ... so carry forward this valued social mission, which in no way conflicts with individual achievement. Enjoy your prestige and comforts. Fulfill your-selves on the terrain of private life.' But because the economic underpinnings of this consciousness were of course *not* unchanging and free of conflict ... the individual pursuit of happiness continued to be a problem ... so it was easy to nourish the suspicion that any perceived lack was one's own fault.[40]

The answer to any problem, then, is not to change society, but to grow up. Social problems are dramatized as personal neuroses, and as plots move towards their resolutions potential unrest is diffused.

Another characteristic of many Canadian canonical plays is their sheer amenability to scholarship. Almost all the plays in the canon are readily classifiable, comparable to 'classics' of their genre, or comfort-ably literary. It is not surprising that academics should privilege the familiar in what occasionally surfaces as a search for 'a national dra-matic *literature*,'[41] but it is perhaps more so that the theatrical process itself as it exists in Canada tends to be logocentric and literary. Director and dramaturge Kathleen Flaherty, describing the processes used in the development of new work in Canada, laments that 'rarely are workshops encouraged to explore the use of sound, setting, dramatic image, audience-actor relationship, or space ... We have a literary tradi-tion which continues to perpetuate itself because of the ways we develop new work.'[42]

The larger social implications of this privileging of literary forms surface in the introduction to Perkyns's anthology when he points out that, in the nineteenth century, 'the quality of popular drama declined to melodrama or farce of little literary merit because theatre managers frequently catered to unruly working-class audiences.'[43] Not only do the privileging of the literary and the classifications 'melodrama' or 'farce' imply particular value judgments and impose particular ways of seeing the work;[44] the very *act* of classifying moves the work into a particular realm of empiricist activity with its own sets of values. Horkheimer and Adorno refer to this as 'that schematization and pro-cess of cataloging and classification which bring culture within the sphere of administration,[45] while Steve Barnet and Martin G. Silverman point out that 'the reproduction of contemporary capitalist society is tied not simply to specific categories, but to the very way we categorize.'[46]

The modern English-Canadian dramatic canon, then, is shaped by the conservative, hierarchical, and nationalistic structures of theatrical production and funding, and by the interests of reviewers, academics, teachers, and audiences who for economic and historical reasons tend to be from the 'professional-managerial class.' The canon therefore tends towards literary realistic or naturalistic plays written in recognizable genres on explicitly Canadian subjects that deal in universalist ways with individual psychology. What is left out? In spite of an apparent liberal pluralism on the level of theme and subject matter – what Frank Lentricchia calls 'the mere pluralization of voices and traditions (a currently fashionable and sentimental gesture)'[47] – the current canon omits virtually all regional, 'ethnic,' native, feminist, lesbian, gay, non-literary, or explicitly political drama that is subversive or 'ex-centric' on a formal or structural level, and that therefore cannot be readily absorbed into the canon.

On the surface, regional voices would seem to abound in the canon, to the point that it has become a cliché to characterize the typical Canadian play as Prairie or Maritime realism. This, of course, is not insignificant. The poetic realism of Michael Cook, an Irishman by birth who continues to draw heavily on Irish dramatic forms and traditions, is no more representative of Newfoundland's anarchic theatre community than is the work of the Newfoundland-born Torontonian, David French. It is a distortion to discuss the work of Cook, French, or Ringwood solely within the context of either realism or regionalism, but the presence of their plays in the canon provides the illusion of national representation without admitting the truly 'ex-centric.' As Barbara Godard argues, 'ex-centricity implies many things – bizarre, fantastic, unconventional, incomprehensible, other – all subsumed by the concept of difference,'[48] and all potentially subversive of established modes and values. Stanley E. McMullin gives Godard's argument an explicitly regional focus when he makes the point that 'the heartland is always concerned with meaning, form, and structure,' while 'the hinterland, in its antithetical response, is eccentric, experimental.'[49] It is not surprising that the 'national' anthologies include Cook's *Jacob's Wake* and *The Head, Guts and Soundbone Dance*, comfortably literary plays in the realist mode, while excluding not only the potent work of Codco or the Mummers, but even Cook's own absurdist monodramas and Brechtian epics. The same pattern applies across the country.

Plays by Canada's native peoples are completely missing from the canon, in spite of the fact noted by Benson and Conolly that 'before the discovery and colonization of North America by Europeans, an indigenous drama of great richness and complexity flourished' in what is now Canada.[50] Native theatrical activity has not, of course, died out, although as Benson and Conolly note, the early native drama 'had little influence on subsequent theatrical developments in Canada, which originated in Europe.'[51] Difficult to classify in European terms, theatrical rather than literary in orientation, the theatre of Canada's native peoples, past and present, has disappeared from the face of the canon.

Not that native peoples are entirely missing. Plays by Ringwood and Ryga place them at centre stage and treat them with a great deal of sympathy. Ringwood, however, in her poetic *Drum Song* trilogy, adapts the Canadian native experience to the forms of Western tragedy, and in 'universalizing' her heroines' suffering flattens and distorts those elements of native language and culture that are unique. Ryga's native peoples in his early one-act play 'Indian' and in *The Ecstasy of Rita Joe* are the combined product of his poetic imagination and his social consciousness, but they are almost indistinguishable from the Ukrainian-Canadian characters in his other plays, as generic representatives of the downtrodden. Both Ringwood and Ryga write from outside the native experience, and both employ recognized European dramatic forms unlikely to do much more than arouse liberal sympathy, or guilt. Interestingly, too, Ryga is the only real representative in the canon of a Canadian ethnic minority, and he is represented only by his plays about native peoples.

Ryga is also one of the few avowedly political writers represented, though his political commitment is generally regarded as something of a liability. W.J. Keith is most explicit about this, finding Ryga's rarely praised *Ploughmen of the Glacier* to be his 'most artistically satisfying' play, 'because its subject ... is more universally philosophical than locally political.' Elsewhere, according to Keith, 'Ryga is limited by his ideological position.'[52] Plays which silently reinforce current ideology, of course, are not considered to *be* political and therefore are felt to be superior as works of non-partisan, universal art.

Ryga's are not the earliest plays to have been rejected or distorted in this way. For years the workers' theatre movement of the 1930s was discounted or ignored by theatre historians because of its avowedly political agenda, and even now, when the power of a play such as *Eight Men Speak* is more likely to be acknowledged, that power is rarely seen to derive from its impassioned political commitment. Benson and Conolly, for example, claim that '*despite* the fact that agitprop theatre championed political rather than aesthetic values, *Eight Men Speak* has a raw dramatic power and employs advanced structural and theatrical techniques foreign to the conventional, bourgeois Canadian stage.'[53] Across the country actively political theatre has received precisely parallel treatment, not only from reviewers and critics, but more alarmingly from supposedly arms-length government funding agencies.

Alan Filewod provides the best account of this in his analysis of the demise of Newfoundland's Mummers Troupe, which folded precisely because of its failure to conform to the dominant aesthetic and ideological structures.[54]

There *are* explicitly political plays in the canon by dramatists other than Ryga, most notably Rick Salutin, who is represented by *1837: The Farmers' Revolt* (with Theatre Passe Muraille); and David Fennario, whose most commercially successful play, *Balconville*, is in Wasserman's collection. These playwrights have both been powerful voices from the left, but the work included in the canon has been neutralized by the processes of production and recontextualization. In the introduction to his anthology, for example, Wasserman undercuts the theatrical impact of *1837*, which is clearly to encourage revolutionary sentiment, by grouping it with other historical plays that depict *failed* revolutions: 'As Canadian history and history plays tell us,' he notes, 'from 1837 to Riel to the FLQ Canadian revolutions don't succeed.'[55] Like other commentators, Wasserman prefers to place *1837* within the context of a developing national mythology.

David Fennario's work has fared even less well. Fennario is a committed communist whose abilities as a writer came to the attention of Maurice Podbrey of Montreal's decidedly middle-class Centaur Theatre before Fennario had even attempted to write plays. Under the tutelage of Podbrey and his directors at Centaur, Fennario learned to channel his skills and beliefs to fit the naturalistic structures that the middle class has always found appropriate for depictions of working-class reality. Fennario was a good student, and his first two plays, *On the Job* and *Nothing to Lose*, were widely praised as powerful portrayals of the lives of English Montreal's working classes. Unfortunately, the political import of the plays was treated in much the same way as we have seen W.J. Keith treat Ryga's politics. Reviewing *Nothing to Lose* in *Canadian Literature*, for example, and praising the play's dialogue, characterization, and theatrical realism, John Ripley finds that 'Marxist rhetoric blunts the play's edge at times, and lends it more than a hint of propaganda. But the author's political bias need not materially mar our theatrical enjoyment or cloud the sensitive insights the play contains. Happily, his more recent *Balconville* is less doctrinaire.'[56]

Balconville, of course, is the play included in the canon, and it is generally considered to be Fennario's best work. It is also, however, the best example of what Golding calls the 'detoxification of potent work.'[57] As produced and published, the play was praised for its sympathetic treatment of convincing characters, and for its not having presumed to suggest social activism as a solution to the characters' problems: 'What *Balconville* risks losing ... as political propaganda, it gains in dramatic resonance. In recognizing and illuminating the human dimensions of a political position he deplores, Fennario has convincingly captured the real complexity of the situation.'[58] According to this argument, the quality of the play derives from Fennario's failure to make his political point.

It is true that *Balconville* largely fails as activist theatre, and that this failure accounts in part for its critical success. Recognizing this, Fennario gave up both on the Centaur and, as is less often remarked, on theatrical naturalism. He returned to his working-class community and mounted productions of non-naturalistic, revisionist history plays that were universally reviled in the mainstream press, and patronizingly regretted by the academic world. But it is worth examining what drove Fennario out of the theatrical mainstream at the height of his success, and what this suggests about the script of *Balconville* that has entered the canon. It seems, from conversation with Fennario, that there was tension between the playwright and his director, Guy Sprung, over the first production of the play, and the source of that tension is suggested in an interview with Sprung published in *Canadian Theatre Review*. In spite of Sprung's claim, made dubious by his subsequent career, that 'David and I share the same political beliefs,' it is clear from the interview that Sprung 'helped' Fennario to fit both *Balconville* and *Nothing to Lose* into aesthetically and therefore ideologically conventional structures. *Balconville* originally opened with a Brechtian sequence of audience address that Sprung cut: 'we started instead with the squealing of tires, some sort of farce, slamming of doors, people shouting and screaming ...' because, as Sprung claims, Fennario has 'no idea of structure; ... he lacks craft.'' Sprung goes on to indicate that the writer character in *Nothing to Lose* had originally expressed many of Fennario's political beliefs, but that 'it was my idea to make the writer a bit of an idiot to balance the play and provide some tension.' Of both plays he says, 'I tried to tell him that the political statement had to come out of either the characters themselves or the situation and that he had to stop trying to verbalize his own solutions.'[59] It seems clear that the naturalistic, well-made-play structure of *Balconville*, together with its political softness, are largely the products of Sprung's intervention. Fennario has not worked with Sprung since, but the play has been absorbed into both the canon and the theatrical mainstream, where it may serve as evidence of the skill of the dominant culture at 'defusing potential hostility by absorption.'[60]

The evidence that actively socialist works are excluded from the canon or neutralized by assimilation through the politics of production, funding, publication, and critical reception is matched by an examination of Canadian feminist theatre. In Canada the search for new forms and languages – what Marcuse calls 'the effort to find forms of communication that may break the oppressive rule of the established language and images ... which have long since become a means of domination, indoctrination, and deception'[61] – has been most persistent among feminist playwrights and collectives, but there is little evidence of this in the national anthologies. There *are* 'plays by women' in the canon, but they include few strong feminist works, and those included, like the political plays discussed above, are recontextualized and their subversive potential thereby effectively defused. Of the playwrights included, only Sharon Pollock and Margaret Hollingsworth have produced work that could accurately be described as feminist, although Erika Ritter's *Automatic Pilot*, using a tight comic structure, capitalizes on a liberal taste for 'soft-core' feminist themes. Pollock is represented by three plays, but two of them, *Walsh* and *Generations*, are early works that are neither feminist in theme or adventurous in form – in fact they are her most conventionally naturalistic plays. The third, *Blood Relations*, while it can be described as feminist, in the context of the canon can as easily be taken as a safely distanced historical costume drama.[62] It has been performed and received this way in regional theatres across the country.

Margaret Hollingsworth, however, is one of an expanding group of women writing and collaborating on Canadian plays who are exploding traditional phallogocentric forms and structures. (Kathleen Flaherty provocatively suggests that theatrical expectations are based on the male orgasm, 'a traditional structure of inciting action, rising action, climax, and denouement.')[63] In plays such as *War Babies*, 'The Apple in the Eye,' 'diving,' and the experimental pieces in her collection *Endangered Species*, Hollingsworth not only writes about 'the ways in which women have been marginalized,'[64] but she uses her own triply marginalized position, as a woman playwright in Canada, as a strength that offers the continuing opportunity of creative formal 'ex-centricity.' Unfortunately, Hollingsworth is represented in the canon by *Ever Loving*, an historical play which is her most conventionally naturalistic and least characteristically subversive script. It is also the only one of her plays to have been adopted into the repertoire of the branch-plant regional theatres, where it is virtually indistinguishable from conventional naturalistic dramas of individual psychological adjustment.

Even outside the realms of marginalization based on geography, race, politics, gender, or sexual preference, the solidification of a dramatic canon necessarily restricts any experimentation or change that does not evolve in a linear way out of existing forms. There is little evidence in the English-Canadian canon, for example, of what Patrice Pavis discusses as the two poles of the theatrical avant-garde, voices (time) and images (space),[65] in spite of the fact that there is a great deal of theatrical activity in these areas. Kathleen Flaherty notes that 'a number of contemporary writers are adapting conventions from film (Lawrence Jeffrey, Sally Clark), from rock videos (Pat Langner, David Widdicombe), from television (John Mighton), from non-white cultures (Tomson Highway, Diana Braithwaite), [and] from performance art (Banuta Rubess) for their theatre writing. These conventions force us to re-think our traditional ideas of staging, scene changes, acting styles, [and] language.'[66] It is this continual process of rethinking, restructuring, and indeed deconstructing the tradition that keeps art alive and allows it to contribute to the ongoing critical project of rethinking, restructuring, and deconstructing our ways of seeing and ordering the world. As Alain Martineau says, 'when the work of art can no longer preserve its critical stance and offer a viable alternative to the irrationality of the world, it is assimilated: it becomes an affirmation instead of a negation of the existing world.'[67] In short, it becomes canonical.

III

What are the alternatives to canon-formation in Canadian drama, given the existing economic and funding structures for theatre in Canada, the traditional audience base, the need for teaching texts, and the current practices of dramaturgy, professional training, journalistic reviewing, and scholarly interpretation? Are there other modes of theatrical production, publication, teaching, or criticism? Critical theorists have attempted to formulate strategies for what Arthur Kroker calls 'the recovery of minority languages, as opposed to the tyranny of the will to truth,'[68] and most of these strategies involve some form of 'relativistic, "interest" theory of value which predicts that different communities will value different things for different reasons.'[69] Many theorists, in fact, argue as Rachel Blau DuPlessis does, for the *privileged* position of the margins, which can speak from outside the restrictions silently imposed on the centre,[70] taking advantage of Marcuse's 'power of negative thinking' to disrupt 'one-dimensional theories of reality.'[71]

The most useful theoretical position for the formulation of alternatives to a traditional canon for Canadian drama seems to me to derive from the points at which aspects of Marxism, feminism, and deconstruction intersect.[72] Each of these projects attacks the logocentric desire to resolve all contradictions; each is concerned with attention to gestures of exclusion and to the extent to which context determines meaning while being itself indeterminate; and each proposes a continuing process of radical heterogeneity. As critical analyses of dominant forms and structures, the Marxist, feminist, and deconstructive projects share a common subject. As Michael Ryan says, 'it seems that thought, sexuality, and political economy form an interlocking network. Capitalism is patriarchal; the metaphysics which legitimates it is phallocentric, and the cognitive operation of equivalence in metaphysics is necessary to the operation of an exchange economy.'[73]

Derrida calls this a 'restrained economy,' and in the positive project that deconstruction can also be said to share with feminism and Marxism, he posits operation within a 'general economy' that is anti-logocentric and that removes the possibility of absolute self-identity and property by pointing towards a 'social' or relational logic of interdependence, inter-relationality and communal non-ownership. For Derrida the project of deconstruction is to produce a way of thinking that accommodates without appropriating alterity and indeterminacy, just as a Marxist utopia posits 'the togetherness of diversity,'[74] and a recent feminist critic a 'multiplicity,' 'mobility and constant change ... beyond a polarization around a unicity she rejects.'[75] As positive projects, each moves towards the need to resist the postmodern malaise by accepting the concept of continually re-centring communities *based* on marginality in order to cultivate concerted difference and radical contingency.

How does this theory translate into practice, particularly in the theatre? What sort of theatre structure can accommodate this type of radical diversity? Ryan, in calling for a new form of *social* organization, describes a structure 'founded ... on participation, self-activity, a diffusion of the leadership function, differences, and radical participatory democracy.'[76] He might be describing certain kinds of theatrical collective, and when he elsewhere points to a political structure based on Marx's description of the Paris Commune, he comes close to describing the operations of feminist theatre companies such as Toronto's Nightwood Theatre and the Company of Sirens. Ryan posits 'a ... form that would be predicated upon the ever-open possibility of a displacement: ... continuous discontinuity, radical difference ... a governmental form that does not pretend to be sovereign, perhaps something like the sort of alternating representation ... in which the representer and the represented are interchangeable because equal, which Marx describes in the Paris Commune.'[77]

The best examples in Canadian theatre of this structural model, however, are the small artist's cooperatives such as The Mulgrave Road Co-op Theatre in Guysborough, Nova Scotia. Mulgrave Road is 'ex-centric' in almost every sense of the word. Located in a small rural community (population 514) in the poorest county of mainland Nova Scotia, the company since 1977 has mounted and toured new Nova Scotian plays on regional, racial, feminist, and political issues to communities throughout the Maritimes and beyond. The Co-op elects its artistic director annually from among its membership, reviews its operations and its mandate biannually in general meetings, and carries out the decisions of those meetings through regular gatherings of a smaller 'workers co-op' made up of members active on current projects. In practice, this structure imposes a continuing process of self-examination – deconstruction – which effectively prevents the linear development or implementation of logocentric artistic or corporate 'visions' for the company.

In his 1988–9 artistic director's letter, Chris Heide made explicit the Co-op's 'ex-centric' role: 'Mulgrave Road is attempting to fly in the face of the dominant forces in Canadian theatre at this moment. Forces which I believe are creating a narrowing of the audience for theatre to professional and high income groups in urban centres. At Mulgrave Road we're referring to theatre of the church hall, not theatre of the parking garage, theatre of the eight-foot ceiling, not theatre of the chandelier, theatre of the margin, not theatre of the automatic centre.'[78] If the company's structure is anti-hierarchical and radically contingent, this manifests itself in a variety of divergent, and usually non-linear, shows, from feminist collective creations such as *One on the Way* to self-reflexive plays such as *Bring Back Don Messer* about the homogenization and commodification of family entertainment. Recent years have seen a rigorously metatheatrical collective creation about the Co-op's relationship with its audience (*Ten Years After*); and a multi-media deconstruction of the relationship between the (mis)use of regional folklore in the media and the acquisition and abuse of economic and political power (*K.C. Superstar*). Each Co-op show develops its theatrical process out of its own needs, and each tries to respond to the company's stated goal, 'to develop innovative *forms* and produce work of a kind and quality which respond to the history, traditions, and culture of North-eastern Nova Scotia.'[79] But few of the Co-op's productions could be expected to show up in the canon as 'regional realism.'

Theatre structures and modes of production shape what audiences experience, but it is the publication of scripts that dictates what is read and preserved and what enters school curricula. Like the organizational and funding structures for theatre, the publishing industry in Canada is both centralized and hierarchical. There *are* specialized collections and regional publishers, but the best model of the anti-canonizing publication of Canadian scripts is provided by the early years of Playwrights Canada (then Playwrights Co-op). Recently, a publishing committee has been established to select scripts for production in a three-tiered system: individual scripts in a 'trade paperback' format; glossy collections of scripts with what is thought to be commercial potential; and computer print-outs of less popular plays made available on request. In its first decade and a half, however, Playwrights Co-op published and distributed staple-bound copies of any professionally produced play submitted to them.[80] It was criticized, of course, for lack of discrimination, but the policy was invaluable in providing individual choice (and demanding individual judgment) on the part of potential producers, readers, teachers, and critics, from a multifaceted, decentred catalogue, and in spite of impracticalities, the move away from the original policy seems to be regressive.

The deconstruction of the canon, of course, has implications for teaching. The new anthologies have certainly facilitated the multiplication of courses on Canadian drama, even if they have also standardized curricula. But there have been other side effects, including what the editor of one of the anthologies calls 'the textual domination of dealing with Canadian drama/theatre in classes,'[81] and the privileging of phallogocentric, literary, and variously naturalistic forms and the ideologies these embody. But deconstruction begins, and belongs, in the classroom. If the academy is to avoid the situation described above by Barbara Herrnstein Smith, in which teaching is seen to ensure the continuity of 'mutually defining canonical works, canonical functions, and canonical audiences,' it must find a new pedagogy. It needs to provide students with a mode of analysis that pays attention to difference; that resists, in Ryan's phrase, 'the desire for conscious categorical mastery,'[82] classification, and ranking by attending to the exclusions on which classifications and hierarchies depend; and that encourages what Barbara Johnson calls 'the careful teasing out of meaning from warring significations within the text'[83] rather than the perception or construction of unities. As afar as it is possible, too, curricula need to be designed on principles of heterogeneity to represent a multiplicity of voices and forms rather than the uniformity of an 'evolving tradition'; and courses on Canadian drama need to resist the textual, literary, and universalist biases inherent in the reading of published texts, by considering *performances* as texts and by taking advantage of opportunities presented by local productions.

Finally, the criticism of Canadian drama and theatre needs to become much more self-conscious, to examine its own discourse and the implicit metaphors and models through which it functions. Even a cursory perusal of the three Canadian theatre journals – *Theatre History in Canada*, *Canadian Drama*, and *Canadian Theatre Review* – together with collections of essays such as Anton Wagner's *New World Visions*, reveals a critical discourse rooted in the same universalist or developmental language, the same focus on theme and content at the expense of form, and the same subject positioning of a generic spectator as we have seen underlying the anthologies, essays, and collections that have provided the basis for this analysis. What Barbara Herrnstein Smith says of American critical theory applies with much greater urgency in the field of Canadian theatre studies to a discourse that has been so long concerned with the construction of a national identity, a theatrical tradition, and a respectable body of criticism, that is has 'painted itself out of the picture':

Beguiled by the humanist's fantasy of transcendence, endurance, and universality, it has been unable to acknowledge the most fundamental character of literary value, which is its mutability and diversity. And, at the same time, magnetized by the goals and ideology of a naive scientism ... obsessed by a misplaced quest for 'objectivity,' and confined ... by the narrow intellectual traditions and professional allegiances of the literary academy, it has foreclosed from its own domain the possibility of investigating the dynamics of that mutability and understanding the nature of that diversity.

Smith goes on to call for an enquiry that 'would consist, at any given time, of a set of heterogeneous projects,' one whose 'conceptual structures and methodological practices' would be historically and otherwise contingent, and which would produce analyses whose value would be 'a function of how well they made intelligible the phenomena within their domain to whoever, at whatever time and from whatever perspective, had an interest in them.'[84]

The result of such a critical inquiry would be to amplify and encourage those marginalized but vibrant voices of 'ex-centricity' that make theatre-going in Canada both exciting and disruptive, while introducing new theatrical forms and new ways of seeing; to provide places and positions from which non-generic spectators might experience and even enjoy theatre without surrendering their deviance from an implied hegemonic social norm; and finally to undermine the very will to consensus and drive towards identity that underly the concept of a developing Canadian theatrical repertoire and stable dramatic canon.

LUCIE ROBERT

The New Quebec Theatre

translated by David Homel

The first problem we encounter in a discussion about literary canon is how to identify it. Which canon do we mean? Where is it to be found? Who defines it? Is it unique or various? Two traditions come into conflict here: the Anglo-Saxon tradition, which mainly sees the canon as an anthology, a collection of texts; and the French tradition, which considers it more as a 'socializing system,' a way of reading texts which transforms it, in the practice of teaching, into a manual of literary history. In this latter way of seeing things, the canon really designates the body of discussion and polemic that created and justified it, the collective procedures that transitively constitute it – or continue to question it – rather than the result of a selection process, a corpus of texts that can be said to be 'canonical.' The French tradition in literary studies prefers the notion of an institution to that of a canon. This way, as well as considering texts, we can attend to the process of their social recognition, as well as the coercive or normative effect exercised back onto writing.[1]

This study looks into the 'new Quebec theatre,' an expression borrowed from Michel Bélair, who used it as a title for his 1973 book, *Le Nouveau Théâtre québécois*.[2] Bélair chose the expression to define a kind of independent theatre, in opposition to 'French-Canadian' theatre, though situated in its traditions, a theatre designed to combat the myth of 'high' theatre used by repertory companies and public bodies. This theatre, argues Bélair, came into being when Michel Tremblay's *Les Belles-Soeurs* was created in 1968. According to Bélair, it is characterized by a purified theatrical space and a 'poor' aesthetic. It brings together

three important currents: a popular or populist tendency, best represented by Tremblay's work; a political tendency, expressed by the
Théâtre du Même Nom (a troupe whose name is both a pun on the
sameness of theatrical forms, be they classical or experimental, and a
satirical joke using the initials of the Théâtre du Nouveau Monde, the
most prestigious Montreal company); and a 'fable' tendency, used to
describe the work of the Grand Cirque ordinaire. The problem Bélair
was addressing in his polemical book was the institutional recognition
of this 'new Quebec theatre.'

A participant in the reality he sought to describe and a journalist
who would soon quit the post of theatre critic at *Le Devoir* because
there was no 'national' theatre to comment on – at least that was his
official reason – Bélair displayed true historical understanding in his
grasp of a double canon in Quebec theatre history: a 'Canadian' and a
québécois one, both existing simultaneously, the first receiving generous
grants and oriented towards performing a repertory in concert with
classical theatrical aesthetics; the second poor and marginal, devoted
to creation and tied into 'combat' aesthetics. What interests me here is
the history of his latter canon, of its emergence and institution as a
national theatre. This presupposes the study of the plays that constitute
it, of the methods used to bring them to the stage, and of the criticism
and cultural policies involved. We will observe the institution of a
'young theatre,' in the shadow of more classical theatrical activity,
which will seek to become a tool to fight 'high' theatre; then, later, we
will see its recognition as a dominant aesthetic code with, as a corollary,
its depoliticization. This is obviously an immense task; we will be
sketching out only the broad lines of this process.

If we want to truly understand the phenomenon's importance, we
must not forget that during the 1950s and early 1960s there had been
a 'Canadianization' of culture in general and theatre in particular.
The driving forces behind this movement were the philosophies and
policies put forward by the Royal Commission on National Development in the Arts, Letters, and Sciences in Canada – the Massey Commission. The Commission submitted its report in 1951, and its
recommendations led to the creation of the Canada Council in 1957.
In Quebec this Canadianization took several forms. At the start, there
was a 'French-Canadian' face, supported by the efforts of three levels
of government. In 1954 the Quebec government created a 'Dramatic
Arts' section in the Conservatoire du Québec, handing over the reins
to Jean Doat. In 1957, for the first time, it gave financial aid to a theatre
group: the Comédie canadienne, headed up by Gratien Gélinas. That

same year, acting on a recommendation from Mayor Jean Drapeau, the City of Montreal created the Conseil des arts métropolitain, whose mandate was to help the performing arts. The 1960 opening of the National Theatre School of Canada, under the direction of Jean Gascon, underscored the federal government's involvement in the cultural sector. And in 1961 Quebec created a ministry of cultural affairs.

Yet these policies were designed to spread 'high culture' of French or British origin throughout Canada, rather than to encourage original, home-grown culture. This explains why cultural policies at the time placed so much importance on training actors in specialized schools, usually under the direction of European-bred maestros. It also explains the massive expenditures for building halls and arts centres, with one government pitted against the other. This kind of investment hit its high point during the celebrations of the centenary of Canadian Confederation, which witnessed the construction of Montreal's Place des Arts, the National Arts Centre in Ottawa, Le Grand Théâtre in Quebec City, cultural centres scattered throughout the regions, and halls belonging to educational institutions, especially colleges and universities.[3]

The situation of the theatrical creator, especially the playwright, was a precarious one. 'Writers for the stage,' Laurent Mailhot pointed out, 'were often novelists and poets: Eloi de Grandmont, Yves Thériault, Anne Hébert. Their texts were read – when they were read – in the context of an overall body of literary work, or of a dimly defined cultural institution.'[4] Seen primarily as works of literary art, home-grown theatre texts were not specifically oriented towards the stage (or if they were, then only by chance), but rather, towards publication as books. Critics rejoiced over certain texts whose writing they considered impeccable, even if they were unplayable. Since no troupes were interested, most theatrical writing ended up on the radio. Hence, the creation during the 1950s of shows like 'Le Théâtre populaire' and 'Nouveautés dramatiques.' Play-writing contests became a regular feature.

It should come as no surprise, then, that young creative groups were outraged by the fate of works that featured enquiry and experimentation. This reaction was felt all across the country: 'Canada was beginning to develop an alternate theatrical model of official culture (Stratford being the prime example in English Canada; Théâtre du Nouveau Monde in Quebec),' observes Don Rubin, commenting upon his years as the *Toronto Star*'s theatre critic. He adds, 'In other cultures, "alternate" tended to mean experiments in form or language; in Canada, "alternate theatre" came simply to be associated with the production of work either collectively created or full-scripted by "Canadian" authors. And "Canadian" was the key.'[5] In Quebec this process was never identified as 'Canadian.' On the contrary. For this generation of young playwrights and actors who identified with a nationalist movement that was becoming ever more independence-minded, 'Canada,' even 'French Canada,' meant, on one hand, the conservative, clerical forces of the past, accused of having left Quebec in poverty and ignorance, and, on the other hand, that generation of Quebec politicians who, in Quebec City and Ottawa, conceived of a Canadian Confederation in a traditional way: men like Pierre Elliott Trudeau, Jean Marchand, Gérard Pelletier, and Jean Lesage.

A two-part process began that was itself based on two centres of interest: first, the specification of a *québécois* identity, distinct from the French, Canadian, or even French-Canadian ones, and second, the specification of a theatrical identity, breaking away from the literary *per se*, especially the literary forms adopted by the repertory of 'high' theatre, forms identified, rightly or wrongly, with minority French-Canadian culture, something almost Third World, and condemned to stay that way forever. The push for autonomy affected simultaneously all components of the theatre: political, cultural, and institutional.

The year 1965 was a crucial one. In February 1965 Quebec's minister of cultural affairs, Pierre Laporte, announced the creation of a Commission de la pièce canadienne (Canadian Play Commission), accompanied by a contest, with the goal of setting down an official catalogue of original plays and creating a general repertory of Quebec theatre. A little later, in the spring, a group of playwrights, including Robert Gurik, Jean Morin, Robert Gauthier, Denys Saint-Denis, and Jacques Duchesne, founded the Centre d'essai des auteurs dramatiques (the Playwrights' Collective), which was to act as both a service organization and a professional association, with two areas of activity: ensuring the development, distribution, and promotion of Quebec plays, and representing Quebec playwrights as cultural workers. That same year, the Festival d'art dramatique canadien (or Dominion Drama Festival) devoted itself entirely to the works of Quebec authors. However, at that same festival a jury unanimously refused to accept a text because of the particular language it used: that was Michel Tremblay's *Les Belles-Soeurs*. The jury members, commented Michel Bélair, were haunted by 'the three myths of High Theatre, High Companies, and High Actors.'[6]

Imposed from above, like the selection of a French-language, Cana-

dian theatre canon, the Commission de la pièce canadienne was a
failure. It disappeared after a short existence (barely two years) without
having accomplished its mandate. The Festival d'art dramatique canadien lived out its last years this way, too. It survived long enough
to see young, experimental, specifically *québécois* plays solidify their
position. On the other hand, the Centre d'essai des auteurs dramatiques, a grass-roots organization created by playwrights themselves,
'both a sign and an agent of change,' as Laurent Mailhot put it,[7] rapidly
attained its first goals and in a few years set up the programs that
assured its success: 'through play-readings and round tables, it became
the pivotal place where new Quebec play-writing got its hold.'[8] We all
know the galvanizing effect of the public reading of Michel Tremblay's
Les Belles-Soeurs on 4 March 1968, which led to the play being staged
at the Théâtre du Rideau-Vert the following August 28, and the publication of the text in the Centre's play series, 'Théâtre vivant.'

Writers for the stage were the first ones to transform the canon by
trying to develop a specifically theatrical language. So many people
have been so sure that *joual* is Quebec's true popular language –
without paying any attention to the regional variations, and even less
to the literary situation in which it is used – that, at the present time,
there is no study of its theatrical formation, composition, or use. Yet
the debate on a literary language specific to Quebec is not new. We
can go back to the nineteenth century and the writings of the poet
Octave Crémazie to find meditations on the constraints on Quebec
writers created by the French language. The attempt to base a literary
language on spoken speech in order to create a popular, 'dialect'
effect is also not new. During the 1930s poet Emile Coderre, using the
pseudonym Jean Narrache, published two collections, *Quand j'parl' tout
seul* (1932) and *J'parl' pour parler* (1939). Reissued in 1961 as *J'parle tout
seul quand Jean Narrache*, Coderre's poems are part of the linguistic
explorations of the group which published the magazine *Parti pris*.
They raised *joual* to the status of a national language, notably through
the publication of Jacques Renaud's novella *Le Cassé* (1964) and Gérald
Godin's poetry collection *Les Cantouques* (1966). Although *joual* had
been used by Eloi de Grandmont in his adaptation of George Bernard
Shaw's *Pygmalion* for the Théâtre du Nouveau Monde in the 1950s, it
did not become a dramatic language until later.

Joual was first refined and readied as a literary language on the stage,
and its fiercest opponents were to be found among theatre critics. 'In
France, the theatre uses written, not spoken, language,' explained
Bernard Dort, commenting on Quebec play-writing and seeing in written language 'one of the problems of French theatre in the twentieth

century.'⁹ Young *québécois* playwrights found their inspiration in spoken language, yet they wanted to turn it into writing and give it graphic representation and a space. '*Joual* isn't used as a dialect or patois, but as dramatic language, either comic, tragic, grotesque, critical, or lyrical, to create the effect of the real, of action and recognition,' wrote Laurent Mailhot.¹⁰ In fact, the very originality of *joual* is to be found, paradoxically perhaps, in its written transcription. Playwrights sought to record spoken language and give written language a theatricality, to write voice into text, to give it movement and breath. Popular language was used to create collective recognition, a sense of identification that would destroy standards of both language and literature, and make any form of Canadian-style bilingualism impossible. Such was the satirical message of Jean-Claude Germain's text *A Canadian Play / Une Plaie canadienne*.

The acceptance of *joual* as a dramatic language was not always easy. Every production of a play by Michel Tremblay was greeted by a storm of controversy in the press. Though it might seem to us today that the Saturnalian aspects of Tremblay's work and the role in it of women and homosexuals are more daring than the language, it was the latter element that was criticized most harshly. One particular episode sums up the collision of two aesthetic codes. In 1972 Jean-Louis Barrault, director of the Théâtre des Nations, received authorization from the Rideau-Vert to stage *Les Belles-Soeurs* in Paris, but the Quebec and Canadian governments refused to give the production any funding. Eighty-three Quebec artists protested to Secretary of State Mitchell Sharpe, who finally approved the grant. Claire Kirkland-Casgrain, however, minister of cultural affairs in Quebec, would not change her position. Instead, she earned the anger of the theatre community by expressing her admiration for a play by novelist Claire Martin, a play 'written in French.' In November 1973 the Parisian public applauded Tremblay's play enthusiastically, catching the minister in her own trap and putting an end to the issue. The following year, the Quebec and Ottawa governments began giving financial support to young theatre groups. But not the City of Montreal, which long remained closed to the innovations in language and cultural 'unpleasantness' so common to experimental theatre. The city even reverted to censorship, notably in the case of Denise Boucher's 1978 play, *Les Fées ont soif*.

This last example is a key one since it concerns a feminist text. Within the same general movement, though working in its own dissidence, feminist theatre also contributed to the formulation of a new dramatic language, expressing women's reality and demanding the transformation of language and the break-up of genres. Where feminism and *joual* meet – the exact location of Denise Boucher's play – is where the new theatre was attacked most violently.

In their attempt to theatricalize the text, young playwrights challenged classical aesthetics within the text of the play itself. Besides creating a dramatic language, these texts also presented the literary canon in a kind of on-stage theatrical critique, a literary critique at the theatre. Playwrights undertook to theatricalize literary tradition using the methods of translation and parody, as Annie Brisset has shown in her studies. This operation can take several forms. One is through titles (*Manon Lastcall, Emile et une nuit, L'Alphonse fait à Marie*), whereby works of the French literary canon are mocked, without the work itself being used elsewhere in the text. 'The Québécois work rests on the fame of the foreign masterpiece not only by way of identification and equation, but also by way of antithesis: the classic becomes an object of derision to the audience of the new play as it appears invalid or "outdated" in the sense that it has become an inappropriate vehicle for the expression of *la québécitude* of the Québécois status.'[11] Mocking adaptations and translations (examples are *Le Cid maghané* by Réjean Ducharme and *Hamlet, Prince du Québec* by Robert Gurik) work to distance the canonical text by using *joual* as the audience's shared language, a referential displacement which gives texts a local, contemporary feel. The result is a feeling of distance towards high culture, itself an object of parody, and towards literature, which is oralized and made into theatre.

This distancing also found expression in the 1969 production of Jean-Claude Germain's *Les Enfants de Chénier dans un grand spectacle d'adieu* at the Théâtre d'Aujourd'hui. In this important play, the actors/characters bid farewell to classical theatre on-stage. When it comes to the new theatre, Jean-Claude Germain's importance cannot be overestimated. A critic, organizer, author, theatre director, and teacher, he was also executive secretary of the Centre d'essai des auteurs dramatiques from 1968 to 1971, founder of the Théâtre du Même Nom in 1969, and general director of the Théâtre d'Aujourd'hui, the only group devoted exclusively to theatrical creation, from 1973 to 1982.

Publishing was an important part of this new theatre. Whereas the playwrights of the 1950s and 1960s had to settle for the crumbs tossed their way by publishers, or publish in periodicals like *Ecrits du Canada français*, the new generation of authors could count on reaching the public through book form, as well as meeting producers and directors through the Centre d'essai des auteurs dramatiques. Although the Centre, in its magazine *Théâtre vivant* and play series of the same name, published only a few titles, it nonetheless did give the public the chance to read new plays which would have otherwise gone unpublished. In 1968, following this lead, Leméac began the 'Théâtre canadien' collection, followed, a few years later, by two more collections: 'Répertoire québécois' and 'Théâtre acadien.'

Few critics have commented on this triple identity at the Leméac publishing house. The 'Théâtre acadien' collection was actually made up of a single author, Antonine Maillet, and was the corollary of a collection specified as 'québécois.' Acadia was finding its own identity at the same time as Quebec, also in opposition to what had been called 'French Canada.' What interests me here is the simultaneous existence, within the same publishing house, of a *québécois* and a Canadian collection. Readers who remember the 'Théâtre canadien' collection will recall that it was printed on high-quality paper, with illustrations, and with a critical apparatus that included a substantial introduction and the record of press clippings. On the other hand, the 'Répertoire québécois' was a small-format collection, printed on cheap paper, most often without any presentation or introduction. In a stinging article published in 1974, Denis Saint-Jacques pointed out that Quebec playwriting weighed in on an average at only seventy-five pages, while the Canadian collection enjoyed more than one hundred pages. He mockingly remarked that pure verbiage must be filling up all that Canadian space.[12] The double canon was what set apart the two Leméac collections. Denis Saint-Jacques's article appeared in 1974, just as the new theatre was coming into its own, and the two-sided repertory at Leméac soon disappeared. The 'Répertoire' collection was terminated, and the adjective after the word *Théâtre* in the other series was dropped. In 1970 the publishing house launched a collection called 'Traduction et adaptation,' featuring translations and adaptations made in Quebec, thereby recognizing the legitimacy of *québécois* translation, which until then had been neglected.

Despite the work done in this area, critics and commentators alike still spoke of 'the death of the text.'[13] Questioning the literarity of theatre challenged the text itself and, as a corollary, the author. 'Collective creation,' the form that best translated this concern, became more popular. Between 1965 and 1974 there were some 4,720 stagings of some 415 collective creations presented by 1,100 different actors and actresses, reaching approximately 1 million people not generally part of the professional theatre scene.[14] In its strict sense, collective creation as a theatrical form challenges traditional hierarchy. It is called 'collective,' not so much because everyone does everything there is to do, but because every person can do it; non-hierarchical relations also eliminate the directors' and authors' traditional 'authority' over the actors. This type of theatre is founded exclusively on new creations – to revert to a repertory presupposes respect for the authorial world – and each individual can contribute to the text as well as to visual aspects. Sometimes, one person is given the responsibility of writing down the final version of the play or preparing it for publication; in this case, the text is attributed to him or her. This is what happened with most of Jean-Claude Germain's plays. The creative work resides in a popular aesthetics which challenges the division of theatrical work, as well as theatre's social function. There is always a certain hesitation as to its fealty; is it above all theatre, or should it be serving the people instead?

Collective creation is historically important in Quebec theatre because it was linked to the emergence of a new generation of creators who were to play, as Gilbert David put it, the role of 'accelerator for particles of drama and scene.'[15] This generation was trained in the new drama programs added by colleges (called CEGEPs in Quebec) and universities to those of the currently existing schools (the conservatories and the National Theatre School). The theatre major program at the Lionel-Groulx CEGEP was launched in 1968; the Saint-Hyacinthe CEGEP followed a year later. The Université Laval, the Université de Montréal, and the Université du Québec à Chicoutimi offered minors in theatre. Specialized BA programs at the Université du Québec à Montréal and the Université de Sherbrooke were begun in 1969 and 1970 respectively. These programs were entirely divorced from literary studies, and so contributed strongly to the emergence and practice of a specifically theatrical aesthetics. In addition, job creation programs started by the federal and provincial governments – the 'Youth Perspectives' program, the Local Initiatives Projects (LIP), and those of the Youth and Leisure Commission of Quebec (known as the Haut Commissariat à la jeunesse et aux loisirs du Québec) – as well as programs involving student theatre from the Quebec ministry of education, made a variety of adventures in theatre possible and gave professional or semi-professional footing to groups that granting programs would have never recognized otherwise.

Young theatre groups were often labelled as semi-professional, not to belittle the quality of their work, but to refer to their precarious financial situation. Soon these groups began to organize. In 1972 AQJT (Association québécoise de jeune théâtre) replaced ACTA (Association canadienne de théâtre amateur), the latter being more interested in theatre as recreation outside the realm of the professional. The foundation of ACTA in 1958 had been the flip side of the consolidation of professional theatre, creating a parallel 'leisure-time' theatre with a recognized teaching and training function. A conflict between amateur and experimental theatre had a way of breaking out during festival times. During the 1950s and 1960s, experimental groups like Estoc, Mouvement contemporain, Apprentis-Sorciers, and Saltimbanques had been able to exist under ACTA's auspices because of their acceptance of the repertory (even if it was 'absurd') and their classically hierarchical ways of working. But the twin labels of 'Canadian' and 'amateur' soon became unbearable for the young theatre.

The groups which formed the Association québécoise du jeune théâtre were active in popular theatre, and their involvement with their milieu led them into political theatre. They favoured both the decentralization of theatre towards the regions (the Gens d'en bas set up shop in the Gaspé, and the Parminou took up residence in the Bois-Francs region) and the distribution of work along collective lines. These preferences soon brought them into conflict with the ruling political powers, which supported centralization of the theatre and the organizations representing it in Montreal and Quebec City, and the locating of major groups in the cities – exactly one group per city. Despite protests from the Confederation of National Trade Unions (CNTU) and the Union des artistes, the Ministry of Education thought nothing of sacrificing the Estoc, one of the best groups in Quebec City, as well as other regional companies, in order to create a prestige troupe – the Trident – as part of Le Grand Théâtre de Québec.

With the passing of time, the AQJT became radicalized. The popular, fiercely nationalist brand of theatre (the Grand Cirque ordinaire, founded in 1967, is a perfect example) slowly gave way to a young militant theatre linked to far-left causes, such as the Théâtre Euh!, founded in 1970. At the same time, every group was being tested within by the emergence of feminist concerns. The Grand Cirque ordinaire featured an autonomous women's cell for one of its shows, *Un prince mon jour viendra*. The Théâtre expérimental des femmes was born of a schism within the Théâtre expérimental de Montréal. Soon, feminist theatre was creating its own groups and ways of working.

During the first half of the 1970s, the AQJT was torn apart by internal strife, which came to a head in 1975 with a new schism and a manifesto signed by the left-wing and non-conformist troupes. This was the point of no return in the history of new theatre, as certain groups challenged the legitimacy of theatre itself as a cultural practice separated from political life. In North America, this philosophy could only lead down a path where theatre as an aesthetic practice disappears. Some troupes chose this path; notably, the Théâtre Parminou from the Bois-Francs region. The Parminou did not suffer the influence of theatrical currents across the rest of the province nor did it influence them. It was organized along cooperative lines; for instance, all members, including children, received the same salary. This group, which has consistently refused to favour art over politics, continues to produce highly political theatre from a working-class perspective and maintains strong links to Quebec political life. It offers its shows to unions and community groups, for such events as International Women's Day or May Day, and will accept commissions concerning the issue of the hour.

The work of most of these troupes coincided with what playwrights were doing. Even the titles of the two most representative collective creations of the time, *T'es pas tannée, Jeanne d'Arc?* (Grand Cirque ordinaire) and *Cré Antigone!* (Théâtre Euh!), questioned the relation that should be maintained with European literary and stage traditions. The Ligue nationale d'improvisation, which Robert Gravel first developed at the Théâtre populaire d'Alma in 1971, displays another dimension of theatrical creation during these years. Borrowing its rules from hockey, the improvisation league challenges the theatre in two ways: by presenting the theatricality inherent in all performing arts – sports, the circus, dance, to name but a few – and by making theatre into pure performance without any text. Playwrights had already attempted this kind of experiment, though in lesser measure, most notably Claude Levac and Françoise Loranger in *Chemin du roy*. At issue were the borders of a theatre free of literature and seeking other models – or anti-models – for self-definition.

The last phase of the institutionalization of the 'new Quebec theatre' involves theory-building and its co-option into a code of knowledge transmittable in the classroom. The canon has no existence except through pedagogy even if, in order to recognize it, we must return to the process of its creation by the practitioners themselves. In a 1975 article, Laurent Mailhot deplored the lack of historical and theoretical thinking about Quebec theatre, pointing out our dependence on French theory. 'If Parisian journals and Vincennes professors had dissected the poetics of theatre as brilliantly as they had the poetics of narrative, the Quebec critical apparatus would have probably followed their lead, in this area as in others.'[16] As if to spite him, the following years saw the creation of the journal *Jeu* (1976), the Société d'histoire du théâtre au Québec (1978), and the Association québécoise des critiques de théâtre (1984). Playwrights in the young theatre were working to create a specifically *québécois* theatre free from literature, and their work was echoed by the founding of professional organizations which were separate from both literary associations in Quebec and their Canadian counterparts. The creation of advanced programs of theatre study in some Quebec universities meant that this new vision would be passed on and enriched through research.

It was as if we were witnessing the end of an era when Marc Doré from the Théâtre Euh! (founded 1970) and Raymond Cloutier from the Grand Cirque ordinaire (1969), the two troupes most representative in their own ways of the 1965–75 period, were named director of the Quebec City Conservatoire d'art dramatique and director of the National Theatre School in Montreal respectively. We had the same feeling when in 1986 the AQJT became the AQTA, the Association québécoise de théâtre amateur. This corresponded to a new division between amateur and professional theatre, which was confirmed by a conference of 'Les Etats généraux du théâtre professionel' in 1981, and the subsequent birth of the Conseil québécois du théâtre. The feeling became stronger still when the publishing house Herbes rouges began a new theatre collection. A note from series editor Gilbert David at the beginning of every work pointed out that spelling and text presentation had been standardized according to the norms of the French language. The epic period of new Quebec theatre was a thing of the past.

Yet these three events tell us something important: this theatrical revolution is irreversible. Each theatre school, in its pedagogy and its programs, is shaped by its director. The amateur theatre association is still 'québécoise,' in name as in fact. Though standardized for written presentation, dramatic language remains totally theatrical. Quebec plays retain true originality and interest, even in the 'straight' theatres that have made them part of their repertory.

Yet, paradoxically, this is the time playwrights are choosing to return to a more stylized way of writing. The recent work of Michel Garneau, Normand Chaurette, René-Daniel Dubois, and Jovette Marchessault, to name but a few, has moved towards the classical. The major theatre events of the 1980s have revolved around texts by Shakespeare, Claudel, Racine, and Corneille. The 'new Quebec theatre' was ceased to be new. It has become canonical, attained hegemony. In the comfort in which it now resides, no one knows where the next surprise will come from.

Critical Instincts in Quebec: From the Quiet Revolution to the Postmodern Age, 1960–1990

An examination of the founding texts that shaped Québécois criticism, and of the different ways these texts have been used, is a culturally revealing process. A culture says a lot about itself by telling us whom it trusts. While I do not believe any culture can ever be homogeneous, I remain convinced that a culture is grounded in a repertoire of textual examples at different moments of its history. Anglo-American literary cultures refer to this repertoire as the canon; West Europeans in general and francophones specifically prefer to describe it in terms of institutional processes or legitimizing procedures. Over the last two decades the writings of Michel Foucault, Pierre Bourdieu, and Pierre Macherey have helped us understand that the repertoire embodies certain forms of knowledge which have particular conditions for their existence.

The differences between the Anglo-American concept of canonization and the French definition of legitimization may seem negligible when one considers the effect of these concepts, but they are still significant in terms of their cultural premises. Roland Barthes noted that critics do not produce truths but validities or ratifications of the cultures or institutions they choose to support.[1] Such authentications may also provide a means of linking individual works to the different discourses comprising a specific culture.

Barthes's observations have influenced several Anglo-American critics, as is apparent to anyone who has followed the debate prompted by the 1982 publication of Peter Widdowson's collection of essays entitled *Re-Reading English* and continued by W. Lawrence Hogue in *Discourse and the Other* (1986). Peter Hyland identifies a central issue in the debate when he notes that it was not simply a question of rejecting the notion of value held by Leavis and his followers but also one of re-examining 'what has been judged as to be central and what marginal and whether such judgments should be really accepted as absolute.'[2]

In francophone analyses of the repertoire, the notion of what is 'central' is traditionally grounded in a cultural framework, though I should be careful to add that culture should be taken here in its broadest sense. For the structuralists of the 1950s and early 1960s, culture was primarily a linguistic construct, and history had to be understood as a form of textual representation rather than as any expression of an ontological reality. Such reminders are useful when one comes to examine Quebec criticism. Important trends in this criticism appear in the excellent collection entitled *L'Essai et la prose d'idées au Québec* (1985). These essays remind us that criticism in Quebec is historically grounded in cultural determinants. I do not mean to suggest that late nineteenth- or early twentieth-century essayists were all crypto-structuralists but only that such early critics as L'Abbé Casgrain or Camille Roy had strong ties to their culture and history. Each of their essays was as much a judgment on the social fabric of their times as an analysis of literary texts. History – both as social history and as a sequence of political events – was never to be disposed of lightly.

The founders of French-Canadian criticism – Casgrain and Roy – had strong links with Parisian luminaries and academic theoreticians such as Gustave Lanson, Emile Faguet, and Ferdinand Brunetière, yet their personal agendas as essayists had nothing in common with these Sorbonne practitioners. Both Casgrain and Roy had a mission: to found a national literature. When Casgrain writes that 'notre littérature sera nationale ou elle ne sera pas,'[3] he is both programmatic and moralistic; nevertheless, his nationalist views anticipated many of the values that would appear in later criticism.

The period I want to examine is both far removed from Casgrain's times and still unambiguously linked to them; methodological legacies cannot be disposed of lightly. In more than one way, Jacques Godbout takes stock of these legacies and of the Québécois obsession with history as a paradigm when he confesses: 'From the Conquest on we have tried to cure ourselves through the word – be it literarily, religiously or politically. Through discourse. We chose to lie down on History's couch and repeat the same narrative. We tried to occupy a geography through words.'[4]

The period under scrutiny lies between the Quiet Revolution and the postmodern age. The first boundary has been abundantly defined by social historians and scientists; it is generally agreed that it commences around the time of Maurice Duplessis's death.[5] The beginning of the postmodern age requires more scrutiny because there is no consensus among historians, philosophers, critics, and art historians as to what postmodernism is. However, it is still possible to agree that the intellectual maps of European and North American thought, since the late 1960s, have been deeply modified by feminist theory and feminist critical practice and by deconstructionist and post-structuralist problematics. Postmodernism is very much a product of such epistemological questioning. It is indebted not only to French philosophers Jacques Derrida, Jean-François Lyotard, and Michel Foucault but also to the Yale school of deconstructionism (Barbara Johnson, Paul de Man, Geoffrey Hartman), and even more significantly to the critical theories of various feminists (Catherine Belsey, Toril Moi, and Susan Suleiman figure prominently in this context). In short, the intellectual landscape has been transformed by the theories and practices of these thinkers. Postmodernism still is very much a product of Western thought and while its impact on Quebec culture has not yet been fully assessed, Quebec artists and writers have been strongly affected by it.[6]

I am concerned with two questions about the literature produced during the period described above: which critical texts contributed to the institutionalization of specific methodologies and to the exclusion of others? Which theoretical sources did these critics consciously or unconsciously draw from?

As a result of the Quiet Revolution, a secular wind blew over academic institutions and transformed the ecclesiastical and moralistic apparatus that had defined so many legitimizing processes of the founding fathers, including the explicit censorship of the Duplessis era (he was in power from 1936 to 1959, except for the brief interlude of the war years). Two critics writing during the 1960s were influential in their determination to assess their critical culture. They were Gilles Marcotte and Jean-Charles Falardeau. In *Une littérature qui se fait* (1962) and *Présence de la critique: Critique et littérature contemporaine au Canada français* (1966), Marcotte took stock of the critical scene and lamented the lack of authority granted to the critical essay as a form. The main weakness in the prevailing criticism, according to Marcotte, stemmed from the absence of Barthesian qualities of 'un langage personnel et une vision du monde.'[7] It would be tempting to suggest to Marcotte that the excesses of the founding fathers (whose bardic tones were still resonating in many ears) may have made such cautiousness understandable. Jean-Charles Falardeau echoed Marcotte's dissatisfaction.

As a social scientist and a critic, Falardeau argued that the period 1960–74 was defined by critics who had no global vision. Only two critics writing during this time escaped Falardeau's critique: Jean-Louis Major, who contributed an excellent essay on the novelist André Langevin; and Jean Robidoux, who published an essay on the French-Canadian novel. Both appeared in the same volume of *Archives des lettres canadiennes françaises* (1964), a publication from the University of Ottawa which was very much a product both of its times and of the particular kind of intelligentsia in charge of it (academics rather than journalists, polemicists, or men of the cloth). What Falardeau was pleading for in his 1974 collection of essays, *Notre Société et son roman*, was serious scholarship, academic commitment. Falardeau's plea mirrored the critical concerns of his time.

Retrospectively, the 1960s turn out to be doubly interesting. As Jean Fisette has demonstrated in a perceptive essay,[8] that decade witnessed the complex encounter of two opposing schools of thought. The first was the functionalist and rationalist discourse of *Cité libre*, a learned journal whose prominence was due in part to the active participation of Pierre Elliott Trudeau, then theoretician and political scientist. During the 1950s *Cité libre* argued for a functionalist space for Quebec politics and for a new discourse for French Canada, one appropriate to a modern, advanced, capitalist democracy that remained respectful of religious cultural traditions, but resolutely turned its back on the ultramontane authoritarianism which had flourished during the latter part of the nineteenth century. In a way, *Cité libre*'s writers were not only addressing their literary forebears (Casgrain and Roy), but also obliquely undermining more recent discourses, those of corporatist 1930s French Canada, including that of the influential historian and man of letters, Lionel Groulx.

The second form of critical discourse manifested itself in the nationalist discourses articulated by L'Hexagone, *Liberté*, and *Parti pris*. The first two were primarily focused on language and nationalistic issues, while the third took on more overtly political tones in which Marxism and decolonization theories were central. *Liberté* and *Parti pris* articulated theories which conflicted not only with those previously put forward by their predecessor, *Cité libre*, but also with those which European structuralism in general, and its Gallic variety in particular, had helped produce. Fisette demonstrates that by the mid-1960s – a time when structuralism was flourishing in Europe but barely reaching North American shores – its triple negation (that of the subject, history, and referent) conflicted with the cultural expectations of a society in which a new discourse on history, selfhood, cultural identity, and the 'nation subject'⁹ had begun to emerge. One only needs to peruse the writings of Jacques Godbout and Pierre Vadeboncoeur in *Liberté*, or of Paul Chamberland, Pierre Maheu, and Gérald Godin in *Parti pris*, to take the pulse of the 1960s.

What emerges during the period is a dialectical movement between imported structuralism, on the one hand, and a separatist, historicist, Marxist-inspired discourse on the other. The movement is matched by the distinction between *Cité libre* and the younger ideologues of *Liberté*, between a rational state and a utopian one. Fisette skilfully interprets this dialectical encounter by pointing out that the structuralist canon could only establish itself in Quebec when the effects of the Quiet Revolution had eased away – when both *Cité libre* (a product of the late 1950s and early 1960s) and *Parti pris* (which mirrored the mid-1960s) had ceased to hold power in the intellectual market. Such an easing characterizes the 1970s with younger critics well grounded in structuralist skills (Jean Fisette, Pierre Nepveu, Jean-Louis Major, and Jacques Michon) taking an interest in texts that challenged textual, political, and syntactical order, those which consciously or unconsciously expressed a liberationist philosophy. The conflicts which emerged between an imported canon and the cultural expressions of its *langue d'accueil* turned out to be creatively utilized in the end. Quebec's answer to structuralism – cultural semiotics – became its canon of the 1970s. This canon endorsed the recognition of literary history as a constant hermeneutical theory in Quebec. In other words, history as an explanatory paradigm continued to flourish in academic institutions right through the 1970s. Yet, throughout the decade, the pressure exerted by cultural semiotics (in the writings of Iouri Lotman, Pierre Macherey, and Umberto Eco) continued to effect a rapid change in the situation. The young ideologues of *Parti pris*, André Brochu most notably, have matured and grounded their political analyses in textual semiotics.

Two critics' names keep recurring throughout the period: Gilles Marcotte and André Brochu. Marcotte published *Le Roman à l'imparfait* (1976) and with Brochu the brilliant epistolary exchange in *La Littérature et le reste* (1980), which presents twenty-four letters on matters ranging from sports to politics but which is focused primarily on literature. The volume provides an excellent portrait of Quebec criticism taken by two of its best-known practitioners. Marcotte observes that while Quebec writers were calling for an independent Quebec, the very structure of their works was undermining this possibility: because they could not shape history; history had shaped them.

In Quebec the concept of genre underwent serious upheavals during the three decades under examination, but none was as noticeable as that affecting criticism. The binary strategy (reader/text) set by traditional hermeneutics was transformed: complicity replaced critical distance. While the background of these transformations was woven by Bakhtinian intertextual perspectives, whereby a text always converses with many others, including history as text, it was feminist thought during the 1970s which expanded such theory much beyond its initial systemic topos. *Gynocritics/La Gynocritique* (1985), a collection of essays edited by Barbara Godard, eloquently foregrounds these expectations and summarizes ensuing critical developments in both Canadas.

When one focuses on Quebec literary culture during the late 1970s and early 1980s, the relevance of post-structuralist skills needs to be acknowledged. But one needs also to recognize the preponderance of European feminist theoreticians on Quebec's critical scene. Luce Irigaray's *Speculum de l'autre femme* (1974), *Ce Sexe qui n'en est pas un* (1977), *Et l'une ne bouge pas sans l'autre* (1979), as well as Hélène Cixous's *La Venue à l'écriture* (1977), *Partie* (1976), and *With ou l'art de l'innocence* (1981) are texts that had a strong impact on a whole generation of writers from the feminists publishing in *La Nouvelle Barre du jour* to the neo-Marxists gravitating around *Les Herbes rouges*. As well, Irigaray and Cixous gave numerous seminars in Montreal; one of Irigaray's books was published in Montreal as the product of such dialogues with Quebec feminists and psychoanalysts;[10] and Cixous published *La Venue à l'écriture* with another prominent Quebec writer (Madeleine Gagnon) – all indications of an extraordinary exchange of energies and ideas between the two sides of the Atlantic during this period.

During the 1980s two critics loomed over the nexus of such exchanges to greet the demise of the great narratives announced in François Lyotard's *La Condition postmoderne* (1979). They are Philippe Haeck and the late Suzanne Lamy. Feminism and the female subject are high priorities for Lamy. The act of locating both his culture and his psyche in someone else's imagination is important to Haeck. Elective affinities bind them to feminist and phenomenological theory. But it would be reductive to read their interpretations only in that light. Both Haeck and Lamy are sketching a personal and participatory quest. The difference between them and the preceding generations (historicists, nationalists, structuralists, and semioticians alike) is that they are not setting up interpretative skills, waving banners, or establishing the foundations of a scholarly process (they could not care less about Marcotte's and Falardeau's laments). They are not part of the institution, and its overall programming does not concern them. They are not attacking traditional, academic criticism (of either Marcotte's or Brochu's vintage); they are setting it aside. And their new culture, gravitating as it did around *La Nouvelle Barre du jour*, *Les Herbes rouges*, *Nuit blanche*, and *Vice Versa*, infiltrated the institution, worked on it in ways that were subtle and profound. Lamy emphasized the anti-institutional need to dialogue with a text, rather than to analyse it; to be transformed by it, rather than make it fit into a larger system; to be playful, rather than scholarly.

Throughout the 1980s the objective, universal, transcendent reader was slowly disappearing. Two prominent critics at the end of the decade confirm this disappearance: Pierre Nepveu, in his *L'Ecologie du réel* (1988) and Patricia Smart, in her *Ecrire dans la maison du père* (1988). Smart is probably more forceful in grounding her own place as a subject of enunciation than is Nepveu. She explicitly states that one of her most decisive moves as a critic was to take off the universal reader's mask her culture had placed on her and to start reading as a woman. Nepveu is more elusive in situating himself or placing his voice, but still, in the end, he recognizes his position in a postmodern age, his role as a participant in an ambivalent, indecisive, confused society. But the point of both Smart's and Nepveu's admissions cannot be missed: the critic cannot mask his or her own story before articulating his/her reading; subjectivities and 'petites histoires' are just as relevant as their object of study.

In this context is it even possible to speak of theoretical canons? If we are functioning in a world of subjective narratives – each critic has his/her own – is it valid to use the term 'critical legitimacies'? I would suggest that while canons might belong to another age in which humanistic values reigned supreme, legitimacies are still very much among us. They provide one means of making do with small narratives (Bakhtinian, Jamesonian, Kristevan, Irigarayan ...) and of utilizing them for what they can do for us. The difference is that now there is no canon law, no saviour to guarantee the perfection of a hermeneutical culture.

DONNA BENNETT

Conflicted Vision:
A Consideration of
Canon and Genre
in English-Canadian
Literature

I

Almost as soon as English Canadians began writing, they began to try to define Canadian literature.[1] Although a number of canons have been proposed, some of which have gained a temporary consensus, none has been felt to be completely satisfactory and none has gained permanent acceptance throughout the nation as a whole. To understand why this is true, we must understand how canons get constructed and especially how canon-formation has proceeded in English Canada. Central to the attempts to articulate the nature of English-Canadian national literature and to construct its national canon have been questions about influence and region and, most significantly, genre. As critics have sought to identify the most important works in Canadian writing, they have also attempted to define the *genres* that are central to and sometimes unique to English-Canadian literature. They have done so partly because, as they have encountered those works that seem to them the most 'Canadian,' they have found that these texts 'fail' as English forms appropriate to their period; while, at the same time, some of the 'best' works with regard to the generic rules of English literature do not seem well integrated into Canadian culture. As a result, the English-Canadian canonical enterprise contains within it a number of attempts to define genre;[2] moreover, questions of genre-definition also often intrude into critical discussions focused on other matters, so that what appears to be a consideration of regionalism or theme often turns out to be an attempt to define form. These unnoticed moves from canonical considerations to generic ones have kept the Canadian canon unstable, even at this relatively late date.

In this essay I wish to set aside the issue of whether Canadian literature should or should not have a national canon and discuss why formulating one, though often attempted, has thus far been unsuccessful. Although there are other difficulties that have beset the endeavour, I will focus on the way confusion between canons and genres has particularly affected our ability to constitute a national canon. Although this confusion has its roots in the past, I have chosen a recent moment, the 1978 Calgary Conference on the Canadian Novel, as exemplary. However, as we shall see, along with the confusion of genre- and canon-definition, there is a second and related cause of our inability to develop a stable canon – the interplay of genre with region in defining a national canon. To prepare for both of these topics, I must first make some general remarks about the nature of canons and genre.

II

Genre[3] and canon are both abstract notions, not resident in any single text or any group of texts. These concepts function to provide the reader with patterns that simultaneously shape our understanding of individual texts and of the larger structure of literature. A genre is a model, constructed out of a generalized experience of reading by readers and by writers aware of the act of reading. As I have observed elsewhere, 'the ability of a reader to identify a given work as belonging to a genre depends upon his sense that certain complete texts are perceptibly similar in underlying structures, despite variations in subject, character, and setting. The existence *in more than one text* of determining structural patterns allows the reader to abstract a mental construct, a kind of "supertext" which then guides him in recognizing the appropriateness of inclusion or exclusion of additional works in the genre.'[4] But even though genres exist only by agreement, they are not static constructs. Governed by reception of individual texts, they are subject to continual incremental change, as well as, at times, to large alterations.

Genre defined in this way shares a number of features with canon. Like genre, canon exists as – and only as – a mental construct, a collective abstraction. Canons, however, require a greater degree of overt consensus[5] than do genres. Genres can come into existence out of a multitude of private conclusions that may never have been openly or generally discussed. In fact, while genre *can* be discussed in terms of public accord, its existence initially emerges out of private recognition. Indeed, it is conceivable that writers and their audience could never speak of a genre but nonetheless generate and recognize texts in an unnamed generic form. In contrast, canons are, by their very nature, public statements that need to be discussed publicly. The ability to speak critically about a canon is like the ability to discuss a genre, in that it presumes we hold in our minds (as those to whom we speak hold in theirs) a shared list of texts and rules for engendering that list. But any discussion of a canon also presumes a tacit assumption of the existence of a group for which agreement about the canon exists; we must know who the canon-makers are to understand the canon.[6]

There are many different kinds of canons – canons of 'classic' works outside the writing of the cultures that embrace them; canons of contemporary writing, working lists that may allow readers to quickly and usefully survey the texts of a particular field or subject; canons of 'teachable' works; and canons of writing that lends itself to critical analysis. All of these canons are governed by rules of selection and by the dynamics of interaction between texts, and between the texts and the rules themselves.[7] Most canons also have an infrastructure, a shape that indicates the intention of the original canon-maker. I speak of a single canon-maker here because canonical consensus usually arises out of an evaluation first articulated by some one individual – a critic, an anthologist, a publisher, or a leader of a literary movement. The list thus generated must then gain consensus by becoming accepted, in part or in whole, by other interested members of that individual's milieu (who share the same standards of selection) and later by individuals and groups who do not have such a direct and professional commitment to the activity of canon-making. It is this more general awareness that constitutes final consensus, although a professional consensus can be enough to solidify a canon. Created in this way, canons are coherent but never finally fixed – for another canonical statement can undergo the same process and replace or modify one that has previously gained consensus.

While genres gradually emerge from private recognitions, canons, due to their public natures, are *already* institutionalized even as they come into being. New genres regularly displace old ones (the novel takes over the function of the epic) or divide and multiply (the thriller and the tough-guy mystery emerge from and share the domain of the drawing-room mystery) as readers find new literary forms to respond to their changing needs. New canons, on the other hand, have more difficulty establishing themselves against older, entrenched forms, since, consensus having already been gained, a canon is more resistant to revision or replacement. For a new version of the canon to challenge or displace a well-entrenched one is usually indicative of a major shift in values. While genres may change, by slow increments, significantly over time, substantial changes in canons are not the product of a continuous, smooth evolution, but of a punctuated evolution, a relatively sudden alteration. This tendency to resist change is greatest in the kind of canon we usually mean when we speak of literary canons: the national canon. The make-up of the national literary canon is particularly inflexible since it functions to bring into existence a definition of a national literature and is tied to a sense of nationhood.

The notion that a canon is *shaped* also arises out of the relation of canon to national identity, which has been a crucial feature of canons throughout the nineteenth- and twentieth-century eras of nation-building. Coherence is particularly important to most national canons, for their existence is often seen as an outgrowth of a shapely national history. Thus continuity, causality, and development are formative concepts within the structure of the national canon. However, as we shall see shortly, many lists of texts that are considered national canons are really lists aimed at defining national genres – forms that are particularly characteristic of the writing of a country or its regions – rather than at identifying the most important texts in terms of a coherent literary aesthetics. In such lists, aesthetic standards are seen as detached from, and external to, most of the writing of the national culture.

A national canon, the kind of canon English Canadians have been trying to define, is *not* simply a list of texts by itself, nor is it just *any* list. As Hugh Kenner points out, 'a canon is not a list but a narrative of some intricacy, depending on places and times and opportunities. Any list ... is shorthand for that.'[8] The narrative nature of a national canon tells us a complete story of a literature. It has a shapeliness because it contains not simply a list of important texts and the rules that determine literary evaluation but also a list of necessary works and the narrative that engenders selection.[9] These rules include an aesthetics,[10] as well as other values that determine membership, and they also contain guidelines regarding what *kinds* of works should or should not be included and how relatively important these kinds are to the literature as a whole. This question of kind is chiefly a reflection of the genres recognized by a given culture (for some literatures, for example, an essay can be a member of the literary canon but for others it cannot); however, other grids are also possible, based on region, period, audience, and ideology. The canonical list, then, is not a two-dimensional, but a multi-dimensional, structure defining a matrix of subdivisions that may (or may not) overlap and that are not necessarily of equal importance in determining canonicity. Many of these subdivisions or subcanons are broadly generic (such as the canon of lyric poems), but they can also combine place and genre (the canon of Prairie novels) or ignore genre entirely (the canon of postmodernist writing).

Among these subcanons, those based on genre play an important role because they often hold the key to the controlling literary values that define overall canonical standards. (For example, the acceptance in the eighteenth century of mock epic into the English canon tells us much about the aesthetics that governed the English canon as a whole.) This relationship between genre and canon is so powerful that a change in the relative importance of genres within a literature can not only alter the relative representation of a genre within a canon and the specific texts considered canonical, but can also indicate a significant change in the aesthetics that governs the canon as a whole. (The decline of the epic as an important form after the Renaissance precipitated changes of membership in the canon both with regard to specific poems and to the overall proportional representation of epic and lyric.) Thus generic change affects not only new work but also the value assigned to texts from the past.

Although subcanons and genres influence one another, and – like genre and canon in general – share a number of similarities as literary constructs, they are not identical.[11] Clearly, the genre of tragedy is not equal to the canon of tragedy. While each of these constructs generates and contains a list of texts and while these lists share membership in common, their rules differ. Obviously the canon of the American novel is more selective than the genre of the American novel. What is less obvious is that the canon of the American novel may contain work – novels by Vladimir Nabokov and Jerzy Kosinski, for example – not generally admitted to the genre of the American novel, which emphasizes 'American-ness' as one of the defining characteristics. Genres tell us about how one kind of writing differs from others. Because they construct a definition of an idealized form, genres draw on and contain non-canonical works that illustrate the rules of the genre but that are not necessarily artful. Canons, on the other hand, encode criteria to tell us how well works function with regard to some larger standard, such as 'literariness' or 'universal' aesthetics. Even when subcanons seem identical to genres (as, for example, in the case of the canon of the Canadian long poem), these subcanons do not tell us how to define a literary form but provide us with the important texts that are identified with that genre. Often, in fact, the most important texts of a subcanon are not generically the most exemplary ones in the way they follow the rules of a genre, but rather ones that obey the generic rules well enough while also following the larger rules of literariness. In other words, genres define form; canons evaluate texts.

III

In the history of Canadian canon-making, failure to maintain a distinction between genre-definition and canonical evaluation has contributed to the inherent instability of the canon itself. The problems that arise when canon and genre are not well differentiated can be clearly seen in Malcolm Ross's grand attempt at canon-creation,[12] the 1978 Calgary Conference on the Canadian Novel. Ross's goals in organizing this project were twofold. First, by means of polling critics and academics, he sought to produce three canonical lists: one hundred major novels, ten best novels, and ten most indispensable works of any genre. Second, by means of the papers delivered at a separate conference, he hoped to elicit and elucidate the criteria used to formulate these lists.[13] Since the speakers at the conference composed only a small number of those who participated in the poll, Ross's enterprise was built upon an assumption that the 'values' governing the selection of the texts lay *in* the texts themselves and not in the tastes of those being polled.[14]

Before I look specifically at the papers and responses of the panellists, let us consider why this conference focused on one genre, the novel. As we have moved away from the assumption that existed in Canada until the mid-1960s that poetry was the central genre and the one that contained the 'best' Canadian writing to the more recent affirmation of prose fiction as the central form of contemporary literature, our notions about the Canadian canon as a whole have shifted. This change is inevitable since the more central a genre is in a national canon, the greater the relative proportion of texts of that genre considered canonical. As poetry lost its place as the central literary form, there has been both a reduction in canonical lists of poems preserved from the past and some reluctance to admit the work of contemporary poets into the canon. Therefore, by 1978, defining the canon of the Canadian novel was implicitly the first act necessary to defining the national canon. Where earlier canons implied an aesthetics based in poetry, this conference invited a national aesthetics based in fiction.

But one problem in accomplishing this goal lay in the flexible nature of generic definition. The poetic aesthetic previously underlying the Canadian canonical standards had been inherited from England, whose literary values had been formulated at a point in time when notions about generic rules were relatively fixed and when poetry was unquestioned as the primary genre around which the English canon was to be articulated. Attempts to formulate in 1978 a Canadian aesthetics based on prose were hampered not only by the competition of the old poetic aesthetics but also by a lack of contemporary agreement about the nature of fiction. Thus panellist after panellist provided his or her own sense of the novel as a form. The debate at the conference revealed itself as not so much about canonical values as about generic definitions: what was 'the Canadian novel'? what was 'the regional novel'? what was the novel at all? Once critics defined the particular subgenre of the novel that interested them, their canonical goal became one of ensuring that 'neglected' works in this genre would be added to the canon. The lack of accord over what a 'novel' is – although not necessary in the larger scope of literary criticism – undermined the credibility of the canonical lists that had been generated for the conference and of the authority these papers were actually intended to produce. By the end of the conference it was clear that the issue of how to determine a generally accepted canon of the major works of Canadian fiction was almost entirely set aside, and neither a coherent subcanon nor an aesthetics for determining canonicity had emerged from the conference, an outcome contrary to what Ross apparently expected.

We can see from his comments that Ross had hoped an international standard (probably a modernist one) would provide the criteria by which works would be judged: 'What I had in mind was this: are there any Canadian books which we could with confidence put on a course in contemporary fiction which would include writers like Patrick White, Saul Bellow, E.M. Forster; and what kind of authentic, rigid, severe standard can we apply to determine which novels would be suitable to such a context?'[15] Ross was seeking to develop 'a more secure sense of what is really first-class in our fiction, and of what is important to us in assessing our cultural development.' Words such as 'first-class' and 'development' indicate criteria that lie outside a culture and its own writing and point to standards that are extra-national and extra-generic. Such a perspective assumes that evaluative standards

are already understood and that internally derived 'national' characteristics are secondary in canonical evaluation to universal 'literary' ideals.
A national canon from this viewpoint is 'good' writing produced by
writers from a particular country but evaluated by standards that are
extra-national.

When we look at the various papers, we see that the participants in
the conference did not generally share these assumptions.[16] W.J. Keith,
however, did give some support to Ross's notion of identifying a
'universal' aesthetics. Keith's paper begins by suggesting that what
makes a good novel, Canadian or not, is the aestheticizing of humanist
values. To this extent Keith does offer a canonical standard, which is
embodied in his list of the positive characteristics of *Swamp Angel* –
'poise, simplicity, profundity, exquisite control of tone, delicate human
insight, and above all ... compassion' – traits he also finds present in
the novels *Such Is My Beloved* and *Our Daily Bread*. However, even
Keith's paper reflects the prevailing tendency in this conference to
privilege generic arguments over canon-making. Keith suggests that
the works he celebrates have not been sufficiently valued in the study
of Canadian literature – that is, they do not have their proper place in
the canon – because this kind of humanistic writing has not been
sufficiently recognized by Canadian critics as literary. Rather than
arguing that all fiction should have these qualities and that one should
devalue works that do not meet this standard (a canonical argument),
Keith instead seeks to expand the criteria for the literary novel in
Canada; in other words, he is concerned with defining a subgenre of
the novel. Although he does see *Swamp Angel* as a major, and thus
canonical, work, the other texts he examines are represented not so
much as important literary works but as good examples of how the
'humanistic' novel works. This is a revealing strategy because to look
at works that are less than ideal for the purpose of definition is characteristic of generic analysis. By examining these 'neglected' novels, Keith
defines a distinct subgenre of the novel that had been, he feels, invisible
in Canada. In doing so, he is, of course, also attempting to append an
aesthetics to the canon. This tendency to *append* sets of criteria to the
canon is one of the factors that makes the Canadian canon seem
unsatisfactory as a shaped, national canon. At present no overall coherent standard exists that allows us to understand the canon's structure.
Keith's focus is not on the canon as a whole – he neither suggests that
the literary values he found in the texts he examines ought to be the
basis of a governing aesthetics for the Canadian novel (much less, for
all Canadian writing), nor does he present a coherently shaped canon –
but rather on generic structure.

While Keith may have at least begun with an acknowledgment of Ross's desire for a universal standard, the papers more generally representative of the conference were those that did not admit to any universals. When other conferees invoked the idea of a standard, they sought to create a new one derived from Canadian contexts. However, as with Keith's argument, what begins for them as a definition of canonical aesthetics turns into generic considerations rather than canonical ones. In this, Robert Kroetsch's paper is characteristic. It at first seems to put forward both a canonical standard and a canonical list that would reshape the national canon. Kroetsch objects to pre-existing canonical values that privilege content (which he refers to as 'substance'); in place of these he proposes to make the intent of textual construction central: 'the writer [is seen] not as agent, but as something almost the opposite – the inventor of the world.' Kroetsch develops this notion in two ways. First, he is willing to acknowledge all novelists as 'inventors,' which means he is actually offering not a new canonical standard but rather an alternative to prevailing critical methodology, one in which the focus is on the writer rather than the content of the text. Secondly, citing *Under the Volcano* as 'a supreme novel,' he links this idea of world-invention to a more rigorous distinction – one that introduces an aesthetics based on formal invention rather than on semantic or thematic meaning. It is at this point in his paper that his discussion actually becomes a move towards defining a new genre. Works by Hodgins, Harlow, and Wiebe exemplify, for Kroetsch, this new direction in Canadian writing, in which the limits of form and language are tested and emphasis is shifted towards aspects of writing itself and away from older concerns such as setting and character.

In the next part of his paper Kroetsch does return to canonical questions. Here he not only supplies his audience with a canonical list – historical and national – but he also provides criteria for selection. However, Kroetsch's framework is not one that will yield a shapely national canon. Instead he wants to make it possible to identify those works that have the *potential* to influence future writing. He is attempting to 'build' new work and a new culture 'by selecting a few texts.' This goal, to create a tradition out of which new writing can develop, creates a certain kind of canon – a selective canon for the benefit of young writers – but not a national canon. Excellence is not the main criterion for membership in this list. Instead each work has a function, a role to play in the education of readers – and potential writers.

Kroetsch divides his tentative canon into several categories, and each one, we see, has an instructional use: works that are read for their historical value or their ability to define region; works that name past or present Canadian experience, or that reject a previous act of naming; works that take art as subject; works that heal. One finds it hard to identify a controlling aesthetics in these divisions. That the categories are chiefly about naming and its dangers confirms the functional rather than aesthetic nature of his list. And it is here that we can say that this project once more reveals itself as actually generic. These categories are essentially guidelines for looking at Canadian writing in relation to the form of the novel, and especially to Kroetsch's idea of a new form of fiction, the novel as new 'world.' Literary value is made secondary to whether a text furthers this enterprise. Thus Kroetsch provides us in this list with only a partial view of Canadian prose, not an overall perspective on its national character. His list excludes works that hold a place in other canonical lists (by Atwood, Munro, Wiseman, and MacLennan) and redefines the very idea of the novel to allow him to include short stories, non-fiction narratives, experimental poetry, and even a writer in his own person ('George Bowering himself may be a novel'). Like Keith, Kroetsch is more concerned with changing our perspective about what Canadian fiction *is* than in defining a national canon.

The other speakers at the conference made even less attempt to define the aesthetics of the Canadian canon. In fact, the reason that the main speakers and the members of the panels left each other's views unchallenged was not politeness, but evidence of the fact that genre definitions were most often what was really at stake. Because definitions of forms are usually not exclusive and are rather flexible, discussions about generic constructs, to which many variant texts can be accommodated, are allowed a large degree of latitude.[17] Literary excellence is not a criterion for genre; one includes and excludes on the basis of an ever-changing 'fuzzy' standard,[18] which measures how much a work can deviate from 'typical' characteristics and still be taken by readers as of the same 'kind' as other members of a form. Generic definitions are never based on exhaustive sampling; they do not have 'clean' rules for inclusion or exclusion; and, most importantly for our consideration, they do not internalize standards for excellence. These characteristics thus free genres from the restriction that consensus places on canons. For this reason, attempts to deal with canonicity while also defining a generic form – to evaluate for canonical status through the determination of generic features – can blur both genre and canon and produce not a national canon but a set of particularized, generic bibliographies.

IV

One important aspect of the Calgary conference that remains to be considered is its emphasis on region. Of the four main sections, three were shaped around the subject of regional difference.[19] Furthermore, the tendency of speakers who were there from Central Canada to focus on moral and thematic definitions of genres and for Western Canadians to direct their concern more towards defining new forms of fiction writing is characteristic of the roles each region has played in influencing the structure of canon-making.

This conflict between Central and Western Canada in their approaches to the canon has as its source assumptions about genre. Historically Central Canadians have privileged poetry over prose, while Westerners have valued fiction over poetry. Thematic criticism, which has its origins in the beginnings of Canadian criticism, is a methodology much more appropriate to, and less reductive of, a poetry-based aesthetics, particularly when it is governed by stable notions about the lyric. Without narrative and with agreed-upon standards of technique, theme is the natural marker of distinction between writers – and between literatures. In contrast, the early introduction of 'prose' techniques into Western and rural poetry (the adoption of vernacular language; of unrhymed, metrically irregular, or even unmetrical lines; of prose-poem format in which lines are no longer the structural unit; and of a less formal sense of rhetoric and subject matter), coupled with the rise of a realistic fiction in the Prairies, indicates the Western preference for an aesthetics governed by prose. And even though, in the last few decades, fiction has become the primary form of literary writing everywhere in English Canada, the traces of this division remain crucial to the way the canon is perceived and constructed.

The problems connected to the privileging of one literary form over another in formulating the Canadian canon were twofold: the canonical aesthetics governed by one form, poetry, distorted and actually suppressed the significance of another form, fiction, in the canonical hierarchy; and the changes taking place in poetry itself (because the particular structure of English poetics resisted 'new' prose-linked ideas about poetry) were retarded. While poetry was the dominant form of 'literary' writing in Canada until the 1920s, and remained the most valued form long after, it does not follow that at any time satisfactory standards for a national canon in English Canada could be derived principally from the poetic tradition any more than, in 1978, they could be derived from the aesthetics governing contemporary fiction. The consequences of this distortion explain many of the 'failures' of Canadian literature. For example, much Canadian poetry prior to the introduction into poetry of 'prose' techniques has not seemed especially 'Canadian' to either Central Canadians or Westerners. The literary standards of traditional English aesthetics, which provided the rules used to determine canonicity in English-Canadian writing (but not necessarily the rules for writing English-Canadian literature) until at least the 1920s, are based on a poetics of more conventional dynamics, structures, rules, and values than found in the works we now identify as both 'good' and 'Canadian.' In essence, what I am saying is that one of the factors that has made canon-definition in Canada difficult has been the fact that this activity has become important during the period when poetry and fiction have exchanged canonical importance. This shift has made the application of traditional aesthetics problematical, if not inappropriate.

The emergence of prose as a dominant element in English-Canadian writing is one of the punctuated changes that marks a national canon. Along with the introduction of modernism, the development of literary fiction – of, to be more precise, fiction strong enough to change canonical assumptions about what is literary – restructured the rules of canon-making in Canada. This change, however, met resistance in the Central-Canadian literary establishment. To understand this conflict and its importance, let me turn to the history of literary fiction and canonical value in English Canada.

The canonical values that are being called into question at present are largely the outgrowth of English Canada's inheritance of Victorian perspectives,[20] in particular the Victorian sense of historical continuity and evolutionary development, which is the most pervasive structuring pattern in the history of Canadian literary thinking.[21] In the work of critics such as Edward Dewart and William Lighthall, and in later critics, through E.K. Brown and Desmond Pacey, we can see the Victorian framework shaping the kind of genres that are considered literary, and the hierarchical relationship of these genres to one another. In Central Canada, this way of thinking about genre and canon remained in place throughout the modernist period and has only given way in the last two decades. Fiction in English Canada traditionally has been viewed by writers, critics, and readers as a more 'popular' and less literary mode of writing, and early canons of Canadian writing, whether Dewart's or A.J.M. Smith's, comprised chiefly poetry. Prose, on the other hand, although acknowledged, remained largely uncanonical. A.J.M. Smith, for example, compiled his *Book of Canadian Poetry* in 1943 but did not publish *The Book of Canadian Prose* until 1965 – and even that volume contained only pre-Confederation work, clearly selected by standards other than literary ones.[22]

When early critics did judge fiction, their principal 'literary' criterion was an interesting one: they wanted Canadian fiction to be 'realistic.' While 'realism' and 'realistic' are terms that convey a variety of meanings relative to place and period,[23] what these early critics desired was a set of characteristics arising out of Canadian experience and moral ideals. Unlike the twentieth-century realism we later see in the works of Frederick Philip Grove and Margaret Laurence, the 'realism' called for by nineteenth-century critics had more to do with content than technique. They wanted a fiction with *relatively* unmelodramatic plots, with a Canadian setting, with activities that Canadians might be involved in, and with an idealization of social, moral, and political values associated with Canada (usually those of middle-class Britain, often contrasted to those of the United States). Thus the invocation of realist standards[24] was actually an appeal to a certain kind of idealized content; of the *techniques* governing prose writing little was said, and, one suspects, little was expected. As expectations about Canadian fiction (and about what 'realism' is) changed, English-Canadian ideas about literary values began to diverge into two streams, marking the loss of the ideal of maintaining the social codes of English society and the rise of concepts growing out of the experience of the Western settlers and the ethics of the social reform movement associated with non-Anglican Protestantism.

We can see signs of this change in publishing earlier than in criticism. By the 1920s Canadian publishers, while still producing the older idealized 'realism,' began to print a more literary form of the realistic novel.[25] Unlike idealized realism, in which technique was governed not by an aesthetic but by an ethic,[26] this writing sublimated its ethics and began to create an aesthetic consistent with, and as important as, its vision. Though this change can be seen as a move towards modernism, it is also an indication of the emergence of a rural tradition of storytelling, the dynamics of which are found in oral as well as in European aesthetics of fiction.[27] This new realist fiction could be called Prairie realism, for, although this genre is not necessarily about the Prairies or by writers from the Prairie provinces, it does contain a number of important texts that fall into one or both of these categories, and those that do not often have connections with a rural life of

isolation similar to the Prairie experience such fiction usually dramatized. In such novels we see fiction that does not try to idealize experience; rather than embodying bucolic ideals, it responds to a sense of a
world dominated by random forces of nature.[28] These novels attempted
to depict rural life by using the techniques we now identify with
modern realism: a stripped language, deliberate inelegance, and an
unidealized view of experience. Writers of this kind of realism moved
away from older characteristics of Canadian fiction – the genteel 'painting' of idealized landscapes and actions – as they took up a role closer
to that of memoirist or journalist, and chronicled fictional events as
though they were relating their own experiences. This form of realism
reflects, particularly, the influence of journalism upon theories of prose
and poetry in North American writing of this period, which cannot be
underestimated. (Simplicity of syntax, restraint in the use of adjectives,
direct, non-evaluative description, and emphasis on reporting and objectivity are journalistic notions that have been incorporated into North
American modernist techniques and generalized into an aesthetics.)

We can see why this realism had difficulty gaining canonical status
when we contrast its techniques to some of those enshrined in the
English literary tradition. For example, in the Prairie novel, dexterity
with language becomes secondary to achieving the effect of 'truth.'
Indeed in the realist tradition, elegance is often seen as artificial and
distracting from a presentation that serves to intensify such 'non-
literary' values as honesty, which are integral to this kind of fiction.
Thus, because its aesthetics stood in direct conflict with traditional
English evaluative notions about 'good' prose writing – ideas that
applied poetic standards to fiction – the realistic novel was not readily
accorded canonical status.

Although the appearance of Grove, Robert Stead, Martha Ostenso,
and others may have provided an alternative to Victorian literary
values and a challenge to poetically based canonical standards, this
kind of 'realism' did not become institutionalized as part of the canon
until much later. In the early 1930s, realism, both in poetry and fiction,
seemed to gain some critical recognition. However, by the end of the
decade, its importance had faded and its texts had become eclipsed by
more traditional works. The change that made Prairie writing more
recognizably literary came with Central Canada's acceptance of modernism, since modernism, particularly its urban realist strain, took into
its poetry values associated with prose realism and legitimated them
as canonical standards.

In Central Canada, literary responses to new information and the
new ways of seeing that have characterized our century (other than a

resistance to them) seemed to take two forms, both of which were based on poetry as the central literary genre.[29] One group of writers embraced the modernism of T.S. Eliot and sought, by structuring and refining change, to create a new 'civilization,' a response that now looks more and more like a delaying manoeuvre. The other group of writers rejected the need for a 'high' art, a 'literature,' or a 'civilization' as such. In place of this refined writing they espoused the 'realism' of everyday language[30] and, sometimes, elevated psychological 'reality' over that solely governed by pre-formulated social or moral perspectives. Modernism in Canada seems to begin with the first of these groups – made up of Smith, F.R. Scott, Leo Kennedy, and A.M. Klein – affirming a kind of writing that adhered to Eliot's basic precepts. Like Eliot, these writers showed no interest in the fiction that had been making gains both in England and in North America. Since this preference for poetry did not place them at odds with older academic critics, this form of modernism, even though it offered new criteria for the poetry it canonized, did not challenge the values already institutionalized.

Perhaps because poetry kept such a privileged position in the Canadian canon, the other modernist response to Victorian literary thinking is one that did not seem to appear in Canada until after World War II; and even then it seemed to be a special case of the 'realistic' aspect of modernism: it was an urban, proletarian poetry written largely by the children of the middle class. It is with the call for a 'realism' of language and subject in poetry, chiefly in statements made by John Sutherland, Irving Layton, and Raymond Souster, that this kind of modernism became visible in Canada. These writers were the first to identify and support a tradition of realism in Canadian literary writing. They gave attention to the work of poets such as W.W.E. Ross, Raymond Knister, Anne Marriott, and Dorothy Livesay, who already had been working in a 'realistic' vein (but whose work was not yet recognized), as well as encouraging new writers, such as Miriam Waddington, Leonard Cohen, and Al Purdy. Initially these attempts to alter the canon had less success than Smith's, whose criteria for the canon virtually became those of the Central-Canadian literary and academic establishment. One reason for the success of Smith's canon over Sutherland's is that Smith's modernism was closer to the perceived 'realities' of English-Canadian culture. While the political and social structures in English Canada may have been moving away from Victorian ideals, the change was not so great that these structures could accommodate the Montreal-based urban realists' vision – any more than they could that of the Prairie realists.[31]

The difference between the modernism of the Prairie realists and that of either Smith's or Sutherland's groups begins with their differing perspectives on human effectiveness. Writers associated with Smith's *Preview* group and those whose works were featured in Sutherland's publications shared the desire to play the role of social critic. Although they differed on what was wrong and on how to integrate their social ideals into their poetics, these Central-Canadian poets tended to be 'advocates,' writers whose assumptions were based on the idea that writing could effect social change and that social change could take place. In contrast, the writers of Prairie realism were much more intent upon a kind of 'objective' reporting, one that accepts the inevitability of experience. This Prairie realism depicts a 'timeless' existence and contains a bleak vision of an essentially indifferent universe, in which personal effectiveness is unlikely and social ideals largely unreachable. In spite of this dark perspective, Prairie realism expresses not so much a despairing perspective as a resigned one in which human beings can be integrated into their relatively chaotic universe. Although that vision became one that some urban modernist writers later adopted (Layton seems to have moved in this direction by the mid-1950s), the urban modernist aesthetics remained distinct both in its use of a more flamboyant diction and its tendency to produce social criticism. Prairie realism, on the other hand, though it has developed a language-centred branch, has retained its vision and its preference for storytelling techniques.

It is important to grasp the effect upon Canadian canon-making of one segment of Canadian modernist writing remaining virtually unrecognized as aesthetically significant for over twenty years. While the struggle between high modernist values and urban realism is not unique to Canada – for example, following World War II we can see the same split enacted in the United States and in England – the exclusion of Prairie realism from the Canadian canon is another, more Canadian, matter. The fact that the writing of a large section of English Canada was identified by the establishment as subliterary or as failing to achieve literariness is an important feature of English-Canadian literary history.[32] An indicator of the relatively recent adjustment of the canon to the pressures of Western writing may be suggested by Edward McCourt's *The Canadian West in Fiction*, which seemed (and presented itself as) a piece of special pleading when first published in 1949, but by the time of its reissue in 1970 seemed more 'timely.' This marginalizing of a number of significant texts from canonical consideration until, at least, mid-century has had a disastrous effect upon creating a truly national canon, more especially since recognition of this Prairie aesthetic was finally given at almost the same time when English Canada's literary culture began to fragment into ethnic differences. Today the chance for English Canada to consolidate a literary tradition may have already passed, and with it the opportunity to identify even an historic national canon.

Why have the canonical values of the Central-Canadian aesthetic seemed less and less adequate since the war? As well as the rapid change in the last twenty years in the acceptance of a prose aesthetics, which challenged the canonical English-derived aesthetics with its traditional assumptions about the nature and the importance of poetry, there has been a change in the function of the canon itself. While expressions of concern about the need for a canon are a tradition in Canada, the number of people who have been involved with its creation and preservation has been relatively small. Defining the canon has been of real importance to Canadian writers, and to a few academics, journalists, and publishers. However, the growth of governmental interest in the development and maintenance of Canadian culture, an interest that has been translated into funding for the arts, has made the canon an important institution. The expansion of the CBC, the creation of the Canada Council and the provincial arts councils, and the commercialization of things 'Canadian' as socially valuable have all given new and more general immediacy to the questions of what the important works in our literature are and by what standards we make judgments. These institutions have affected not only the canon but the role of region and genre as canonical determinants. For example, the federal mandate to spread cultural support across the provinces has strengthened the position of the Western aesthetic throughout English Canada. Similarly, investment in radio and television broadcasting, has greatly increased the importance of the short story as a canonical form, for writers can gain exposure as well as money by working in this genre. (In contrast, book publication privileges the novel as the only important literary form for financial return.)

With the expansion of the university system during the 1960s and with the expansion of the study of Canadian literature within the university that took place at the same time, Canadian writing has assumed a new role in the market-place. The effect of this change can be seen in the changes in the teaching canon. In particular, the new numbers of students reading Canadian texts in the Prairie universities, and in the colleges and universities of British Columbia, made the under-representation of Prairie and Western writers on canonical lists and the exclusion of the Prairie literary codes from the national aesthetics not only an embarrassment to the academic establishment but an oversight that Canadian textbook publishers rushed to remedy.

The way in which the Prairie literary code has influenced the canonical criteria in recent years is indicative of what happened to the two streams of modernist literary values that once dominated Central Canada. The history of reception of Prairie writing during this period both in Central Canada and in the West is one of reassessment in which characteristics that had been seen as 'flaws' were discovered to be strengths. For example, the history of reception of *As for Me and My House* indicates not only that critics from outside the West had difficulty accepting the 'artfulness' of this book until the last two decades, but that its acceptance into the Central-Canadian-defined canon came only after the book was interpreted – with a shift in emphasis onto the unreliability of the narrator – in a way that aligned its techniques with those of modernist literary criticism. What had bothered earlier critics – repetition, the claustrophobic perspective, and the relative lack of drama and dramatization – became virtues, and new values were discovered in the text: irony, psychological intensity, and a vision blurred by ambiguity. As Morton Ross observes, in his essay on the canonization of this novel, these later readings of the book are partly efforts to deregionalize it. However, what Ross does not notice is that beneath the long debate over whether the book is, as Roy Daniells believed, a minor work or, as later critics have claimed, one of the great Canadian novels, lies hidden the dispute over the Prairie realist aesthetic that has long troubled the waters of canonicity.

The values that contemporary Canadian critics brought to fiction (and poetry) – values centred on irony, parody, and ambiguity – emerged out of both the high modernism that Smith embraced and the urban realist response to the twentieth century. By the end of the 1950s both streams of modernism had lost the authenticity of their visions of reform and had refined ironic detachment into a value system of its own. This detached perspective of late modernism made it easier for the Prairie aesthetic to be accepted in, and revised for, Central Canada since an important topic in Prairie writing has long been the inadequacies of any vision.[33]

V

If we look again at the Calgary conference in light of this history of value systems in twentieth-century Canadian writing, we see more clearly why the conference took the shape it did and why it failed to produce a canon. Because of the history of fiction in Canada, Malcolm Ross's instincts were right when he thought that the area in which canonical lists needed to be made and standards needed to be discussed was the novel. Even his decision to locate the conference in the West made sense. However, not only did his methods of deriving lists keep the choice of books on the level of popular writing, not only was it unwise to have a value system articulated separately from the selection process, and not only was the conference's focus distracted by question of genre, but the very framing of canonical standards was generally blocked because of regional associations with literary values. The participants in the conference did not have a shared history of aesthetics. The Westerners wanted an aesthetics governed by form, language, and the structures of storytelling, while the Central Canadians chiefly wanted one that, whether grounded in Victorian or in modernist ways of seeing, would evaluate works not only in terms of technique but also in terms of topic and moral vision.

The question remains: Is it possible to define a national canon in English Canada? Given the diversity of aesthetics that are in play today both in new texts and in contemporary critical theories, a single vision seems impossible to generate and may not be desirable. And yet this response to the question of canon is not satisfactory. National canons give us both the literary vision that influences the shape of newly articulated work and the narrative of aesthetic values that expresses how a culture locates its writing within its larger history. While we may not be able to produce a stable canon that will supply Canadian writers and readers with a single tradition, we may still seek to shape one that will show us the aesthetic history of our literature and, in so doing, will show us the standards that have emerged from our conflicted literary values.

Calgary, Canonization, and Class: Deciphering List B

I

Critics, sixty years from now ... will no doubt smile condescendingly at our judgments. For we are engaged in a kind of pantheon-making among the living. We occupy the most treacherous ground.

Robert Kroetsch, in *Taking Stock*, 13

More than ten of the sixty years have passed since Robert Kroetsch made these remarks at the Calgary Conference on the Canadian Novel in 1978. The 'kind of pantheon-making' to which he refers is the self-conscious fashioning of a Canadian literary canon; the Calgary conference produced tangible evidence of this enterprise in the form of three lists: of the most 'important' one hundred works of fiction, ten novels, and ten 'works of various genres.'[1] So far, very few people are smiling condescendingly at these judgments. In a recent article, Robert Lecker observes that 'while some did (and still do) take issue with the list distributed at the conference, that list remains the single most prominent and thorough indication of what the Canadian canon has become.'[2] Whether we as individuals like it or not, we know which works comprise the canon. So far there is absolutely no evidence that the 'ground' occupied by the participants in the Calgary poll is at all 'treacherous,' as Kroetsch claimed.

But there is also, as Lecker has noted, a near absence of discussion of the justification for the content of the canon: 'We do not know why the Canadian canon includes certain texts and excludes others. No one can account for the taste informing the list of the 100 "most important" novels chosen at the Calgary conference' (Lecker, 659). What I propose to do here is somewhat more modest than to provide such an account: to investigate the possible reasons for the choice of the *ten* 'most important' novels, with a view to illuminating the more general issue of 'why the Canadian canon includes certain texts and excludes others.'

The list (hereafter referred to as 'List B' as it was at the Calgary conference) is as follows:

Laurence	*The Stone Angel*
Davies	*Fifth Business*
Ross	*As for Me and My House*
Buckler	*The Mountain and the Valley*
Roy	*The Tin Flute*
Richler	*The Apprenticeship of Duddy Kravitz*
Watson	*The Double Hook*
MacLennan	*The Watch That Ends the Night*
Mitchell	*Who Has Seen the Wind*
Laurence	*The Diviners*

(TS, 153–4)

This list, like the other two, is the result of 'a mail ballot completed before the conference began' (TS, 150). The ballot was sent, according to Malcolm Ross, who devised it, to 'teachers and critics across the country' (TS, 137) – not a random sampling, but only to those invited to attend the conference.[3] Nowhere in *Taking Stock*, the published proceedings of the conference, are the criteria for being invited explained. Apparently organizers and participants alike believed it to be self-evident that they constituted an elite capable of making such legislative gestures.

And certainly there is nothing in *Taking Stock* to explain why this mysteriously chosen elite made their own choices. The structure of the conference would have made this nearly impossible, in any event. The results of the balloting were not revealed until the morning of the last day, leaving time for only a brief panel discussion about their significance – a discussion recorded in fewer than ten pages of *Taking Stock*.

This discussion is not helpful to anyone seeking an explanation. Henry Kreisel says that the novels on List B 'constitute a respectable list' (TS, 143). Antoine Sirois does not comment directly on List B, though he notes the general absence of 'some very important French-Canadian novels' (TS, 145). W.J. Keith, observing that 'the top ten never stays the top ten for very long,' says that he is 'prepared to approve moderately, without taking it too seriously, the tentative drawing up of such a list' (*TS*, 143). But neither Kreisel nor Keith offers a rationale for the selection of the specific group of texts constituting List B.

Neither does perusal of the rest of *Taking Stock* result in enlightenment on this score. The most obvious starting point is the proceedings of the opening session of the conference, comprising Robert Kroetsch's paper, 'Contemporary Standards in the Canadian Novel' and responses by three critics. Kroetsch mentions about thirty-six novelists, including all nine represented on List B, but provides no hint as to how their work might be distinguished from that of the other twenty-seven. Barry Cameron, in his response, mentions five novelists, none of whom appears on List B. William H. New mentions no novelists by name. Warren Tallman focuses on American writers, mentioning only Morley Callaghan and Kroetsch as Canadians. No clear line of relation can be drawn between the conference presentations and the works appearing on List B.

But perhaps no explanation is needed. Is it possible that the objectively identifiable characteristics of the works on List B simply replicate the characteristics of the larger pool of works from which they were chosen? I think not. Consider a possible alternate List B:

Cohen, L.	*Beautiful Losers*
Wiebe	*The Temptations of Big Bear*
Kroetsch	*The Studhorse Man*
Atwood	*Lady Oracle*
Hood	*White Figure, White Ground*
Cohen, M.	*The Disinherited*
Hodgins	*The Invention of the World*
Ondaatje	*Coming through Slaughter*
Gallant	*The Pegnitz Junction*
Levine	*From a Seaside Town*

Of this group, only the first five placed in the top one hundred at Calgary, with *Beautiful Losers*, in thirty-second place, coming highest. Yet how different would a neophyte's impression of Canadian fiction be if he or she were to read these works in the belief that *they* are the ten 'most important' published up to 1978. What is it that makes the works on the *real* List B more important than these?

One obvious feature distinguishing List B from my alternate version is that List B is characterized by a conservatism, even timidity, of technique. As Lecker has noted, 'nine of "the first ten novels" selected at the Calgary conference were clearly works that operated according to ... mimetic conventions' (Lecker, 664). He comments on the general tendency of Canadian critics to evaluate individual works 'according to their ability to record time and place' (664) and links this tendency to nationalism. In what follows I will take for granted the accuracy of this perception. What I wish to do, however, is to consider the *nature* of the nationalism implied by the way in which time and place are recorded in these works. It would be easy enough, after all, to find ten other novels governed by mimetic conventions, whether from other works in the Calgary conference's top one hundred, or from those excluded from the Calgary lists, that would equally well sustain Lecker's thesis. What, in other words, is so special about this particular group of ten? Or, more precisely, what did the voters canvassed before the Calgary conference perceive to be special about it?

II

I was asked to discover from my colleagues which one hundred
Canadian novels seemed more useful in the classroom ... I asked
for a choice of one hundred titles and a short list of ten novels which
seemed most important – not great, mind you, *important*.

Malcolm Ross, in *Taking Stock*, 137

It is surely not an accident that the novels deemed to be 'most useful in the classroom' are those from which the 'most important' ones are to be drawn. The works selected for canonization at the Calgary conference were selected with a particular practical value in mind. 'Useful' to whom? Irresistibly, the question of the class interests of those who teach Canadian literature in post-secondary institutions raises itself.

What, exactly, *are* these interests, and how do they affect the selection of works to be canonized?

If the reader thinks this sort of enquiry frivolous or impertinent, I would refer him or her to a provocative essay by Richard Ohmann, 'The Shaping of a Canon: U.S. Fiction, 1960–1975.'[4] In it, Ohmann traces the process by which an American novel of the period came to be accepted as 'eligible for canonical status' (378). This process, he argues, occurs in two stages, the first involving book buyers, agents,

editors, advertisers, and reviewers, whose work, collectively, constitutes a screening process which resulted in the identification of a
relatively small number of novels as 'compelling, important, "talked-
about" ' (382). The second stage involves the separation of the novels
that 'were never regarded as serious literature,' such as *Love Story* and
The Godfather, from those that 'survived and continued ... to attract
buyers and readers for a longer time, and ... still do' (382). A novel in
this second group invariably received a certain kind of attention from
an elite group of about eight journals; this attracted the interest of
academics, and finally the novel would become part of the university
curriculum: 'the college classroom and its counterpart, the academic
journal,' Ohmann argues, 'have become in our society the final arbiters
of literary merit, and even of survival' (384).

Ohmann goes on to observe that everyone involved in this process belongs to what he calls, somewhat uneasily, the 'Professional-
Managerial class,' which is characterized by 'its conflicted relation
to the ruling class,' its 'equally mixed relation to the working class,'
and its 'own marginal position with respect to capital' (387). Members
of the Professional-Managerial class work for the ruling class yet long
for autonomy; have authority (in theory benevolent) over the working class, yet in exercising this authority promote the interests of the
ruling class; and are relatively well off financially but still need to earn
their living.

In postwar America, Ohmann argues, members of this class were in
many ways led to believe that social, economic, and political conflict
in their society was becoming less and less significant. If something
seemed to be going wrong with one's life, it was reasonable to conclude
that this must, in some sense, be one's own fault. The members of the
Professional-Managerial class concerned with selecting novels for pre-
canonical status tended to choose, naturally enough in Ohmann's
view, works which feature versions of what he calls the 'fiction of
illness' (390) – works which 'transform deep social contradictions into
a dynamic of personal crisis, a sense of there being no comfortable
place in the world for a private self' (395). Examples of the fiction of
illness include '*Franny and Zooey, One Flew Over the Cuckoo's Nest, The*
Bell Jar, Herzog, Portnoy's Complaint, and Updike's *Rabbit* series' (390),
and other works by Pynchon, Vonnegut, and Heller. Ohmann finds in
these works certain common denominators (too numerous to detail
here), concluding that, in choosing these works as candidates for canonization, the Professional-Managerial class 'shapes culture in ways
that express its own interests and experience' (397).

For the Canadian reader of Ohmann's article, several observations suggest themselves. One is that the process by which a Canadian work achieves 'pre-canonical status' is very much simpler. Ohmann's first stage, preliminary commercial success, need not occur at all (*As for Me and My House*), or if it does, there need not be a demonstrable connection between best-sellerdom and canonization (*The Mountain and the Valley*). Nor is the first part of Ohmann's second stage, the singling out of the novel by an elite group of trend-setting journals, relevant. Virtually all of the action in Canada occurs at the very end of the process, the simultaneous embracing of a work by the classroom and the academic journal.

So, in Canada, it is a relatively small group that makes the decisions about what books are fit for canonization: university teachers of English who specialize or dabble in Canadian literature. It may be useful to draw an analogy between this group in the microcosmic society of the Canadian university English department, and the Professional-Managerial class in American society, as Ohmann characterizes it.

The 'ruling class' in this context, those in control of Canadian English departments, comprised scholars and teachers devoted to the study of British (especially) and American literature. During the late 1970s, at the time of the Calgary conference, these academics tended to be from the United States or the United Kingdom (or elsewhere in the Commonwealth) – people whose own life experience may not have led them to be particularly sympathetic to the aspirations of their Canadianist colleagues. It was, of course, possible for some born and/or educated in the United Kingdom or the United States to become interested in Canadian literature, and many did, but to make this transition, as W.J. Keith reports (in an article published eight years after the Calgary conference), is to become painfully conscious of the gulf separating the two academic 'classes': 'I became a critic and scholar of Canadian literature ... after I had made a modest reputation for myself in another area of English studies. The same is true of a number of Canadianists, and all of those to whom I have spoken agree that they are conscious of a lowering of the temperature when they cross the boundary into Canadian studies. The standard of scholarship seems less rigorous, the level of criticism and commentary less disciplined and sophisticated; even the quality of the writing appears slacker, less precise.'[5] No doubt we all have our own thermometers in these matters. But certainly Keith's weather report about the lower intellectual temperature on the Canadian side of the boundary indicates something pertinent about the perceptions of the 'ruling class' in Canadian

English departments of the 1970s. The Canadianist, whether native or naturalized, had something to prove to his or her presumptively superior colleagues.

The 'working class,' in this analogy, would of course be the students. The teacher of Canadian literature certainly experienced the 'mixed relation' that Ohmann argues is characteristic of the interaction between the Professional-Managerial class and the working class: like the students, the instructor is Canadian by birth or adoption; he or she wishes to exercise authority benevolently by putting the students in intellectual touch with their own culture. But he or she is also promoting the interests of the 'ruling class,' using the Canadian texts as samples of literature – literature as epitomized by the British and American canons. The Canadian texts must be shown to have the same sort of literary value as the others, and the critical techniques employed must be identical to those used in other courses. Otherwise, academic standards would suffer.

Hence the third part of the analogy, the 'marginal position with respect to capital' experienced by the Canadianist. The 'capital' here is of course the perceived value of one's own subject area, and the stocks and bonds have names like International Shakespeare, Milton, Inc., Consolidated Melville, JoyceCo. The 'ruling class' can live comfortably off their capital: there need be no time wasted in justifying the study of these authors. The position of the Canadianist is somewhat different: 'they didn't have the wealth to sit back and clip coupons,' as Ohmann says of the Professional-Managerial class, 'but they had ready access to credit' (Ohmann, 387). Canadianists could teach their courses, publish in their journals, and so on. But there was, I would suggest, something akin to an aura of affirmative action surrounding the enterprise, a sense that, if the study of Canadian literature deserved a place in Canadian English departments, that place was at the margin.

If the analogy I have just drawn is at all accurate, we might expect to find some relation between the 'class interests' of teachers of Canadian literature and the novels chosen for List B at the Calgary conference. A glance at this list is enough to establish that it does not yield up anything parallel to Ohmann's 'fiction of illness.' There is no obvious common denominator in terms of subject or theme. But it would be hasty to conclude that there is no connection between the usefulness of these novels in the classroom and the class interests of those who use them.

III

> The purpose of the list of ten important books was to determine the
> difference between the general approval of a large number of
> novels, and a very careful, narrow selection. What I had in mind was
> this: are there any Canadian books which we could with confidence
> put on a course in contemporary fiction which would include writers
> like Patrick White, Saul Bellow, E.M. Forster; and what kind of authen-
> tic, rigid, severe standard can we apply to determine which novels
> would be suitable to such a context?
>
> Malcolm Ross, in *Taking Stock*, 138

For Malcolm Ross, apparently, the main concern with respect to List B
was, to use my adaptation of Ohmann's language, to please the ruling
class, to convince sceptical colleagues that Canadian fiction possesses
the complexity and sophistication characteristic of a certain kind of
internationally recognized writing. I leave it to others to determine
whether this is true of the novels on List B, but I would suggest that
it is not clear that these novels display such qualities in greater abun-
dance than, say, those on the alternate list that I proposed in the first
section of this essay – though one could find many other grounds on
which to distinguish the two lists. And I leave to others also the task
of deciding what standard that is 'authentic,' 'rigid,' and 'severe' might
be applied to the novels on List B. Instead, I would like to determine
what portrait of Canada, what implicit definitions of what it is to be a
Canadian and what a Canadian novel is emerge from an examination
of these works.

  Before embarking on this endeavour, I would like to make a case for
excluding Gabrielle Roy's *The Tin Flute* from the discussion. It is not
clear what inspired the mostly Anglo academics invited to the conference to think, first, that they were capable of assessing literature written
in French at all, and second, that they were capable of making a
reasonable evaluative comparison of such works with English-Canadian texts. The result was, predictably, an embarrassment, as at least
one of the participants, the ubiquitous W.J. Keith, had the grace to
recognize at the time: 'I would like to dissociate myself from the way
Quebecois texts were treated,' he said. 'How on earth ... can we ...
make a value judgment about Quebecois fiction, whether we read it in
translation or stumblingly in French?' (TS, 146). The Calgary conference

in fact paid only token attention to Québécois writing (in only one of the five sessions did it receive equal treatment), and it is clear that it is the English-Canadian canon that is really at issue for its participants. The question of why English Canadians perceive the literature of Quebec and other francophone communities in the country as they do is an interesting one, but not the same as the question of why the English-Canadian canon has assumed the form that it has.

Examination of the nine English-Canadian novels on List B reveals a remarkable degree of homogeneity in their composite depiction of what it means to live in Canada, a remarkable degree of agreement about what needs to be said and what needs to be left unsaid. To say this is not to pass negative judgment on any of these works – after all, they were not written so that they might be included on List B! It is, rather, to suggest that there are reasons other than their achievement of some 'authentic, rigid, severe standard' that have made these novels fit candidates for canonization.

Let me establish a rough paradigm by examining the earliest-published novel to appear on the list, Sinclair Ross's *As for Me and My House*. The story of Philip Bentley and his journal-keeping wife is well known to all students of Canadian literature. Bentley is a minister in a small Prairie town during the 1930s. His life is desiccated, emotionally and spiritually. His Christianity has no power to inspire him, and its institutional manifestation sickens him with its narrow-mindedness and hypocrisy. He is apparently incapable of real intimacy with his wife, whose own emotional life is correspondingly impoverished. They are childless. Nevertheless Philip struggles, almost despite himself, to find some sort of fulfilment: through his drawing, through the temporary adoption of a twelve-year-old boy, and through an affair with a young woman, who dies giving birth to their child. At the novel's end, there is some hope for the Bentley family: Philip has decided to leave the ministry to run a bookstore near a university, and the Bentleys will rear the child born of his adulterous relationship. The ending is mutedly upbeat.

The novel is clearly in the realist tradition, yet it is remarkable that so much of what realism normally includes has been edited out of Ross's depiction of the Bentleys' lives. Dick Harrison, describing a number of novels he discusses under the rubric of 'prairie realism' (and including *As for Me and My House*), makes this observation: 'Once we begin to look for what is missing from the prairie realism we discover some surprising gaps. During the 1930's two national political parties were formed in Saskatchewan and Alberta, yet ... these novels give us practically nothing of the very active political life of the time. And where are such staples of prairie life as the cooperatives, grain growers' associations, and other farm organizations? Where is the Prairie Farm Rehabilitation Administration? The radio? The *Winnipeg Free Press*? Where, in effect, is the outside world?'[6] Where indeed?

I wish next to sketch the general pattern which can be abstracted from this brief discussion of *As for Me and My House*. In the world of the novels on List B, the following statements are usually true. The central character struggles to find meaning, purpose, authenticity, identity (or something that can be expressed by some other congruent term), and it is, in principle, possible for him or her to complete this quest successfully. That is, whether the protagonist is successful or not, the reader can easily perceive how one could have achieved this sort of success in the novel's world. The significance of the protagonist's experience is *personal*; that is, it is to be understood in terms of his or her individual growth, development, identity (or whatever). Social and political reality may hardly exist at all (as in the case of *As for Me and My House*), but in any case this reality has no importance beyond the way in which it affects the protagonists' lives. There is no serious examination of political and social issues, no indication that collective action may be as interesting or important as individual action.

The conservative technique that characterizes most of the works on List B is ideally suited to deliver narratives about this sort of world. The fact that hardly any of these novels make use of such a staple of twentieth-century fiction as multiple points of view is startling, but understandable, given the premises that the experience of the individual is what is of primary importance, and that the meaning of this experience can be presented without ambiguity. The texture of the realism (usually – though not always – grimly, humourlessly mimetic) discourages the reader from questioning suspiciously simple presuppositions about character or theme. This is how the world is, these novels tell us. There are no postmodernist or metafictional tricks to remind us that the narrative is playfully and subjectively structured by its author, no suggestion that the notion of identity has in our time itself become problematic, hardly a hint that one way to render the richness and complexity of the world is to present it through the eyes of two, three, or more equally important characters, rather than one.

To summarize, the world of the English-Canadian novels on List B is a world in which the main issues are personal, are clearly defined, are resolvable. To be a Canadian is to cultivate one's own garden – and to have the opportunity to do so according to a clear, simple set of rules. To write a Canadian novel is to ignore much about the way the art of fiction has developed in the twentieth century; it is, however, to use time-honoured literary techniques to point the way to some secular analogue of salvation – to write, as it were, a good gardening manual.

Is Canada not, after all, the best of all possible worlds?

IV

My simple conclusion is that we are in some danger in this country, as our attempt to find the ten best Canadian novels might also suggest, in assuming that there is one right way for criticism, of declaring an orthodoxy from which no variation is allowed.

Laurie Ricou, in *Taking Stock*, 98

Of course some of the works on List B deviate to some extent from the paradigm outlined in the last section. Nevertheless, the word 'orthodoxy' is not out of place in discussion of this group of novels. Brief synopses should be enough to establish this point. Consider the near-uniformity of attitude towards character and theme to be found in these works.

In *Who Has Seen the Wind*, Brian O'Connal begins to grow up in a small Prairie town (the story ends when he is twelve), where he learns to reject the ways of both the hypocritically religious Mrs Abercrombie and the amoral Bens. Instead, he begins to synthesize what is good in civilization with the values he has learned from studying the natural world, in the process preparing himself for what promises to be a happy and productive adult life.

In *The Mountain and the Valley*, David Canaan grows up in the Annapolis Valley. His ambition for his intense imagination never expresses itself in mature artistic creation. He dies a failure, but not before a final moment of insight reveals to him that the reason for this is his inability to find a central focus, a means of interpreting the myriad impressions that comprise the potential material for his art. Had he been able to discern this central meaning, he would have become an artist who could have enriched the lives of others by giving voice to a community characterized by its collective inarticulateness.

In *The Apprenticeship of Duddy Kravitz*, the protagonist becomes a success in material terms, but his life is to be judged a failure by the reader, as Duddy internalizes the values of survival-of-the-fittest capitalism and, in so doing, rejects the more humane values represented by some of the novel's minor characters.

In *The Watch That Ends the Night*, George Stewart moves towards self-knowledge and affirmation of the value of life, largely as a result of his relationships with his wife, Catherine, and the charismatic Jerome Martell, both of whom, in different ways, undergo profound suffering. As one commentator pus it: 'George is the main character; the central theme is his confrontation with death and a rejection of nihilistic despair. That is, Catherine's illness and Jerome's torture seem to happen only so that George can reach a plateau of understanding he could not otherwise have attained.'[7]

In *The Stone Angel*, Hagar Shipley, near the end of her long life, recognizes the way in which pride has isolated and imprisoned her; before she dies, she comes to understand that she should have given her allegiance to a different, more humane set of values which would allow for compassion, charity, openness, rejoicing.

In *Fifth Business*, Dustan Ramsay throughout his life rather smugly distances himself from the shallow materialism of Boy Staunton and finally comes to reject his Calvinist heritage of guilt. This enables him to join a community of self-selected elite who have achieved a state of profound self-understanding in accordance with the theories of C.G. Jung.

The two novels I have not yet discussed, *The Diviners* and *The Double Hook*, do not fit my paradigm quite as neatly as the others. But their deviation from it is far from radical.

In *The Diviners*, Morag Gunn achieves self-knowledge based on her acceptance of her personal and cultural past. This is almost the only novel on List B to attempt to engage directly social and political issues, as dispossession and injustice are major themes. The love of Morag's life is a feckless Métis named Jules Tonnerre; their daughter, Pique, embodies the union of traditional racial enemies. But this dimension of the novel remains subordinate to its interests in portraying Morag's character (she is the centre of consciousness throughout) and in creating a sense of what one commentator has called a 'mythical timelessness' invoked 'through literary and biblical allusions.'[8]

In *The Double Hook*, the narrative focus is, for once, not on the growth and development of an individual; the story is told from the points of view of a number of characters of approximately equal importance. In other respects, however, the novel is well within the bounds of (to use Ricou's word) 'orthodoxy.' The individual characters almost all move from an initial sense of isolation from others and from their own authentic being to a deeper sense of a self and a commitment to a renewed idea of community. Although the figure of Coyote is in many respects ambiguous, there is no doubt as to which values the novel affirms. Its implicit didacticism is as strong as that of the others on List B.

I should add here that I am aware that some of these others do deviate in minor ways from the general pattern outlined at the end of the last section. Margaret Laurence, it can be argued, does flirt timidly with certain 'postmodern' techniques in *The Diviners*. Some chapters of *The Mountain and the Valley* are presented from the point of view of characters other than David Canaan. And so on. But in the main, these works conform to the requirements of the List B paradigm.

In order to demonstrate the extent to which this is so, one need only point to the alternate list that I proposed in the first section of this essay. Consider some of the ways in which the 'orthodoxy' of List B could have been challenged by the inclusion of some of these other works. The mimetic realism dominating List B could have been called into question by the presence of several works that make use of techniques which, in various ways, draw attention to their own provisional, artificial nature as works of literature: *Beautiful Losers, The Temptations of Big Bear, The Studhorse Man, Coming through Slaughter, The Invention of the World*. Some of these novels, *Lady Oracle* especially, question the unitary nature of the self, something taken for granted in the works on List B. Others also question the hypothesis that personal fulfilment, authentic identity, or the like can be achieved by choosing to live according to the appropriate system of values. (In *From a Seaside Town*, for example, the protagonist cheerfully resigns himself to the fact that any such gesture on his part would be quixotic.) Others, through the use of multiple points of view, implicitly question the doctrine that the experience of a single individual should be the primary focus of interest in fiction: *The Temptations of Big Bear, The Disinherited, The Invention of the World*. While there is a certain comic element in such List B novels as *Fifth Business, Who Has Seen the Wind*, and *The Apprenticeship of Duddy Kravitz*, the predominant tone of List B is grim seriousness; consider how this might have been altered by the inclusion of such works as *Beautiful Losers, The Studhorse Man, Lady Oracle*, or *The Invention of the World*. The alternate list would have provided other forms of variety, as well. *White Figure, White Ground* is a novel whose protagonist is an intelligent, educated man who is also a Christian, a phenomenon absent from List B. *Coming through Slaughter* and *The Pegnitz Junction* are set in countries other than Canada, and their protagonists are not Canadians – features that presumably more or less automatically disqualify them from the list of 'most important' works.

Before concluding this section, I wish to return to the question of realism, and the treatment (or avoidance) of political and social issues. Dick Harrison's observations about *As for Me and My House* and other Prairie novels, ending with the question 'Where, in effect, is the outside world?' (181), can be made *mutatis mutandis* (and without reservation) with respect to *The Mountain and the Valley, The Double Hook*, and *Who Has Seen the Wind*, and, with only minor qualifications, with respect to nearly all of the other works on List B. If the 'outside world' is more prominent, as it is in, say, *Fifth Business* or *The Watch That Ends the Night*, its primary purpose is to provide a certain kind of context for the protagonist's identity quest. Even in *The Diviners*, the novel in which political issues are closest to the surface, we must be content with statements no sharper or more insightful than that implied by the relationship of Morag and Jules: the union of Celt and Métis produces a child whose identity synthesizes conflicting elements from the cultural past. All will be well if people who live in Canada will regard each other as members of the same family.

Compare this sort of approach with what we find in *The Pegnitz Junction*, with its subtle and delicate probing of the sources of Nazism in the personal life. Compare it with the way in which *The Temptations of Big Bear* radically questions received interpretations of Canadian history, with the way in which *The Disinherited* examines traditional Canadian attitudes to the land, or with the way in which *The Invention of the World* explores the nature of community in Canada. *The Pegnitz Junction* deals with themes that are important to any thinking person alive in our century. The other three works deal with themes that one would expect to be central to Canadian literature. But these themes are either under-represented or absent from the works on List B.

V

The University of Toronto Graduate Department of English is the largest graduate training department in Canada. For the year 1970–71 it offered graduate students choice from 106 courses. One, only, of the 106 was concerned with Canadian literature ... What is the situation today? ... In 1977–78 it offered seven courses involving u.s.

literature figures significantly [sic]. It listed three, largely survey, courses in Canadian literature.

Robin Mathews, *Canadian Literature: Surrender or Revolution*, 175–6

What the conference articulated above all was the maturity and richness of Canadian fiction ... In poorer times fictionally, a consensus might well have been reached simply in self-defence, but there was a comfortable feeling here that at last no apologies and no explanations had to be offered.

Hallvard Dahlie, in *Taking Stock*, 3

In 1978 no explanations had to be offered – if you were attending a conference of your fellow Canadianists. But the aura of self-congratulation that emanates from the pages of *Taking Stock* cannot obscure the fact that the study of Canadian literature in Canadian universities was not nearly as respectable as those attending the Calgary conference appeared to believe. As Robin Mathews has documented, even to *be* a Canadian in a Canadian university English department during the 1970s was to make a political statement: 'Before aliens began taking Canadian citizenship because of the loud airing of the citizenship issue,' Mathews reports, 'about ninety per cent of the U.B.C. English Department's more than thirty assistant professors were non-Canadians.'[9] It would be extremely naïve to think that, in such circumstances, the *teaching* of Canadian literature would not carry with it some heavy political cargo. Yet there are few hints of this in *Taking Stock*.

And it would be equally naïve to think that there is no connection between the 'class interests' of those who were teaching Canadian literature in 1978 and the group of novels selected for List B. I would like to conclude with a couple of speculative suggestions about such a connection. I began this essay by noting the conservatism of technique that characterizes List B, a fact immediately evident when my suggested 'alternate' list is placed alongside it. I went on to suggest that, during the 1970s, the teacher of Canadian literature was (to use Ohmann's analogy) in a 'marginal position with respect to capital,' that is, in constant need of justifying his or her existence to powerful colleagues who regarded their own work as (to use some of Keith's adjectives) more 'rigorous,' 'disciplined,' 'sophisticated,' and 'precise' than that of the Canadianist. I would like now to hypothesize that these two facts may be causally connected. That is, that the professional insecurity of the Canadianist may have led to a privileging of texts that are unremarkable with respect to technique: texts which are safe from being ridiculed as too ambitious, risky, obscure, or pretentious, texts which in more ways than one can be said to 'know their place.'

Respectable and inoffensive, the novels on List B (or at least many of them) can be read with profit by an intelligent fourteen-year-old. If any of them aspires to difficulty, it is in the modest manner of *The Double Hook*, constantly tugging its forelock to Modernist Tradition. (Essay topic: Wasteland Imagery in *The Double Hook*.) I'm only a foot-note, this novel says, a remote colony. It is as if List B were calculated to elicit chuckles of amused condescension from the Canadianist's wealthy cousins, the Faulkner scholar and the Beckett specialist. 'These novels aim low,' one of these might have said to the other, 'but, on balance, they achieve their aim.' Far better for this sort of judgment to be made of the works on one's syllabus than that they attempt too much and fail.

I would like, finally, to suggest the parallel possibility of a causal connection between the 'class interests' of the Canadianist and the *content* of the novels on List B. Conservatism of technique is not, after all, their only common denominator. As I have attempted to show, these novels tend to focus almost exclusively on the growth or develop-ment of an individual. The protagonist's success or failure turns on his or her ability to make correct choices according to a set of values which may vary slightly form novel to novel but is always (in the broad sense) humanist and is always clearly spelled out for the reader. Social or political reality, if it exists at all, is no more than a backdrop for the protagonist's quest for self-knowledge, self-fulfilment, or self-something-else.

Why would such novels be attractive to Canadianists of the late 1970s? One possible reason is that the emphasis, in these works, on making correct choices in one's personal life can be used to establish a strong link between CanLit courses and the general curriculum of the English department. A critical approach which concentrates on analysis of theme underscores the presence in these works of the 'values' of which English departments have such vast supplies, and thereby implicitly legitimizes itself: Margaret Laurence can be com-pared to Shakespeare, Ernest Buckler to Joyce. Questions of artistic merit – which would seem to provide another possible link to the rest of the curriculum – can be downplayed or ignored, since the implicit didacticism of these works upstages everything else.

But there may be a second, complementary answer to my question.

To present one's students with a vision of Canada from which political reality has virtually been effaced is to avoid a potential source of embarrassment. In the world of Canadian academe described by Robin Mathews, the professional survival of *Canadians* was a live issue, as much so as the development of the study of Canadian literature. It would have taken a courageous Canadianist indeed to have devised a syllabus giving prominence to questions of political power. Safer, perhaps, to choose works for which, in the words of Hallvard Dahlie, 'no apologies and no explanations had to be offered.'

Culture and Its Values: Critical Revisionism in Quebec in the 1980s

In some ways, the terms of the discussion relating aesthetic judgments to socio-political pressures have remained remarkably stable in the Quebec literary tradition. While critics have been far from unanimous on what it is that novels represent or how they go about representing, the articulation of the link between representation and value, between literary and social configurations, remains the persistent core of critical activity. Revisionist assault on the canon (those works deemed to most fruitfully effect this articulation) comes less in the form of an alternate list of works than in a shift in the site at which this essential link is discerned.

Perhaps the most important single issue which has emerged during the 1980s concerns the definition of the 'culture' which the novel is charged to convey – or challenge. It is surely something of a truism to say that Quebec has entered a crisis of culture as it passes from an ideal of a homogeneous, collective identity to a more problematic and heterogeneous conception of social and symbolic union. Increasing diversity in the representations of cultural space reflects the plurality of discourses and interests which seek expression *within* the borders of Quebec culture.

This diversity is to be seen as well within literary theory and criticism. This paper will examine two important revisionist readings of the Quebec novel – those of Pierre Nepveu and of Patricia Smart – in the light of the new correspondences they draw between the text and images of social space. In evoking two quite different configurations, in attempting in very different ways to redefine cultural identity, their work comes to crystallize issues in the contemporary debate concerning the *grounds* of literary value. While the feminist and postmodernist paradigms they use are (relatively) new to Quebec criticism, their attention to the institutional constraints and conflictual interests which underly critical activity is not. This tradition reaches back to the very first versions of the dialogue between the novel and social values in Quebec.

A History of Negativity

From the start, the novel in Quebec engages in a conflictual dialogue with aesthetic and moral value. 'Ceci n'est pas un roman': 'what you have before you is not a novel and I am not a real writer,' say the plentiful prefaces to nineteenth-century historical fiction in Quebec, enjoining readers to exercise prudence in engaging with the text.[1] Coy or sincere, the disclaimers show the novels to be navigating between two kinds of judgments, two potential modes of legitimation. By disqualifying themselves on *aesthetic* grounds (they do not dare consider themselves candidates for literary glory), they nicely avoid dangerous confrontation with the *moral* prohibitions of institutional authority.

Gilles Marcotte, at the start of his own book, which in turn inaugurates modern criticism in Quebec,[2] underlines the ambivalence of Quebec's first novels, their simultaneous acceptance and taunting of 'the fearful theology of the 1870s.' The hesitations of these first novels, their uncertain status as literature, become a haunting and persistent motif for the critics of the early 1960s. Doomed to incompletion and mediocrity because of the very society it confronts, the novel becomes the basis of a paradigm of failure which informs much of the most powerful critical writing of that period.

For these critics, the 'novel,' in fact, became a term of value in itself, a positive term situated between two poles of exclusion. It took on existence and value in opposition to what it was not: on the one hand, the failed novel (which was tainted by didacticism and which was really an essay); and, on the other, poetry. The first criterion would allow critics to take the nineteenth-century prefaces at face value and to dismiss a substantial portion of the corpus of Quebec novels as non-literary. Expelled from the realm of the Quebec novel, these problematic texts (like Gérin-Lajoie's *Jean Rivard* or the more controversial *Les Demi-civilisés* [*Sackcloth for Banner* in English] by Jean-Charles Harvey) were relegated to the category of contentious or simply uninteresting essays. It is something of a paradox that one of the most substantial pieces of modern Quebec criticism, André Belleau's *Le Romancier fictif*, is devoted to a corpus of novels which Belleau himself admits to be of questionable literary value.[3]

These exclusions on aesthetic grounds are just one part of the heritage of negativity which the novel brought with it to the 1960s. Marcotte, van Schendel, and others will complain that the relative failure of the novel in Quebec up until the 1960s is in reality a political failure; the Quebec novel does not 'measure up' to the standards which would make the literary form (and the society it expresses) fully realized. How painful it is to read these critics as they speak of the refusals and incapacities of the novel, the alienation and impossibilities it expresses. But beyond this aesthetics of failure is the hope of change: 'We are led to believe that the French-Canadian novel will reach the age of value (both moral and aesthetic value) when a certain number of ideas and principles will have been inscribed in our existence and in our milieu.'[4] The very poverty of the genre (in comparison to what it could be, in view of the master works which are yet to come) becomes a political accusation and a rallying cry.

The dialogue between the novel and poetry, also launched during the 1960s, has a rather different critical function. Here critics ask what forms of representation are most appropriate to social needs. Some held that poetry is an expression of ideals which the novel (because too tied to material reality) cannot express (Georges-André Vachon and Michel van Schendel in 1964); others maintained that only the novel can express with maturity a modern society (Jacques Brault and Marcotte).[5] André Brochu suggests quite recently that poetry is perhaps above all a kind of affirmation and the novel a kind of criticism.[6]

This kind of discussion, we know, has venerable roots in Continental speculative philosophy and the various schools of criticism which evolved from it. From the Aristotelian typologies of lyric, dramatic, and epic through to the theories of Lukács, Bakhtin, and others, literary form has been given specific functions and values. The novel has more often than not been considered a factor of progress in the history of literature and thought. Its very polymorphism, causing perpetual difficulties of definition, has been interpreted positively. 'If the word "roman" has throughout the centuries, resisting its own semantic challenges, continued to designate a genre perpetually renewing itself, it is surely because the revolutionary and transformational element implied in the word "roman" as well as the idea of a new literary language, were more important than the content of the works.'[7] Surely the prize for the largest extension of 'novelness' should go to Bakhtin, who ascribed novelness to any text which would work to undermine the official or high culture of any society.[8]

While generic criticism of the idealistic sort has generally fallen into disrepute ('genre' is dead, as the title of a recent volume of Quebec criticism reminds us),[9] the question has not entirely lost its pertinence for Quebec critics. Indeed, there are important echoes of these issues in two recent and significant works of criticism, Pierre Nepveu's *L'Ecologie du réel* and Patricia Smart's *Ecrire dans la maison du père*,[10] which in two quite different ways bring to the critical forefront new formulations of the question of representations of the novel and culture in Quebec. Neither of these two formulations seems entirely satisfying. But both books are important and influential efforts to rethink national-cultural paradigms. It would seem appropriate to examine them – their differences and similarities – against the backdrop of the social and intellectual currents from which they emerged.

Revising the Tradition

Despite the very obvious differences between Smart's feminist project and Nepveu's postmodernism, their books, both published in 1988, offer a few surprising similarities. Both are *books* in the strong sense of the word, works which progress from a significant beginning moment to a conclusive end. This kind of volume is rather rare in Quebec criticism, where major critics regularly publish collections of essays making little claim to a coherent overall interpretation of Quebec literature. And while several recent critics (André Belleau and Suzanne Lamy, for example) have offered strong new critical tools for reading Quebec literature, they have not systematically 'applied' their perspectives to a large and varied corpus. Both Nepveu's and Smart's books are teleological in form and orientation: they isolate a moment *ab initio* from which the movement of interpretation will draw its force (for Smart, Laure Conan's *Angéline*; for Nepveu, the literary figures who became the founding myths of the 1960s); and they conclude by identifying so-called marginal works as the true centre, the significant core, of contemporary Quebec writing. In addition, both books are concerned less with presenting new critical objects than in a revisionist view of the tradition. This orientation has the double effect of augmenting the weight and substance of the tradition (what Smart calls the 'Quebec cultural text,' a scroll unfurling from 1884 to the present day) at the same time as it confirms what René Payant has defined as the essentially revisionist nature of the postmodern 1980s: 'We understand then that postmodernism is probably not the production of new objects, that it does not derive from the progress of Techno-culture, that it is not a question of style. It concerns interpretative and evaluative systems, in other words reception. The postmodern condition is the ... disappearance of stable and absolute frames of reference.'[11]

The two books confront this increasing relativity of frames of reference in quite different fashions. Smart's forceful reading of the Quebec cultural text from a feminist perspective remains tied (as her title announces) to the conceptual world it opposes. Feminist values are defined as oppositional; they presume a solid cultural edifice against which they come into existence. Nepveu's cultural world is more like a ritualized mixture of signs and discourses, which literature comes to mimic, finding its truth in the expression of the forms or formlessness of culture. Nepveu challenges the myths which since the 1960s have made literature an expression of collective certainties. His rereading of the critical 'fictions' generated from the literature of the 1960s on seeks to restore to this material its reality as 'inner exile,' as 'catastrophe.' Exchanging progress and affirmation for an ethics of pluralization and doubt, Nepveu confronts but cannot resolve the dilemma of value. It is at this blocking-point that Nepveu's project is particularly instructive.

As a final preliminary remark, I might add that my focus will be exclusively on the formulation of critical concepts by Smart and Nepveu, not on their readings of individual texts, which in both cases are admirably strong and illuminating.

A New Realism

Smart's reading of the emergence of the feminine voice in Quebec literature proposes a dramatization in which two separate trajectories – masculine and feminine – are pitted one against the other. The masculine voice is dominated by the themes of tragedy, wandering, blackness, exacerbated mysticism; the feminine voice is oppositional, preferring texture to structure, eros to logos, rhythm to affirmation. In an extremely coherent reading of Quebec novels from *Angéline de Montbrun* on, Smart uses the figure of the Oedipal triangle as the matrix of her reading of the rivalries in the 'father's house' of language and culture.

Though Smart distances herself from essentialist feminism in the introduction to her book, the extremely wide use she makes of 'the feminine' tends to disqualify those precautionary terms and imposes a sense of the feminine as a value in itself. The analysis of Quebec novels moves from the inaugural gestures of Laure Conan to a paroxysmal moment of quasi completion in the work of France Théoret. The feminine and the real are conflated: the coming into being of the feminine in language is also the movement towards an 'authentic realism' (323).

The concept of realism turns out to be extremely important to Smart. Realism, like the feminine, is proposed as a value because it assumes a certain responsibility and direction in literary representation. 'The question of the representation of reality – and therefore of the *novel* – remains persistent and involves moral and political as well as aesthetic choices. Remaining open to marginal and dispossessed voices without fitting them into the socio-cultural and historical fabric, is this not to remain an eternal 'little girl' in the House of the Father? If the voice comes from everywhere, where is the unity and responsibility?' (303).

Smart appeals to the concept of realism as the anchor which will signify the insertion of the 'modern' subject within her society. Despite the evident modernity of a writer like France Théoret, she becomes for Smart a 'realist' writer in a tradition directly inherited from Gabrielle Roy. She is a writer in the tradition of realism because she has sought to bring into words a hitherto unspoken reality.

In fact, the use of the concept of realism here is almost purely rhetorical.[12] Smart could have used any number of other terms, more commonly associated with modernism, to draw attention to the mechanisms by which the difficulties of the modern feminist subject are shaped. But by using this term specifically, she defines Théoret's work as a progression in a line stretching from Laure Conan to Gabrielle Roy at the same time as she situates her own work within a critical tradition inherited from Gilles Marcotte. Referring in her conclusion to Marcotte's imagining of an impossible 'novel of maturity' for Quebec in 1976, Smart identifies *Nous parlerons comme on écrit* as 'almost' the realization of this (perhaps illusory) dream.

But this new realism will not be a 'masculine' realism. It will try not to 'capture' reality but to 'approach it gently, being attentive to its nuances – in other words, to respect all the otherness that the gesture of writing brings to language' (304). Have women not too quickly relegated realism 'like all other "discourses of mastery" to the dusty shelves of literary history'? In breaking with realism and mimetic representation, in abandoning the possibility of a totalizing vision or a stable point of view, does the novel not risk 'losing at the same time its ethic, moral and political dimension,' the possibility of suggesting a 'direction in the infinite density of signs'? (305).

Smart's archaeological exploration of the Quebec cultural text ends with a determination to impose femininity, realism, and action as positively connoted values – as the order and direction which the novel should furnish to its readers. With its oracular call for action and its ultimate appeal to feminine reality as a transcendent authenticity, Smart's conclusion sets a confident agenda which seems somewhat removed from the pluralism and conceptual doubts of the hyperconscious '80s. (In fact, Smart's coverage of the masculine 'contemporary novel' ends around 1975.) While Smart's book has the immense merit of imposing gender as a constitutive element of culture – a perspective long overdue in historical studies of Quebec literature – it tends to de-emphasize the heterogeneity of feminine subjectivity and experience.[13] At the same time it offers a vision of an 'emergent' literature which renews a venerable Quebec topos.

Hierarchies

Pierre Nepveu's *L'Ecologie du réel*, in contrast, circulates in a hyperconscious, exacerbated contemporaneity. Beginning by defining the feeling of an 'after' which he calls 'post-québécois' culture, Nepveu quickly leaves the 'then' of literary history for the 'now' of interpretation and myth. 'I am convinced that the situation of culture in the 1980s ... offers the possibility, beyond a sometimes salutary nostalgia and pessimism, of rereading the Quebec tradition, of displacing it and questioning it from new angles' (9–10). Nepveu's book is an ambitious and complex attempt to work out the increasingly problematic dynamics between literature and culture. He directs textual analysis to the realization that Quebec has over the past ten or fifteen years (and especially after the defeat of the referendum) changed its view of itself. Culture has become an accumulation of spaces, references, and pulsations, the very opposite of the rather monolithic entity to which earlier critics could refer.

If Patricia Smart's book (in parallel, of course, with the prominent and abundant body of feminist writing and theory) can be said to have emerged out of the social context of feminism in Quebec – both as a social movement and as a long-term creative struggle to redefine the place of women within the symbolic world – one can place Pierre Nepveu's book against the backdrop of a more diffuse but significant series of recent productions which point to new conceptions of collective cultural space. A heterogeneous and cursory list of such productions might include those novels of the 1980s which take the form of laid-back, often ironic 'quests' for identity (the novels of Jacques Poulin,

Yvon Rivard, and Dany Laferrière, or even Anne Hébert's *Le Premier Jardin*), Denys Arcand's sardonic comment on the sense of collective destiny in the *Decline of the American Empire*, the plurilingualism and intercultural themes of playwright Robert Lepage's *Dragon Trilogy*, the infatuation with Shakespeare which overtook the Montreal theatre scene during the summer of 1988, the continued popularity of Bakhtin in literary studies as a reference for culture as dialogue and contradiction, the new passion shown by Quebec social scientists for Quebec's minority communities[14] – these are just a few signs of the de-centring of nationalist paradigms in contemporary thought.

It is precisely the way the contemporary novel comes to configure this reconceptualization of social space which interests Nepveu. Nepveu's readings of Villemaire, Brossard, and Poulin concentrate on the textual structures which underscore the difficult relationship between the density of cultural signs and the individual desire to make sense of the cultural order.

Though not, properly speaking, itself a work of socio-criticism, we can consider Nepveu's book to be a response to the evolution of socio-critical perspectives of the last decade. The unproblematic relationship between literature and national culture which seemed so natural to such writers as Jean Royer or Marcel Rioux (respectively criticized by Jean Larose and François Ricard)[15] is here deliberately blown wide open. But rather than avoiding the national question altogether as many thinkers might have been tempted to do during the last decade (Ricard: 'Quebec is no longer an object of thought'),[16] Nepveu's book throws itself energetically into the void left by the death of a certain nationalist criticism.[17]

At the same time, Nepveu's focus on the spatial and conceptual patterns of the novels appears to be one more displacement in the history of recent socially oriented *textual* criticism. While much Quebec socio-criticism has given a great deal of attention to external institutional or ideological constraints in the production of literature and literary value,[18] some critics, like Suzanne Lamy and André Belleau, have sought to combine a concern for social pressures with internal analysis. And so Suzanne Lamy created categories of feminist writing ('bavardage,' litany, dialogue) which occupied a space *between* oral and written forms, between the anonymous murmur of tradition and the articulations of modernist writers,[19] and André Belleau showed the novel to be a conflictual space traversed by the differing cultural norms and codes which inform the society at large.[20] Nepveu also seeks in textual patterns architectures of social space, but these patterns are no longer exclusively discursive – as they were for Belleau and Lamy. Language gives way to metaphors of space: the archaeologies of Francine Noël and of Régine Robin, the gestures of ritualization in Jacques Poulin and Yolande Villemaire, the figure of the angel, the dialogue of translation in Poulin and Nicole Brossard. Dialogue immediately loses its linguistic dimension to become a figure for a social space in which 'dialogism,' a 'strong, non-fusional pluralism,' will not dissolve into relativism but exist as an 'unceasing problem, a disorder which must be assumed and surmounted otherwise than through dogmatic appeals to unity, identity, recentring' (215).

Minorities at the Centre

The chapter which Nepveu devotes to the writing of Marilù Mallet, Régine Robin, Jean Jonassaint, Naïm Kattan, Fulvio Caccia, Marco Micone, Anne-Marie Alonzo, and others, is significant for a number of reasons. It is the first important overview of Quebec minority writing by a major Quebec critic. In addition to the important critical dimensions of Nepveu's analysis, this chapter tells of the changing institutional emphases of literary research in Quebec over the last few years.

Two tendencies have been most important in opening up the field of critical investigation in Quebec over the past decade. On the one hand, the semiotics of culture created a vast new range of critical objects. On the other, the great quantity of research, both conceptual and empirical, generated by the concept of the literary institution focused the attention of researchers on areas traditionally 'excluded' from mainstream considerations. In consequence, there has been a perceptible move towards the exploration of literary margins. Topics until now ignored by Quebec criticism – translation, French-language minority writing in Quebec, Montreal as a pluralistic cultural space – have become the objects of new and general interest.[21] Nepveu's chapter, however, is the first global appropriation of this corpus within a book devoted to the Quebec tradition in general.

It is doubly significant then that 'l'écriture migrante' both becomes for Nepveu an echo of the Quebec tradition which since the 1960s defines itself in terms of exile, the absent country, negativity, an 'excentric' space, and also coincides with the postmodern aesthetic – a return to history and representation in the hybrid, plural mode. This pluralism 'opens a new relationship to what is "here," a relationship expressed first by exiles and immigrants but which could well belong to any contemporary Quebec consciousness' (206).

To measure the distance between Nepveu's equation of centre and margins in Quebec literature and the judgments of past critics, we might recall a bizarre footnote which Gilles Marcotte adds to the last page of his *Roman à l'imparfait* (1976). Discussing the Quebec novel's difficult relationship to history, Marcotte mentions Mordecai Richler's work as the successful counter-example to the failure of novels like Gérard Bessette's *The Brawl*. Marcotte 'explains' this difference by the fact that Richler 'belongs to a culture in which the historical order conserves its powers.' In other words, Marcotte seems to attribute Richler's success in portraying the life of Montreal to his Jewish culture. This association of a successful realist aesthetic (inspired by a Lukácsian ideal?) with a specific historico-cultural tradition is certainly surprising – especially as it neglects the considerable aesthetic distances among Jewish writers (Kafka and Bellow, Canetti and Malamud). Nepveu's project avoids any such potentially reductive generalizations by leaving aside the traits which divide one cultural group from another in favour of an all-englobing concept of marginality. The concept of 'inner exile' is elevated rather to an exemplary status, to be discovered at the centre of Quebec writing.[22]

But while Nepveu sees in 'écriture migrante' a positive materialization of all Quebec writers' difficult relationship to place and memory, as well as the valorization of difference and cultural pluralism, he is also fearful of the (im)morality of absolute relativism, which might be the logical conclusion of such an aesthetic position. Despite, however, the numerous provisos and conditionals he sprinkles throughout his text, Nepveu has no real critical defence with which to elude such a conclusion. He has scuttled any conceptual appeals to authenticity or ultimate grounds. And so he says of the writing of Yolande Villemaire that it is 'a writing of migration at the centre of here,' linked in an essential manner with the experience of exile, the emptiness, the whiteness which is at the heart of Quebec experience but which also suggests the 'ultimate reduction of all differences' (191). It is here that we begin to wonder what is to separate Nepveu's own critical appraisal from the words he quotes from one of Villemaire's characters: 'Everything is in everything' (169)? Nepveu seems to suggest that the dispersion of signs and the energetic irrationalism of Villemaire's writing are at once an accurate transcription of an overcharged cultural environment and a challenge to the very possibility of order and direction. Rather than appealing, as Smart does, to a redeeming concept like realism, Nepveu accepts the difficult paradoxes of texts (and worlds) devoid of centre.

The 'Case' of Villemaire

The 'case' of Yolande Villemaire rather dramatically marks the limitations of Nepveu's refusal to create a hierarchy of textual practices. The writing of Villemaire, along with that of Jacques Poulin and Nicole Brossard, define exemplary responses for Nepveu to an identical cultural situation. Reacting to a certain 'ideological exhaustion' (159), to the 'loss of meaning of history, the problematic nature of reality itself, the fragmentation of the territory of culture, the loss of social solidarities and the attempt to redefine them,' these writers pose the question of 'energy, englobing and even swallowing up the question of meaning' (165). Questioning the notion of culture as a 'global field of references and identifications' (162), *La Vie en prose* demonstrates 'one of the most profound and decisive changes in our relationship to literature and to the totality of culture: a relationship which no longer gives priority to meaning (because it is too multiple, too infinitely differed) but which is centred on force, on energy' (166). While Nepveu shows that he is aware of the 'worst regressions' suggested by this 'neo-primitivism,' this coupling of meaning and force, he does not condemn it. Rather, returning to this theme in his conclusion, he offers 'energy' as one of the figures of ritualism which define the response of literature to the ethical and aesthetic confusions of contemporary thought.

One senses in Nepveu's pondered remarks a certain uneasiness. He uses a vocabulary of mysticism and irrationality ('angelism,' 'pollution,' 'energy,' 'form-force') while recognizing its real conceptual and moral dangers. At the same time he refuses to judge negatively what he clearly considers to be an accurate representation of the 'cultural stress,' 'disorder,' and 'ritualization' of contemporary culture.

Had Nepveu chosen to analyse Villemaire's next novel, *La Constellation du cygne* (he refers to it in passing as an 'end-point,' the extreme limit where multiple identities and cultural mixtures tend to melt into total undifferentiation [201]), he would no doubt have had to take a position on Villemaire's narrative strategy – if only because the book has given rise to some (but surprisingly little) debate. Suzanne Lamy has delivered a multi-pronged attack on the novel, to which Caroline Bayard offered a measured and perceptive response.[23]

It might be useful to recall here that *La Constellation du cygne* tells of an erotic relationship between a Jewish prostitute and a Nazi soldier and ends with an oneiric cremation scene at Auschwitz. Suzanne Lamy's objections to the novel concern the writer's responsibility both to history and to feminist consciousness; she explicitly rejects the structuralist bias which has turned the referent into an 'effect of reality.' Lamy notes the inconsistencies of the story and its historical improbability, grounding her critique in the regained legitimacy of the referent in critical theory.

Lamy argues for a feminist position which takes into account the social realities of author and reader. She is seconded in this by Caroline Bayard, who in a finely argued response concurs in affirming the novel's responsibility to the past (the ethics of history) – if not to the future (the ideals of feminism).

It is significant that criticism of Villemaire's novel should come from a feminist position, especially as *La Vie en prose* was enthusiastically greeted as an important feminist work. In arguing against the trivialization of history and the confusion of passion and titillation, critics of Villemaire's work find themselves of course in the very midst of the postmodern debate. While it may be true, as Linda Hutcheon persuasively argues, that postmodern historical metafiction can have an important function as political critique, this aesthetic can also easily fall into self-parody or, as Janet Paterson worried, 'narcissism' and 'neo-mannerism.'[24] Nepveu's reluctance to take a position is consonant with his conceptual approach: culture is not constructed as continuity or as value (here again in opposition to Smart) but rather as a problematized space.

Rewriting Culture

By drawing to their extremes the two positions we have traced – creating a somewhat artificial and perhaps tendentious dichotomy – we find the novel to be, on the one hand, the expression of a culture on the way to recovering its suppressed truth; on the other, a revelation of irrecoverable loss, the passage from the security of totalizing truths to the potentially infinite relativity of pluralism. These diagnoses are based on two different conceptions of social and textual space: on the one hand, the dyadic relation of alterity (which risks the polarities of essentialism); on the other, the plurality of difference (which is threatened with the vaporous mysticism of total undifferentiation). By giving our two positions the value of exemplary sites within the spectrum of contemporary thought, we can see in them the conflicts which are at the heart of the debate on postmodernism, on conceptions of the subject, and specifically on feminism's 'difficult alliance' with postmodernism.[25]

Such neat dichotomies exist only to be transcended, however. The

very different responses of feminist critics to the dilemmas of postmodernism are revealing of the wide range of theoretical and conceptual assumptions which already inhabit literary feminism today.
Feminist theory has become increasingly attentive to the necessary
heterogeneity of concepts of gender, and feminist cultural analysis of
the 1980s and 1990s has undertaken to confront the complexities of
social pluralism which Nepveu's perspective takes into account. It has
indeed become clear that all cultural critique must include gender as
a fundamental conceptual category through which the narratives of
culture are constructed.[26]

Most illuminating among the insights offered by the divergences
between conceptions of social space in these two studies, however, is
the way in which literature comes to make evident the complex and
problematic nature of culture itself. Both are instrumental in exposing
the way in which the novel represents the mechanisms of cultural
production, the process by which social reality takes on conceptual
form, by which the realm of the symbolic comes to inhabit all aspects
of material existence. Their very disagreements show how the cultural
arena is in fact a field of overlapping and competing versions of reality –
and that power consists precisely in the ability to create and sustain
representations and their interpretations.

Normalizing the Subject: Linda Hutcheon and the English-Canadian Postmodern

We were told over and over again that theory was really in bad taste.

George Bowering, *Future Indicative*, 18

We are, of course, still being told that theory – a mere fashion, a dis/ease – is in bad taste and that literary study in English Canada will soon return to 'normal,' to the world of community, shared values, mutual illumination, health, and moral well-being, values which have prevailed – in fact, become canonic – in English-Canadian literary criticism for more than a century.

Nonetheless, something else appears to be happening as well, for not only have individual Canadian theorists pursued their destabilizing craft, but 'theory' as a discipline, in spite of the negative polemic often accompanying its incursions, came to be widely known in Canada during the 1980s, primarily in association with postmodernism. In fact, to the extent that Canadian theory has achieved recognition outside its own disciplinary boundaries at all, it is largely a result of the widespread circulation and popularity of books like Linda Hutcheon's *The Canadian Postmodern* (1988).[1]

Evidently written primarily for a Canadian college and university audience, *The Canadian Postmodern* may interestingly be compared with Hutcheon's *A Poetics of Postmodernism* (1988),[2] which, though published in the same year, addresses a very different audience. No longer at pains to clarify technical terms or even to explain her own allusions as she was in *The Canadian Postmodern* (e.g., TCP, 75, n. 14), Hutcheon is free in the second book to construct a more complex, historically embedded argument and to draw on theoretical materials which she assumes will be well known to her readers. The differences in Hutcheon's rhetoric from one book to the other no doubt result, at least in part, from the different circumstances of publication: the Toronto office of Oxford University Press in the first case and the international house, Routledge (formerly Methuen), in the second. But one cannot, of course, fault Hutcheon for the perennial attachment of Canadian academic publishers, presumably including Oxford, to the belletristic tradition. Nor can one exclusively fault the publishers since they frequently rely on subsidies from the Canadian Federation for the Humanities' Aid to Scholarly Publication Programme,[3] which itself has the perhaps unintended but nevertheless very real effect of maintaining the status quo in a given field. In what is whimsically still known as 'English,' that levelling effect tends to exclude serious theoretical work from publication, at least without 'revisions' tantamount to mutilation of a theoretical text written in any of the languages (deconstruction, semiotics, etc.) of the discipline. However, the extent to which *both* of Hutcheon's books, despite the levelling of lexicon and restriction of focus in the first, express precisely those communitarian values which many still take to be the norm in Canadian 'literary criticism' is an index of Hutcheon's acceptability, thus accessibility and canonic status in the Canadian literary market-place.

Less radical than the longer-canonized Northrop Frye, Hutcheon balances on the edge of English-Canadian acculturated intolerance of speculative thought, redeeming herself at every possible lapse through invocation of the official values enshrined in our literary tradition. In fact, so close to the rhetoric of the great Canadian hermeneutic/realist paradigm does Hutcheon's poetics of postmodernism come that co-optation by the still dominant Tory tradition seems almost inevitable. Subjecting Canadian as well as international modernism to a normalizing influence, domesticating deviance and inscribing it within her postmodern paradigm, Hutcheon converts danger into safety, the marginalized into the mainstream, the non-referential into the referential. Presenting a classically 'anti-modern, pro-postmodern'[4] position, Hutcheon undertakes what Robert Kroetsch has called a 'righting of the culture'[5] which returns it to its long-held values, its code of civility, and privileging of clarity, good taste, and 'standard English.'

An 'enabling violation,'[6] this 'righting' reinscribes the code of accessibility/community/conformity across the destabilizing codes of theory; reinscribes a hermeneutics of word and world, of illumination, affirmation, and progress as strategy of control, containment, legitimation of what might otherwise disrupt the hegemonic balance of a *Realpolitik* founded on good taste and liberal-humanist assumptions about the correct construction of the world, the text, and their points of interface. As Hutcheon, following Wolfgang Iser and Stanley Fish, stresses, readers define genre, and reading strategies 'co-create' (*TCP*, 27, 83) texts. All the more important, then, that readers learn politely to perform as autonomous subjects in the parlour game of liberal postmodernism, having their reality strategies parodically inverted, their metaphysics of the present historiographically transmuted via the 'grand narrative'[7] of metafiction and restored at the end to normal. However, if the Formalist/speech-act assertion of the association of the performative with literariness is to be set aside – as Hutcheon does – in favour of a theorizing of performance as hyphen between art and life, then we must question with greater urgency what doctrine of life is inscribed across this call to text-processing, what concept of reality – or, as Umberto Eco puts it, what theology[8] – legitimates this performance.

Taking *The Canadian Postmodern* and *A Poetics of Postmodernism* as focal texts, then, I propose in this paper to consider 'the text's long degeneration toward the normal'[9] in recent Canadian theory, and to explore some aspects of the canonic rhetoric of co-optation which has subverted the work of deconstructive theory in English Canada at points of greatest visibility for academic practice. Given that *The Canadian Postmodern* is essentially a thematically restricted and simplified version of *A Poetics of Postmodernism*, I will also be considering points of contact and similarity between these two texts and their respective delineations of implied readers, Canadian and international. The third in a series of studies of the canonic rhetoric of Canadian criticism/ theory which I have undertaken, this paper relies particularly on 'The Discourse of "Civility": Strategies of Containment in Literary Histories of English Canada' and, to a lesser extent, on ' "Maps and Tales": The Progress of *Canadian Literature*, 1959–87,'[10] both undertaken in association with the 'History of the Literary Institution in Canada' (HOLIC/HILAC) project at the University of Alberta. In those studies it became apparent that the seemingly communitarian values denoted by such code-words as *strength, fidelity, clarity, sincerity, vitality,* and *accessibility* have from at least the 1880s to the present been used as strategies of containment in English-Canadian literary criticism of Canadian writing. Whether in a canonic journal like *Canadian Literature* under the editorial supervision of George Woodcock (from 1959 to 1977) or, more recently, of W.H. New (from 1977) or in a history of

Canadian literature such as W.J. Keith's *Canadian Literature in English* (1985), this rhetoric of sharing and mutuality has been used as a device of exclusion, casting beyond its pale the work of all those who choose other values, other styles. That these rhetorical strategies of containment should continue to operate is predictable; that a leading exponent of postmodernism can be accommodated to them is perhaps less so. Situating her work in metonymic relation to canonic strategies of containment, Hutcheon herself shares in the great Canadian attempt to normalize the subject through sheer force of decorum and civility.

In a much-quoted statement first published in 1974, in *Boundary 2*'s special issue on Canadian literature, Robert Kroetsch maintains that 'Canadian literature evolved directly from Victorian into Postmodern.'[11] As Linda Hutcheon has herself pointed out, however, this statement 'tends to underplay the strong *continuing* tradition of realist fiction in English-Canadian writing as well as the fact that Canadian postmodernist fiction presupposes the existence of dominant realist conventions in order to effect its parodic postmodern challenges' (*TCP*, 182, Hutcheon's italics). Thus just as modernism constitutes the necessary ground for postmodernist refutation, so Victorian realism constitutes the necessary ground for modernist refutation via modernism's emphasis on form, structure, technique in and of itself, and rejection of the Victorian humanist ideology of the subject (Freud its greatest proponent) and of progress (Darwin et al.). Before we can consider Hutcheon's concept of postmodernism in detail, we need therefore to provide ourselves with a sketch-map of modernism. Andreas Huyssen provides a convenient list of canonic notions of the modernist art work exemplifying the major characteristics of international or so-called 'high' modernism:

- The work is autonomous and totally separate from the realms of mass culture and everyday life.
- It is self-referential, self-conscious, frequently ironic, ambiguous, rigorously experimental.
- It is the expression of a purely individual consciousness rather than of a Zeitgeist or a collective state of mind.
- Its experimental nature makes it analogous to science, and like science it produces and carries knowledge.
- Modernist literature since Flaubert is a persistent exploration of and encounter with language.
- The major premise of the modernist art work is the rejection of all classical systems of representation, the effacement of 'content,' the erasure of subjec-

tivity and authorial voice, the repudiation of likeness and verisimilitude, the exorcism of any demand for realism of whatever kind.

– Only by fortifying its boundaries, by maintaining its purity and autonomy, and by avoiding any contamination with mass culture and with the signifying systems of everyday life can the art work maintain its adversary stance: adversary to the bourgeois culture of everyday life as well as adversary to mass culture and entertainment which are seen as the primary forms of bourgeois cultural articulation.[12]

However, with the emergence of dada, surrealism, and constructivism, as Huyssen points out, modernism undergoes a mutation, and the art work's privileged autonomy as well as its exclusivist separation from mass culture disappear.[13] While the work's aversion to bourgeois culture sometimes remains, in the defining case of open modernism in English, that of James Joyce, bourgeois Bloom and HCE refute the charge while both *Ulysses* and *Finnegans Wake* joyously exhibit the integration of popular and so-called 'high' cultural forms as well as the polyvocal call to performative enactment which characterizes the Joycean or so-called 'experimental' tradition[14] in international modern writing from Stein, Beckett, and Borges to Zukofsky, Niedecker, Calvino, Eco, Jane Bowles, Lyn Hejinian, and so on into the 1990s.

Taking its primary model from postmodernism in architecture, Hutcheon's theory retains for literature those characteristics of architectural history which Paolo Portoghesi emphasizes in a passage used as an epigraph in *A Poetics of Postmodernism*. 'Those who fear a wave of permissiveness,' Portoghesi writes, 'would do well to remember that the ironic use of quotation and the archaeological artifact as an *objet trouvé* are discoveries of the figurative avant-garde of the twenties that have landed on the island of architecture sixty years late' (*PP*, 32). Displacing dada and surrealism from modernism, Portoghesi takes the absolutist emphasis on, as Hutcheon says, 'social reform through purity of structure' (*PP*, 30) as definitive of the modernist movement in architecture. Setting aside precisely the Bauhaus/constructivist principle of form following function which is exemplified in the work of such modernists as Le Corbusier and Mies van der Rohe, Hutcheon maintains that postmodern architects like Portoghesi, Venturi, and Jencks have 'turned from pure form to function and to the *history* of function' (*PP*, 39, Hutcheon's italics). But the history of modernism is more complex than such neat oppositions will permit. In splitting off function from form, Hutcheon succeeds temporarily in bracketing what she calls 'formalism' with modernism. However, not only the history of architecture but also that of literary theory make the whole picture vastly more complex. 'Formalism,' after all, is not simply a random accretion of the noun *form* plus suffix *-al* plus suffix *-ism*, and the history of Russian Formalism, Prague structuralism, and French structuralism cannot logically be subsumed, as Hutcheon tries to do, under the simplistic equation of 'structuralist/modernist/formalism' (*PP*, 52) without at least exploring Hutcheon's own indebtedness to Formalism with a capital *F*.

Consider, for example, Hutcheon's use of Roman Jakobson's concept of the dominant with reference to what she calls the dominant culture (*TCP*, 182) or ideology (*TCP*, 35). Jakobson defines the dominant as 'the focusing component of a work of art: it rules, determines, and transforms the remaining components. It is the dominant which guarantees the integrity of the structure.'[15] Further, 'the dominant specifies the work ... [it] specifies a given variety of language [which] dominates the entire structure and thus acts as its mandatory and inalienable constituent dominating all the remaining elements and exerting direct influence upon them' (82). Jakobson maintains that the dominant may be sought 'not only in the poetic work of an individual artist and not only in the poetic canon, the set of norms of a given poetic school, but also in the art of a given epoch, viewed as a particular whole' (83). Bringing all of this contextual information to bear upon the reading of a particular text, Jakobson's 'reader of a poem or ... viewer of a painting has a vivid awareness of two orders: the traditional canon and the artistic novelty as a deviation from that canon. It is precisely against the background of that tradition that innovation is conceived. The Formalist studies brought to light that this simultaneous preservation of tradition and breaking away from tradition form the essence of every new work of art' (87).

For Hutcheon, postmodernism has become the dominant over against modernism while remaining thoroughly implicated in modernist conventions and ideology. In postmodernism, she maintains, 'what is both instated and then subverted is the [modernist] notion of the work of art as a closed, self-sufficient, autonomous object deriving its unity from the formal interrelations of its parts' (*PP*, 12). Postmodernism is precisely visible against the background of modernism, simultaneously preserving and breaking away from it and taking the energy of its canonizing convictions from the dominant of modernism. Or, as Jurij Tynjanov put it in 1929, a 'literary system is first of all *a system of the functions of the literary order which are in continual interrelationship with other orders'*[16] in a given cultural system or what Hutcheon refers to as 'the cultural dominants of today' (*PP*, 222).

Hutcheon derives two other crucial aspects of her theory of post-modernism from Russian Formalism: her evolutionary model and her concern for the 'enunciating act' (*PP*, 78). Not only a rethinking of modernism (*PP*, 81), postmodernism is, for Hutcheon, also an aspect of the progress, the development, of literature and thus – given her neo-Formalist alignment of artistic, broadly cultural, and social-political models of meaning-production – of society as a whole. As the conclusion of *A Poetics of Postmodernism* puts it, 'the questions that will make any answering process even possible are at least starting to be asked' (*PP*, 231). Similarly, her book is conceived to be a stage in an evolutionary process towards an understanding of postmodernism in the form of a poetics which is also a 'problematics' (*PP*, 226). And postmodernist art itself constitutes a 'challenge to analytico-referential [i.e., modernist/formalist/structuralist] discourses' repression of the entirety of the enunciating act and its agents' (*PP*, 78). Invoking Terry Eagleton's 'rough three-stage periodization of the history of modern theory,' Hutcheon argues that it 'corresponds *grosso modo* to the literary changes of the last hundred and fifty years': (1) 'preoccupation with the author' – Romanticism and the nineteenth century; (2) 'exclusive concern with the text' – New Criticism; (3) 'marked shift of attention to the reader' – postmodernism (*PP*, 78). Working back through the repression of the speech situation, the postmodern text thus also works back through these three stages of literary theory, reintegrates them, and begins the development of a fourth stage, that of enunciation or what Hutcheon calls 'process.'

Although this 'concern for the production process, rather than the product, is actually inherent [sic] in Saussurian theory,' it was, Hutcheon argues, 'suppressed in the more mechanical formalist model of structuralism' (*PP*, 82) and is only now being brought to the fore once again. This curious assertion not only belies Saussure but also conceals another debt to Russian Formalism. In 'The Theory of the Formal Method' (1927), Boris Eichenbaum emphasizes the historical concerns of the Formalists, their interest in speech, and their study of 'literary evolution as the dialectical change of forms.'[17] In the course of a 1923 study of Anna Akhmatova, Eichenbaum participated in the development of a theory of the linguistic characteristics of verse (an ongoing concern of the Formalists) and specifically contrasted an ordinary language situation with a literary one in which 'lateral meanings, disrupting the usual associations of words,' are formed, a property which he takes to be the chief aspect of verse semantics.[18] From these concerns with the literary citation of speech there developed an equally strong interest in what speech-act theorists were later to refer to as 'uptake' in the reception and processing of an utterance. Thus Bakhtin's emphasis in an early essay like 'Discourse Typology in Prose' (1929) on such verbal devices as 'stylization, parody, *skaz* (in its strict sense, the oral narration of a narrator), and dialogue' and his assertion that all of these devices have one feature in common: 'in all of them discourse maintains a double focus, aimed at the referential object of speech, as in ordinary discourse, and simultaneously at a second context of discourse, a second speech act by another addresser.'[19] From such a simple assertion comes the theory of dialogism or 'double-voiced discourse' (181), which in turn gives rise to a theory of irony and parody of which it is a core principle. As Bakhtin writes of 'stylization,' 'a conventionalized utterance is always a double-voiced utterance. Only what was once perfectly serious and nonrelative to another point of view can become conventional. What was once a straightforward and nonconventional value now serves new aims' (181). Thus 'stylization stylizes another style in the direction of its own projects. All it does is make those projects conventional' (185). But whereas in Bakhtin's agonistic theory of parody 'the second voice, having lodged in the other speech, clashes antagonistically with the original, host voice and forces it to serve directly opposite aims' (185), Hutcheon's allows for a more generous spirit of indebtedness and, sometimes, homage. Her understanding of the 'ex-centricity' (*TCP*, 3; *PP*, 12) of metafiction's creators is, however, precisely in line with Bakhtin's distinction between periods in which conventionalized discourse holds sway and those in which 'parodic speech in all its varieties' (195) becomes dominant. The former arises when 'a given social group has at its disposal an authoritative and durable medium of refraction' (195), while the latter arises when such conditions are absent.

From parody as a neo-Bakhtinian speech genre to 'historiographic metafiction' and thus postmodernism (the former being the ultimate expression of the latter in Hutcheon's theory) as the fulfilment of Benveniste's theory of textual enunciation and Kristeva's of novelistic enunciation is not the logical leap it may at first seem to be if one remembers – as Hutcheon sometimes does – Saussure on speech. For it is precisely Saussure's emphasis on sound, on meaning as that which the speech community sanctions from among all possible permutations and combinations of sounds uttered with the human tongue, lips, teeth, palate, which both generates and restricts the arbitrariness of language as phonological system or as what Umberto Eco refers to as the encyclopaedia of a culture.[20] And it is Saussure's rejection of the Indo-European philological tradition with its persistent efforts to bind printed words, reified through the false logic of writing privileged over speech, which motivates his radical assertion of paradigmatic and syntagmatic orders and thus of language as what Michael Halliday calls a 'social semiotic.'[21] Because of time, 'language is no longer free,' Saussure writes, 'for time will allow the social forces at work on it to carry out their effects. This brings us back to the principle of continuity, which,' he concludes, 'cancels freedom.' But continuity necessarily implies change, varying degrees of shifts in the relationship between the signified and the signifier'[22] and so language as a system is not static but in constant transformation interfacing with all of the other systems, all of the 'interlocutory relationships,' in Kristeva's phrase,[23] in which it participates.

In its novelistic form, this situation of performance or enunciation is 'a compromise between testimony and citation, between the voice and the book. The novel will be performed within this empty space,'[24] its performance being, as Benveniste says of the performative in general, 'self-referential, [having the quality] of referring to a reality that it itself constitutes by the fact that it is actually uttered in conditions that make it an act. The act is thus identical with the utterance of the act. The signified is identical to the referent.'[25] Self-referential, self-reflexive, the novel is performed, uttered, the reading a speech act which is performative in and of itself. 'The utterance *is* the act,' writes Benveniste; 'the one who pronounces it performs the act of denominating it.'[26]

Hutcheon thus derives from Kristeva and Benveniste an understanding of novelistic discourse in general which she then grafts onto a theory of postmodernist discourse in specific, characterizing postmodernism in terms which are provided by dynamic models of the reading process developed by such theorists as Bakhtin, Eichenbaum, Tynjanov (not to mention Lotman's theory of a dynamic semiotics and his concept of literature as a 'secondary modelling system')[27] and by speech-emphatic/performative models of language and novelistic processing from Benveniste, Kristeva, and many others, ranging from Ricoeur to Zukofsky.[28] Nonetheless, Hutcheon asserts in *A Poetics of Postmodernism* that 'when the locus of meaning shifts from author to text to reader, and finally, to the entire act of enunciation, then we have perhaps moved beyond formalism and even beyond reader-

response theory *per se*. We may be on the road,' she confidently concludes, 'to articulating a new theoretical model adequate ... to the self-
reflexive art of today' (*PP*, 86).

That model is, in its own terms, not only antithetical to 'formalism ...
[which is] the defining expression of modernism,'[29] but also to residu-
ally formalist trends in contemporary literature. Consider, for example,
Hutcheon's assertion in *The Canadian Postmodern* that Margaret
Atwood's 'formalism ... is even more noticeable [in her public state-
ments] than her politics' (*TCP*, 138) and her citation of Atwood's statement that 'what people fail to understand about poetry and novels
and criticism is that they are hypothetical, and they are patterns of
words and ideas' (*TCP*, 138–9). Attributing this 'formalist' statement
(which is completely in keeping with Huyssen's criteria for the modernist text) to Atwood's studies with Northróp Frye at the University
of Toronto, Hutcheon not only assimilates Frye to her structuralist/
formalist/modernist equation but also implies an antithetical association of the non-hypothetical and the non-patterned, on the one hand,
with the non-'formalist,' on the other. As the context makes evident,
the non-formalist is for Hutcheon the postmodern.

But how can the language and, for that matter, the logical status of
a literary text be characterized as non-hypothetical? If an equation is
implicitly being made here between non-hypothetical and referential
uses of language, then we may provisionally conclude that for Hutcheon literature operates referentially. Since 'formalism'/modernism
stresses pattern/structure, 'the effacement of "content," the erasure
of subjectivity and authorial voice, the repudiation of likeness and
verisimilitude,'[30] if Hutcheon is to recuperate Atwood for postmodernism, she must attach Atwood's 'formalist concerns' (*TCP*, 157) to a
referential *Realpolitik* or lose her to the 'hypothetical.' Hutcheon solves
this problem via what she refers to as postmodernism's 'metafictional
paradox' whereby 'art' is attached to 'life' as 'product' is to 'process,' an
attachment which she sees as grounded in 'contradictions underlying
both' pairs of opposites (*TCP*, 140).

The paradigm becomes clearer in *A Poetics of Postmodernism*, where
Hutcheon refers to the 'hermeneutic process of reading' (*PP*, 156) and
argues that 'historiographic metafiction's emphasis on its enunciative
situation – text, producer, receiver, historical, and social context –
rcinstalls a kind of (very problematic) communal project' (*PP*, 115).
Problematic or not, that project in Hutcheon takes on all the typical
characteristics of the traditional hermeneutic enterprise, including the
emphasis on process and community, on the importance of the (post-

modernist) text's 'being understood' and 'meaningful to the public' (*PP*, 34); [31] on the contextualizing of literary meaning through social, political, and historical data; and, as we have seen, on the 'entirety of the enunciative act.' Analysed separately as traces from Saussure, the Formalists, Benveniste et al., these terms can be assimilated, albeit in a contradictory fashion given their impetus in Hutcheon's theory, into the history of modern theory and its co/incidence with modernism.

What happens, however, when the paradigm is viewed as a unit is very different, for that aspect of Schleiermacher's hermeneutic which he classified as the 'divinatory'[32] and which becomes in Dilthey the apparently secularized version of Schleiermacher's 'hermeneutic circle'[33] retains the trace of the search for transcendental meaning in Scripture which is the foundation of Judeo-Christian hermeneutics. From Augustine to Stanley Fish, the condition of that access to meaning and understanding has been faith, belief. In *De doctrina christiana* Augustine cites 2 Corinthians 5.7: 'If you will not believe, you shall not understand'; [34] in *Is There a Text in This Class?* Fish consoles interpreters by advising that 'what they are searching for is never not already found' by those, we might add, with the canonic eyes of faith or, as Fish puts it, by those for whom 'the text as it is variously characterized is a *consequence* of the interpretation for which it is supposedly evidence.'[35] Those meanings which are sanctioned by an interpretive community are thus already the ones which are accessible to and understandable by that community since those are precisely the conditions of recognition and validation. As the Formalist axiom has it, context defines meaning. The ascent to contextual knowledge is, quite precisely, a process characterized by sequentiality, cumulative knowledge, and community engagement in the 'radical provisionality, intertextuality, and fragmentation' (*PP*, 116) of *any* text.

It is not surprising, then, that in *The Canadian Postmodern* Hutcheon restores via Robert Kroetsch 'the conventions of both humanist ideology and realist fiction' to postmodernism, interpreting this move as yet another 'postmodern paradox' (*TCP*, 174). Thus, given her subsequent – and, I think, historically accurate – ascription of realism to the nineteenth century (*TCP*, 201) rather than to modernism, it is apparent both that Hutcheon agrees with Kroetsch's leap from Victorian/realist/ humanist to postmodern/neo-realist/deconstructive and that she rejects that sequence in favour of a definition of postmodernism which clings to linguistic referentiality while ascribing a special status to art. This normative assumption serves a threefold purpose: (1) it contains the subversive, anti-humanist drive of modernism as formulated by

Huyssen; (2) it legitimates 'art' by providing an ethical foundation for the aesthetic, enabling the hermeneutic assertion of such values as health and morality through art; and (3) it reinscribes the subject, guarantor of the norm, across a bourgeois reality characterized by the possibility of personal autonomy within the strictures of a reality game whose rules are determined by bourgeois convention.

It becomes apparent why Hutcheon's resolutely thin descriptions of 'formalism' and her recirculation of post-structuralist theory via 'formalism' / modernism / Victorian realism are necessary to her program. Texts, 'reading and reception,' she argues, are 'safer' for 'modern critical writing' to deal with than authors, 'writing and production' (TCP, 83). Opting for the less safe study of 'writing and production' while retaining a bourgeois humanist ideology, Hutcheon recuperates Atwood for precisely what, in Frank Davey's words, 'is refused throughout ... [her] work ... liberalism.'[36] Borrowing Pierre Macherey's Marxist lexicon of writing as production, text as product,[37] Hutcheon attempts to empty these terms of their ideological significance and to expropriate them for reinscription in a canonic postmodernism which, grounded in 'life' as process, returns to Presence, to a normative theory of the utility value of 'art' – a product rendered processual via the theory of the performative – in the service of 'life.'

Hutcheon's reader, then, may co-create text but only to the extent that she or he operates within the rules of the realist ideology of liberal humanism, bound to the hermeneutic fulcrum of meaning as Presence and the Subject (whether reader or writer) as well-mannered practitioner of the game of life and art. It is no accident that Hutcheon's Atwood is a novelist more than a poet (as Hutcheon remarks, 'Atwood is *also* a poet' [TCP, 139, my italics]) and that the poems are discussed only insofar as thematic linkages between the two genres can be identified in Atwood's practice. Canadian poetry in this century has always been less attached to the realist/humanist paradigm and the hegemony of the subject,[38] while canonic prose has tended to adhere to realist convention, or – to put it another way – only those texts which adhere or could be made to seem to adhere to realist convention have been canonized. Hutcheon's postmodernism simply continues this canonic operation, producing the new thematic conventions of 'paradox' and 'historiographic metafiction' where once we had survival, landscape, and region. For Clara Thomas the paradigm could be summed up under the heading *Our Nature, Our Voices*;[39] for Hutcheon, 'nature' has become 'art' but the subject remains unchanged. History, after all, is still 'process *in progress*' (TCP, 216, my italics).

How, then, can Michael Ondaatje's *Coming through Slaughter* or *Running in the Family* be said to be 'compromised – that is, it is both historical and "performative" ' and 'thus accessible' (*TCP*, 83)? If performativity is the criterion of accessibility – perhaps in the sense that any reader who performs (enacts, engages in enunciation of) the text must already have gained access to some basic level of competence in performance or the text would be inaccessible to him/her – then the historical aspect of the text may be 'compromised' by every co-creating reader who moves the static text into dynamic enactment just as the author (since reader and author are, for Hutcheon, both creators) moves historical materials (whether Ondaatje's family history or Buddy Bolden's) into enactment in the process of writing them into/through an/other text which the reader then processes, renders performatively in and through enactment. But what is *compromised* here is surely the moment of origin either in its written form (the 'original' family diaries, photographs, and so on) or in its precedent oral form since, according to Hutcheon, metafiction meets 'oral history' (*TCP*, 213), oral tale meets written chronicle, in Canadian postmodern metafiction.

What is risked here is thus precisely the point of origin towards which textual/authorial enactment moves but which can never be attained.[40] What is adjusted or settled in this dispute between the parties of origin and author/text or text/reader is precisely the fictive weight of origin in balance against the metafictive pressure of 'creation' in this co-creating process. 'Creation' must then be that point at which the balance shifts and oral becomes print, origin becomes succession, and the weight of inheritance moves, impelled by historical process which – for Hutcheon – is progress, towards the present moment of creation.

This is the moment emblematized by the Nigel Scott photograph on the cover of *The Canadian Postmodern*, the moment when 'Julie diving' in 'June 1986' becomes forever transformed into 'Maillot Noir et Blanc,' becomes a work of 'art.' But, as Hutcheon says, Scott's parodic image, like parody itself, 'contests both the authority of that tradition [of realism] and the claims of art to originality' (*TCP*, 8). However, like Ondaatje's moment of compromise, Scott's moment of parody is as thoroughly implicated in what is parodied as in the instant of parodic transformation: we must recognize both in order to function as competent readers of the text.

Origin/ality, author/ity, tradition, creation: these are the coordinates of a Romantic aesthetic; their response, a hermeneutics of revelation, Truth, authenticity, Schleiermacher's 'divinatory' mode towards which the exegete, empowered by 'facts' and contextual knowledge, might move if, entering the hermeneutic circle, he (seldom, if ever, she) were lucky. Returning, his prophecy would utter meaning, in/form life, heal the weary traveller. These are the expectations of an exegetical theology grounded in Biblical texts – expectations of consonance,[41] of accurate recognition of rules, of behaviour bound by rules to which prior assent is given by the interpretive community. It is precisely this communitarian model of decorous behaviour in text and life, both grounded in a higher wisdom towards which the community has committed itself through the act of interpretation,[42] upon which Hutcheon's theory of postmodernism is predicated. Serving the same ideological purpose as the thematic tradition of survival/landscape/nature of which it is the most recent exemplar, Hutcheon's theory is a strategy of containment which, in its 'anti-modern, pro-postmodern' stance, moves seamlessly 'from the aesthetic to the ultimate defence of,' as Jameson puts it, 'family and ... religion'[43] or, perhaps more accurately in this case, the terms of the canon: propriety, Canadian collectivity, humanist hegemony in 'art' and 'life.'

The price that this latest Canadian inscription of a kind of 'Defence of the Realm Act' pays is not only the subversion of Canadian modernism with, as Huyssen maintains of international modernism, its critique of 'subjectivity and authorial voice ... its repudiation of likeness and verisimilitude ... [its] exorcism of any demand for realism of whatever kind,'[44] but also the domestication of theory into thematics and – ironically, given Hutcheon's apparent championing of theory – its containment at the level of both process and product.

But there is a logic to this move of Hutcheon's, this transformation of process as practice into an aesthetics of inaction, a logic which Huyssen's account of the relation of post-structuralist theory to modernism helps to define.[45] For if 'process' is validated as theme in Hutcheon, her aestheticism ironically delineates its own literariness in the act of dismissing 'formalism.' Yet it is precisely that dismissal which prevents Hutcheon from attaching her concept of art as product to life as process other than by glossing the problem as paradox. That the non-referential literary text operates processually and performatively is no surprise since its very literariness dictates not only its semantic non-referentiality but also its performativity as sole condition of meaning. However, its performance is necessarily conducive neither to health nor to morality,[46] both notions which Hutcheon appears to associate with the hyphenated relation of art to life. Thus her aestheticist theory may be construed in terms of a transposition of 'art' to the realm of 'life' such that the performance of a postmodern text paradoxically resolves the seeming tension between the two, rendering the text referential in apposition to its own processual enactment by the reader.

Grounded in Hutcheon's implied theory of origin, this transportation evidently serves to reinforce the exchange of meaning in a community of readers whose competence meshes with the semantic and ideological demands of the text. In Derridian terms, this dynamic of reinforcement is an 'always already' condition which ensures the mirroring relation of world and text, and thus the liberal humanist ideology of the transparency of reality.[47] Mirroring humanist operations of world-construction, Hutcheon's principle of readerly 'co-creation' bypasses Fish's understanding of the literary as readerly game strategy and opts instead for the canonic equation of mimesis/referentiality/accessibility encoded in processual operations which are explicitly *not* performative but, rather, capitalist/humanist strategies of object production.

Hutcheon's argument is, then, fundamentally concerned not to defeat modernism/formalism/structuralism but, via the equation of postmodernism/realism/hermeneutics, to reinscribe the conditions of communal understanding, the *boundaries* of the interpretive community, in the face of deconstruction's assault on the liberal-humanist subject. Reinscribing the literary, Hutcheon's postmodernism is no longer marginalized by modernism but demarginalized 'through confrontation with the historical' (*PP*, 108). Not the 'political self-marginalization' of modernism (according to Hutcheon [*PP*, 23]), then, but the political inscription/centring and thus canonizing of postmodernism. Not the transcendence/Presence of modernism (*PP*, 19, 42), but the engagement of postmodernism. Not the 'isolation of art from the social context' (*PP*, 35), but its reinscription at the heart of that context. Not the 'referential agnosticism' (*PP*, 157, quoting Christopher Norris) of modernism, but the referential in/fidelity of postmodernism. *Faith* bounds the exercise; it is a contest for faith, open to all, meaningful to all, reflecting the norms of the community (linguistic, political, social, historical) and the struggle to *find answers* (*PP*, 231). Reinscribing the archive, as she says, Hutcheon has also reinscribed the order of things: Protestant hermeneutics, liberal-humanist style.

What has been canonized is, as always, what can be absorbed with least resistance or noise in the institution. One result is that Canadian modernism, like the dissenting tradition in Canadian social and political thought with which it is strongly aligned, has still not been considered in Canadian theory nor has Canadian theory, for the most part, yet taken the challenge of deconstruction seriously. 'To deconstruct ... is to do memory work,'[48] work which may never – in fact, *can* never – be 'in good taste' but which must be undertaken nonetheless, even if for no other reason than to construct a critique of 'good taste,' whether its products be accessible or not to those who insist on the colonial standard of 'plain English' and the universal criterion of semantic referentiality. There is much to reclaim, to find, to remember, to think, before Hutcheon's metafiction of modernism, this hermeneutic of clarity in disguise, wins the contest for theory in Canadian language departments, and theory is, once again, lost.

Notes

LECKER Introduction

1 The phrase is from Paul Lauter, 'Society and the Profession,' PMLA 99 (1984), 417.
2 Alastair Fowler, 'The Selection of Literary Constructs,' New Literary History 12, no. 1 (1975), 41
3 Paul Lauter, 'History and the Canon,' Social Text 12 (1985), 94, 95
4 John Guillory, 'Canoncial and Non-Canonical: A Critique of the Current Debate, ELH 54, no. 3 (1987), 483
5 H. Aram Veeser, ed., The New Historicism (New York: Routledge 1989), xi. Veeser's collection of essays brings together the work of nineteen writers who are prominent in the new historicist arena.
6 Linda Hutcheon, The Canadian Postmodern: A Study of Contemporary English-Canadian Fiction (Toronto: Oxford University Press 1988), 189, 108
7 See Barbara Godard, ed., Gynocritic: Feminist Approaches to Canadian and Quebec Women's Writing / Gynocritiques: Démarches féministes a l'écriture des Canadiennes et Québécoises (Toronto: ECW Press 1987); and Shirley Neuman and Smaro Kamboureli, eds., A Mazing Space: Writing Canadian Women Writing (Edmonton: Longspoon/NeWest 1986).
8 Frank Davey, Reading Canadian Reading (Winnipeg: Turnstone Press 1988), 5
9 Louis Montrose, 'Renaissance Literary Studies and the Subject of History,' English Literary Renaissance 16 (1986), 6
10 Stephen Greenblatt, 'Introduction,' Genre 15 (1982), 6
11 John Guillory, 'The Ideology of Canon-Formation: T.S. Eliot and Cleanth Brooks,' Critical Inquiry 10 (1983), 195

12 Annette Kolodny, 'The Integrity of Memory: Creating a New Literary History of the United States,' *American Literature* 57 (1985), 291. All further references to this work (Kolodny) appear in the text.

13 Barbara Herrnstein Smith, 'Contingencies of Value,' *Critical Inquiry* 10 (1983), 10

14 Guillory, 'Canonical and Non-Canonical,' 503

15 Montrose, 'Renaissance Literary Studies,' 6

16 See Bernard Andrès, 'L'Institution et l'avant-garde poétique au Québec,' *Littérature* 66 (1987), 24–33; André Belleau, 'Le Conflit des codes dans l'institution littéraire québécoise,' *Liberté* 134 (1981), 15–20; Richard Giguère, 'Evolution de l'horizon d'attente de la poésie du terroir: Le cas de la réception critique d'*A l'ombre de l'Orford* d'Alfred DesRochers, 1929–1965,' in *Problems of Literary Reception / Problèmes de réception litté-raire*, ed. E.D. Blodgett and A.G. Purdy (Edmonton: University of Alberta 1988) [hereafter cited as 'Blodgett and Purdy'], 102–25; David Hayne, 'The Concept of "littérature" in Nineteenth-Century Quebec,'' in Blod-gett and Purdy, 126–35; Kenneth Landry, 'Comment la réception des œuvres littéraires pourrait venir à la rescousse de l'histoire de la littéra-ture: L'Exemple du discours critique au début des années soixante-dix sur le corpus québécois,' in Blodgett and Purdy, 9–23; Maurice Lemire, ed., *L'Institution littéraire* (Quebec: Institut québécois de recherche sur la culture and Centre de recherche en littérature québécoise 1986); Jacques Michon, 'La Réception de l'œuvre de Nelligan, 1904–1949,' in Blodgett and Purdy, 77–92; Lucie Robert, 'L'Emergence de la notion de "littérature canadienne-française" dans la presse québécoise (1870–1948),' in Blodgett and Purdy, 136–43; and Sherry Simon, 'Alli-ances stratégiques: Le féminisme et les revues littéraires au Québec,' *Questions of Funding, Publishing and Distribution / Questions d'édition et de diffusion*, ed. I.S. MacLaren and C. Potvin (Edmonton: University of Alberta 1989), 93–102.

17 See Douglas Barbour, 'Re: Viewing: Giving and Receiving in Canadian Poetry; or, The Role of Reviewing in the Reception of Poetry in English Canada in the 20th Century,' in Blodgett and Purdy, 49–60; Wilfred Cude, *A Due Sense of Differences: An Evaluative Approach to Canadian Literature* (Lanham, Md.: University Press of America 1980); Davey, *Read-ing Canadian Reading*; Margery Fee, 'English-Canadian Literary Criti-cism, 1890–1950: Defining and Establishing a National Literature' (PHD diss., York University, 1981); August J. Fry, 'Periods, Canons and Who Wants to Get into *The New Yorker* Anyway?' in *Literatures in Canada / Littératures au Canada*, ed. Deborah C. Poff [*Canadian Issues* 10 (1988); hereafter cited as 'Poff'], 57–65; Carole Gerson, *A Purer Taste: The Writing and Reading of Fiction in English in Nineteenth-Century Canada* (Toronto: University of Toronto Press 1989); Pauline Greenhill, *True Poetry: Tradi-tional and Popular Verse in Ontario* (Montreal: McGill-Queen's University

Press 1989); Paul Hjartarson, 'The Literary Canon and Its Discontent: Reflections on the Cultural Reproduction of Value,' in Poff, 67–80; Hutcheon, *The Canadian Postmodern*; Patricia Jasen, 'Arnoldian Humanism, English Studies and the Canadian University,' *Queen's Quarterly* 95 (1988), 550–66; W.J. Keith, 'The Quest for the (Instant) Canadian Classic,' in *The Bumper Book*, ed. John Metcalf (Toronto: ECW Press 1986); 155–65; Robert Lecker, 'The Canonization of Canadian Literature: An Inquiry into Value,' *Critical Inquiry* 16 (1990), 656–71, with 'Critical Response I: Canadian Canons,' by Frank Davey (672–81) and Lecker's 'Critical Response II: Response to Frank Davey' (682–9); Rota Herzberg Lister, 'What Is a Classic? The Case for Canadian Drama,' in Poff, 81–92; I.S. MacLaren, 'Defusing the Canon: Against the Classicization of Canadian Literature,' in Poff, 49–55; Lawrence Mathews, 'Hacking at the Parsnips: *The Mountain and the Valley* and the Critics,' in Metcalf, ed., *The Bumper Book*, 188–201; John Metcalf, *What Is a Canadian Literature?* (Guelph, Ont.: Red Kite Press 1988); Walter Pache, 'Tradition and the Canadian Talent: Dilemmas of Literary History in Canada,' in *Carry On Bumping*, ed. John Metcalf (Toronto: ECW Press 1988), 85–100; Morton L. Ross, 'The Canonization of *As for Me and My House*: A Case Study,' in Metcalf, ed., *The Bumper Book*, 170–85; David Staines, 'Reviewing Practices in English Canada,' in Blodgett and Purdy, 61–8; Maria Tippett, *Making Culture: English-Canadian Institutions and the Arts before the Massey Commission* (Toronto: University of Toronto Press 1990); Tracy Ware, 'Notes on the Literary Histories of Canada,' *Dalhousie Review* 65 (1985–6), 566–76; and Lorraine Weir, 'The Discourse of "Civility": Strategies of Containment in Literary Histories of English Canada' in Blodgett and Purdy, 24–39.

18 The two volumes are Blodgett and Purdy, and MacLaren and Potvin, eds., *Questions of Funding, Publishing and Distribution*, both cited in full in note 16, above.

SURETTE Creating the Canadian Canon

1 This is the title of Carl Ballstadt's extremely useful edition (on historical principles) of essays addressing the question of the nature and function of Canadian literature, *The Search for English-Canadian Literature* (Toronto: University of Toronto Press 1975).

2 The trilingual, and therefore tricultural, nature of the Swiss state is an important, but unstressed, component of Burckhardt's motivation as well as a further parallel with Canada.

3 Jacob Burckhardt, *Force and Freedom*, trans. James Hastings Nichols (New York: Meridian Books 1955), 77

4 I take this characterization of Hartz's position from H.D. Forbes, 'Hartz-Horowitz at Twenty: Nationalism, Toryism and Socialism in Canada

and the United States,' *Canadian Journal of Political Science* 29 (June 1987), 287–315, especially 289–92. Forbes is also my authority for the canonical status of Horowitz's adaptation of Hartz to Canada.

5 Forbes, 287–9. I cannot enter into the controversy, but note that Horowitz had already answered some of Forbes's criticisms in 'Notes on "Conservatism, Liberalism and Socialism in Canada," ' *Canadian Journal of Political Science* 11 (June 1978), 384–99. I am indebted to my political science colleague John McDougall for references to these articles.

6 Quoted by E.K. Brown, *On Canadian Poetry* (Toronto: Ryerson 1943), 2

7 See Northrop Frye, ' "Conclusion" to *Literary History of Canada*,' in *The Bush Garden* (Toronto: House of Anansi Press 1971), especially 232–3 and 250–1.

8 See F.M. Barnard, *Herder's Social and Political Thought: From Enlightenment to Nationalism* (Oxford: Oxford University Press 1965). Barnard attributes the modern conception of the nation state to Herder's elaboration of the German Pietistic Enlightenment. In particular Herder attached language and race to culture, and identified all three with nationhood: 'Those sharing a particular historical tradition grounded in language Herder identifies with a *Volk* or nationality, and it is in this essentially spiritual quality that he sees the most natural and organic basis for political association' (57).

9 Burckhardt, *Force and Freedom*, 125

10 I recognize that Canada and America are both internally heterogeneous on Herderian grounds. We both have indigenous non-European populations of alien culture on any measure, as well as largely assimilated African and Asian citizens. Canada has in addition a large unassimilated French-speaking population, and the United States has an almost equally large unassimilated Spanish-speaking population. These factors complicate the story but do not alter the general picture of both countries as fragments of European culture employing English as their language of expression.

11 'Here Is Us: The Topocentrism of Canadian Literary Criticism,' *Canadian Poetry: Studies, Documents, Reviews*, no. 10 (Spring/Summer 1982), 44–57

12 The Jews, incidentally, were the model case for Herder of a *Volk* maintaining its identity and spiritual heritage *without* either political or territorial integrity. He chose the Slavs, rather than the Germans, as a *Volk* who could in the future rise to political maturity as a unified nation.

13 See, for example, Lionel Stevenson, *Appraisals of Canadian Literature* (Toronto: Macmillan 1926). Stevenson claims that Canada's unmodified, primeval, primordial landscape produces an 'instinctive pantheism' (11–12); and later remarks, 'In Canada the modern mind is placed in circumstances approximating those of the primitive myth-makers' (39). Although a little more sophisticated, Tom Marshall's history of Canadian poetry, *Harsh and Lovely Land* (Vancouver: University of British Columbia

Press 1979), retains both the topocentric axiom and the model of a reprise of European cultural history in a new place.

14 Northrop Frye's denigration of the realistic bourgeois novel in favour of 'prose romances' in *Anatomy of Criticism* is, of course, an important factor. Most of the Canadian fiction of the past forty years has been written under Frye's influence. Frye himself participates in topocentrism and nineteenth-century cultural theories (see 'Here Is Us'). Hence Frye's criticism is both a symptom of the forces producing the dominance of romance and mythopoeia in Canadian fiction, and a contributing causal factor.

15 T.D. MacLulich, *Between Europe and America: The Canadian Tradition in Fiction* (Toronto: ECW Press 1988), 251

16 See Dick Harrison, *Unnamed Country: The Struggle for a Canadian Prairie Fiction* (Edmonton: University of Alberta Press 1977) for an elaboration of this motif.

17 John Metcalf's spirited attack on T.D. MacLulich's outline of the 'central Canadian tradition' in *What Is a Canadian Literature?* (Guelph, Ont.: Red Kite Press 1988), 37–44, helps to keep one cautious when generating such taxonomies of the canon. Metcalf, for example, rejects Richler from the canon on the grounds that Richler 'belongs to a tradition of North American Jewish writing' (39).

Mordecai Richler and Rudy Wiebe are two novelists who fit neatly into neither of my two groups. Both belong to the realistic bourgeois tradition, but in very different ways from one another and from Callaghan, MacLennan et al. Richler's urban, earthy, Jewish satire is worlds away from Wiebe's rural, *volkisch* historical fiction. With respect to the Guelph/Ghibelline division, Richler is clearly a Ghibelline, and Wiebe a Guelph. (Incidentally, although published in Guelph, Metcalf's book is more Ghibelline than Guelph.)

18 Margaret Atwood, *The Journals of Susanna Moodie* (Toronto: Oxford University Press 1970), 63–4

19 The inversion of the Demeter-Persephone-Pluto myth is a recurrent motif for Atwood. Her heroines – like Susanna Moodie and Catharine Parr Traill – are commonly threatened by all that is sacred to the Earth goddess, and feel safe in chthonic depths. The short story 'Death by Landscape' (*Saturday Night*, July 1989) makes this motif explicit. In the story a thirteen-year-old Lucy simply disappears while she and the narrator, Lois, are having a pee in the woods at summer camp. The elderly narrator meditates on the meaning of it all. She cannot – like Wordsworth for *his* Lucy – take comfort in the thought that *her* Lucy is rolling round in earth's diurnal course with rocks and stones and trees. Instead Lois imagines that Lucy is in the Group of Seven paintings hanging on her apartment wall, which 'open inwards on the wall, not like windows but like doors. She is here. She is entirely alive.'

Atwood's Lucy is *killed* by the landscape, in contrast to the arduous survival of Traill's lost children in *The Canadian Crusoes*. See Carl Ballstadt, *Catharine Parr Traill and Her Works* (Downsview, Ont.: ECW Press [1983]).

20 A.R.M. Lower, *Canada: Nation and Neighbour* (Toronto: Ryerson 1952), 56

21 Robert Kroetsch, 'The Exploding Porcupine,' in *The Lovely Treachery of Words: Essays Selected and New* (Toronto: Oxford University Press 1989), 109–10

22 Robert Kroetsch, *Badlands* (Toronto: General 1975). All further references to this work appear in the text.

23 As Robert Lecker puts it, Kroetsch 'concentrates on the chaos of origins' (*Robert Kroetsch* [Boston: Twayne 1986], 19).

24 Quoted by MacLulich, *Between Europe and America*, 134

25 Margaret Laurence, *The Diviners* (Toronto: McClelland and Stewart 1974), 84 (Laurence's italics). All further references to this work appear in the text.

26 It is not part of my story, but it is impossible to pass silently over Laurence's slur on Traill's bourgeois values reflected in her listing of threatened property, before tacking on the children as an afterthought. By contrast the Gunns carried all of their possessions on their backs, and Morag had a child in the womb. There is a very strong element of class conflict in *The Diviners*, which I cannot pursue.

Despite the rather rough treatment Catharine Parr Traill receives here, Margaret Laurence picked Traill's Tory settlement of Lakefield, Ontario, as her place of residence in the same year that *The Diviners* was published (1974).

27 Susanna Moodie, *Roughing It in the Bush* (1854; reprint, Toronto: Coles 1980), xv. Notice the presence of the motif of self-improvement here – too early to be Arnoldian, and too Tory to be Methodist.

28 One of the other reasons is the radical undermining of storytelling itself described by Lecker (*Robert Kroetsch*, 82–3). Lecker does not make the point, but Kroetsch's radical, postmodern deconstruction of story and history alike undermines the mythopoeic solution to the problem of Canadian identity necessary for both Ghibellines and Guelphs, and which Kroetsch himself has pithily expressed in the phrase 'the fiction makes us real.' Another reason is the complete absence of the Arnoldian and Methodist theme of self-improvement already mentioned.

MCCARTHY Early Canadian Literary Histories and the Function of a Canon

1 Claudio Guillen, *Literature as System: Essays toward the Theory of Literary History* (Princeton: Princeton University Press 1971), 5

2 See Leon Surette, 'Here Is Us: The Topocentrism of Canadian Literary

Criticism,' *Canadian Poetry: Studies, Documents, Reviews*, no. 10 (Spring/ Summer 1982), 44–57.

3 Northrop Frye, 'Conclusion,' in *Literary History of Canada: Canadian Literature in English*, ed. Carl F. Klinck et al., 2d ed. (Toronto: University of Toronto Press 1976), 2:338

4 Edward Hartley Dewart, ed., *Selections from Canadian Poets, with Occasional Critical and Biographical Notes, and an Introductory Essay on Canadian Poetry* (1864; reprint, Toronto: University of Toronto Press 1973), vii. All further references to this work (*SCP*) appear in the text.

5 Thus, what Klein later laments in 'Portrait of the Poet as Landscape' is a long history of failed complementarity, or of the culture's failure to fully accept the poet's participation in its most valued activities and therefore to share the cultural power which accrues from such participation. That apparently canonic poem is canonic because of its repetition of a traditional lament in Canadian literary history, a repetition, however, which is read as novel and/or radical by its own period.

6 William Douw Lighthall, ed., *Songs of the Great Dominion: Voices from the Forests and Waters, the Settlements and Cities of Canada* (London 1889), xxi; all further references to this work (*SGD*) appear in the text. Lighthall's anthology must be read in the context of the cultural nationalism that developed throughout the British Empire from 1880 up to the outbreak of World War I. It was intended to be read along with a companion Australian anthology and is dedicated 'To / That Sublime Cause / The Union of Mankind / Which the British Peoples, / If They are true to Themselves and courageous in the / future as they have been in the past, / will take to be / The Reason for Existence of their Empire.' For a discussion of the cultural nationalist movement, see John Eddy and Deryck Schreuder, eds., *The Rise of Colonial Nationalism: Australia, New Zealand, Canada and South Africa First Assert Their Nationalities, 1880–1914* (Sydney: Allen and Unwin 1988).

7 John George Bourinot, *Our Intellectual Strength and Weakness* (1893; reprint, Toronto: University of Toronto Press 1973), 4

8 Ray Palmer Baker, preface, *A History of English-Canadian Literature to the Confederation: Its Relation to the Literature of Great Britain and the United States* (Cambridge: Harvard University Press 1920). This work is hereafter cited as 'Baker.'

9 He acknowledges that Rosanna Mullins (Mrs Leprohon) has 'a right to contest Richardson's primacy as the first Canadian novelist,' describing her as the 'leader of a distinct Canadian School' (Baker, 139).

10 Since French only wrote three chapters (16, 17, and 21), I will refer to Logan as the main author and guiding theoretical/ideological intelligence in the work.

11 See Northrop Frye, *Anatomy of Criticism: Four Essays* (Princeton: Princeton University Press 1957), 3.

12 J.D. Logan and Donald G. French, *Highways of Canadian Literature: A Synoptic Introduction to the Literary History of Canada (English) from 1760 to 1924*, 2d ed. (Toronto: McClelland and Stewart 1928), 5–6. All further references to this work (*HCL*) appear in the text.

13 Guillen, *Literature as System*, 6

14 Ibid.

15 Ibid.

16 Ibid., 377

17 Lionel Gossman, 'History and Literature: Reproduction or Signification,' in *The Writing of History: Literary Form and Historical Understanding*, ed. Robert H. Canary and Henry Kozicki (Madison: University of Wisconsin Press 1978), 29

18 Ibid., 32

19 Ibid., 17

20 Frye, 'Conclusion,' 359–60

21 Charles Altieri, 'An Idea and Ideal of a Literary Canon,' in *Canons*, ed. Robert von Hallberg (Chicago: University of Chicago Press 1984), 57

22 Barbara Herrnstein Smith, 'Contingencies of Value,' in von Hallberg, ed., *Canons*, 23

23 Rene Wellek and Austin Warren, *Theory of Literature*, 3d ed. (New York: Harcourt, Brace 1977), 257

24 Herrnstein Smith, 'Contingencies of Value,' 23, 27, 29

25 Ibid., 32–3

26 T.S. Eliot, 'Tradition and the Individual Talent,' in *Selected Prose of T.S. Eliot*, ed. Frank Kermode (New York: Harcourt Brace Jovanovich 1975), 38–9

27 Northrop Frye, 'The Archetypes of Literature,' in *Fables of Identity: Studies in Poetic Mythology* (New York: Harcourt, Brace and World 1963), 12, 14

28 Margaret Atwood, ed., *The New Oxford Book of Canadian Verse in English* (Toronto: Oxford University Press 1982), xxvii

29 Eliot, 'Tradition and the Individual talent,' 38

30 Guillen, *Literature as System*, 453

31 Her remarks on the number of women poets in the anthology, and in the Canadian canon, are interesting in this respect.

32 Eliot, 'Tradition and the Individual Talent,' 38

33 Edward W. Said, *Beginnings: Intention and Method* (New York: Basic Books 1975), 285

34 Lorne Pierce repeats this judgment, and language, but about Roberts's first book, *Orion*: 'An authentic voice had been heard, and at last Canada had become articulate'; 'Here at last was the authentic prophet of the new day.' See *An Outline of Canadian Literature (French and English)* (Toronto: Ryerson 1927), 71, 236.

35 Guillen, *Literature as System*, 437

36 Archibald MacMechan, *Head-Waters of Canadian Literature* (Toronto: McClelland and Stewart 1924), 234, 85

37 Pierce, foreword, *An Outline of Canadian Literature*
38 Lionel Stevenson, *Appraisals of Canadian Literature* (Toronto: McClelland and Stewart 1926), v–vi. This work is hereafter cited as ACL.
39 Louis O. Mink, 'Narrative Form as Cognitive Instrument,' in Canary and Kozicki, eds., *The Writing of History*, 137
40 However, Stevenson's 'emplotment' of Canadian literary history as the liberation struggle of an inappropriately civilized national imagination leads him to describe the conditions faced by the twentieth-century Canadian writer in terms which, from the vantage point of the post-modernist 1980s, seem remarkably prophetic; see ACL, 39 40–1. For 'emplotment,' see Hayden White, *Metahistory: The Historical Imagination in Nineteenth-Century Europe* (Baltimore: Johns Hopkins University Press 1976), 1–42; or 'The Historical Text as Literary Artifact,' in Canary and Kozicki, eds., *The Writing of History*, 41–62.
41 Altieri, 'An Idea and Ideal,' 41, 59

GERSON The Canon between the Wars

Research for this paper was supported by a grant from the Women and Work Strategic Grants Program of the Social Sciences and Humanities Research Council of Canada.

1 See Carole Gerson, 'The Changing Contours of a National Literature,' *College English* 50 (1988), 888–95.
2 Terry Eagleton, *Literary Theory: An Introduction* (Minneapolis: University of Minnesota Press 1983) 11
3 Terry Lovell, *Consuming Fiction* (London: Versa 1987), 132
4 See the first chapter, 'Masterpiece Theatre: The Politics of Hawthorne's Literary Reputation,' in Jane Tompkins, *Sensational Designs: The Cultural Work of American Fiction, 1790–1860* (New York: Oxford University Press 1985).
5 In many ways, this essay is a continuation of my earlier paper 'Anthologies and the Canon of Early Canadian Women Writers,' in *Re (Dis)covering Our Foremothers: Nineteenth-Century Women Writers*, ed. Lorraine McMullen (Ottawa: University of Ottawa Press 1989).
6 The term enters Canadian feminist criticism of the canon from Sharon Nelson, 'Bemused, Branded, and Belittled: Women and Writing in Canada,' *Fireweed* 15 (1982), 65–102, who takes it from Lewis A. Coser, Charles Kadushin, and Walter W. Power, *Books: The Culture and Commerce of Publishing* (New York: Basic Books 1982), who in turn borrowed it from Diana Crane, *Invisible Colleges: Diffusion of Knowledge in Scientific Communities* (Chicago: University of Chicago Press 1974).
7 In Pierce's *Outline of Canadian Literature* (1927), Logan and French's *Highways of Canadian Literature* (1924, 1928), and Rhodenizer's *Handbook of Canadian Literature* (1930), Duncan is not treated as a serious novelist but

is given several pages in a chapter on humorists. In Logan and French, Crawford receives five pages in the chapter on 'Incidental Pioneer Literature,' while in Rhodenizer she is given three pages in the chapter on 'Early Poets,' and in MacMechan's *Head-Waters of Canadian Literature* (1924), she is not even mentioned. In contrast, both Rhodenizer and Logan and French devote full chapters to Roberts, Lampman, Carman, Scott, Campbell, F.G. Scott, W.H. Drummond, and Pauline Johnson, the latter being the sole woman thus dignified.

8 Paul Lauter, 'Race and Gender in the Shaping of the American Literary Canon: A Case Study from the Twenties,' *Feminist Studies* 9 (1983), 435–63

9 For a good example of how the masculine academy came to dominate Canadian letters during this period, see *Canadian Literature Today*, a 1938 series of CBC broadcasts later published by the University of Toronto Press. The contributors were Professors E.K. Brown, Arthur L. Phelps, W.E. Collin, Edgar McInnis, J.F. Macdonald, and Watson Kirkconnell, with the non-academic community represented by authors Philip Child and Frederick Philip Grove, and bookseller William Tyrell.

10 This term also comes from Nelson (70, 79) and enters the field from Dale Spender, 'The Gatekeepers: A Feminist Critique of Academic Publishing,' in *Doing Feminist Research*, ed. Helen Roberts (London: Routledge and Kegan Paul 1981), 186; and Dorothy E. Smith, 'A Peculiar Eclipsing: Women's Exclusion from Men's Culture,' *Women's Studies International Quarterly* 1 (1978) 287.

11 The chronic inadequacy, on the part of national institutions, in providing serious and consistent funding for the collection, preservation, and detailed cross-indexing of unpublished materials relating to the history of English-language Canadian literature – except on a single-project basis (e.g., the Lorne Pierce Collection at Queen's University, the Deacon Collection at the University of Toronto, and the Dorothy Livesay papers at the University of Manitoba) – can itself be read as a canonical statement about the value of literary and cultural history in the minds of those who determine funding and priorities at the national level.

12 Marguerite Anderson, 'Subversive Texts: Québec Women Writers,' *Studies in Canadian Literature* 13, no. 2 (1988), 127. Note also Rosemary Sullivan's claim that 'Canada has produced an unusual, even a predominant, number of women writers' ('Introduction,' in *Stories by Canadian Women* [Toronto: Oxford University Press 1984], ix).

13 Margery Fee, 'Lorne Pierce, Ryerson Press, and The Makers of Canadian Literature Series,' *Papers of the Bibliographical Society of Canada* 14 (1985), 51–69

14 Information on the Master-Works series is found in Garvin's correspondence with W.D. Lighthall, 27 Dec. 1922–20 March 1923, (Lighthall Papers, National Archives of Canada, MG 29, D93, vol. 2); Lorne Pierce Correspondence and the Hale-Garvin Papers, Queen's University

Archives; and W.D. Lighthall Papers, Rare Book Department, McGill University.

15 E.K. Brown, *On Canadian Poetry* (1944; reprint, Ottawa: Tecumseh Press 1973), 64

16 Lorne Pierce, ed., *The Selected Poems of Marjorie Pickthall* (Toronto: McClelland and Stewart 1957), 21

17 Diana Relke, 'Demeter's Daughter: Marjorie Pickthall and the Quest for Poetic Identity,' *Canadian Literature*, no. 115 (Winter 1987), 28–43

18 An undated letter written during the war (Brown to Pelham Edgar, Edgar Papers, Pratt Library, Victoria University) suggests that Mackenzie King (b. 1874) was being courted to write the introduction to one of her books.

19 Hugh Eayrs to Frank Dodd, 2 Sept. 1936, Macmillan Papers, McMaster University, box 78, file 8

20 Edgar to MacPhail, 22 Oct. [1930], MacPhail Papers, National Archives of Canada, MG 30, D150, vol. 15. Sandra Campbell, in 'The Canadian Literary Career of Professor Pelham Edgar,' (PHD diss., University of Ottawa, 1983), 233–51, details Edgar's literary relationship with Brown during the 1930s.

21 Brown to Hugh Eayrs, 13 June 1934 and 18 July 1934, Macmillan Papers, McMaster University. See E.K. Brown's comment on her lack of development, in 'Letters in Canada,' *University of Toronto Quarterly* 7 (1937–8), 342.

22 Brown to Scott, 30 June 1944, Scott Papers, National Archives of Canada, MG 30, D100.

23 She thought she was the first, but she was preceded by Mazo de la Roche in 1938. Her other predecessors constitute a check-list of the canonizers and canonized; only the female recipients lacked earned or honorary degrees: 1926 – Charles G.D. Roberts; 1927 – D.C. Scott; 1928 – Bliss Carman; 1929 – Camille Roy; 1930 – Andrew MacPhail; 1931 – Adjutor Rivard; 1932 – Archibald MacMechan; 1933 – no award; 1934 – Frederick Philip Grove; 1935 – Edouard Montpetit; 1936 – Pelham Edgar; 1937 – Stephen Leacock; 1938 – Mazo de la Roche; 1939 – Wilfrid Bovey; 1940 – E.J. Pratt; 1941 – Léon Gérin; 1942 – Watson Kirkconnell; 1943 – George Clarke.

24 Until rescued by Rosemary Sullivan in *Poetry by Canadian Women* (1989).

25 Lyn Harrington, *Syllables of Recorded Time: The Story of The Canadian Authors Association, 1921–81* (Toronto: Simon and Pierre 1981), 264–5

26 Deacon to Clay, 13 March 1940, Clay Papers, National Archives of Canada, MG 30, D 30, vol. 1. It is tempting to speculate which book would have prevailed if McDowell had authored *Waste Heritage*, and also what effect winning either the Governor General's Award or the Guggenheim Fellowship would have had on Irene Baird's future literary career.

27 Clara Thomas and John Lennox, *William Arthur Deacon: A Canadian Literary Life* (Toronto: University of Toronto Press 1982), 249

28 Deacon to Clay, 13 March 1940

29 This is what Eayrs paid him in 1937 for reporting on Louise Morey Bowman's *Characters in Cadence*. See Ellen Elliott[?] to Pratt, 22 Dec. 1937, Macmillan Papers, McMaster University, box 76, file 7.

30 Macmillan Papers, McMaster University: Pratt to Mrs Brook, 19 March 1934, and Pratt to Ellen Elliott, 24 Feb. 1936, box 123, file 10; Eayrs to Bowman, 31 Dec. 1937, box 76, file 7; Pratt to Eayrs, 23 Jan. 1937, box 121, file 4. As individual letters in the Macmillan Papers are not indexed by author or topic, the extent of Pratt's involvement can be discovered only by investigating each file.

31 Doris Ferne to Hugh Eayrs, 2 Dec. 1937, Macmillan Papers, McMaster University, box 93, file 9. Pratt seems to have had less influence on Margaret Duley's novel, *Novelty on Earth*, as she refused to omit phrases to which he objected. See Alison Feder, *Margaret Duley: Newfoundland Novelist* (St John's: Harry Cuff 1983), 89.

32 In 'Anthologies and the Canon of Early Canadian Women Writers' I describe A.J.M. Smith's winnowing out of women authors in the second and third editions of his *Book of Canadian Poetry* during the 1940s. In a paper presented at the University of Alberta (11 Nov. 1989) on the role of women in Canadian little magazines, Pauline Butling speculated that the fact that *Contemporary Verse* (1941–52) was founded by four women (Anne Marriott, Dorothy Livesay, Floris McLaren, and Doris Ferne) may be responsible for its low profile in recent histories of Canadian literary magazines.

33 Kathryn Colquhoun to R.A. Hood, 2 April 1940, Hood Papers, University of British Columbia

34 Sandra M. Gilbert and Susan Gubar, *No Man's Land: The Place of the Woman Writer in the Twentieth Century* (New Haven: Yale University Press 1988), 153–5. Gaye Tuchman's *Edging Women Out: Victorian Novelists, Publishers, and Social Change* (New Haven: Yale University press 1989) presents a sociological and economic analysis of women's loss of power in the literary world towards the end of the nineteenth century.

35 'Intimations of Mortality' [Eleanor Wachtel interviewing Phyllis Webb], *Books in Canada* 12, no. 9 (Nov. 1983), 14

SCOBIE Leonard Cohen, Phyllis Webb, and the End(s) of Modernism

1 This introduction is 'polemical' in the sense that it makes some sweeping generalizations for which this paper does not have the time or space to offer detailed support. I am well aware that, like all generalizations, they admit of many exceptions, nuances, and modifications. However, they are advanced here as a broad framework for the main argument of this essay.

2 Margery Fee, *Canadian Poetry in Selected English-Language Anthologies: An Index and Guide* (Halifax: Dalhousie University School of Library Service 1985)

3 Frank Davey, *From There to Here* (Erin, Ont.: Press Porcépic 1974), 264. All further references to this work appear in the text.

4 Leonard Cohen, *The Energy of Slaves* (Toronto: McClelland and Stewart 1972), 112

5 Pia Southam, 'Hot Lunch,' *V*, Dec. 1988, 110

6 Phyllis Webb, *The Vision Tree: Selected Poems* (Vancouver: Talonbooks 1982), 150

7 George Woodcock, *Northern Spring: The Flowering of Canadian Literature* (Vancouver: Douglas and McIntyre 1987), 258

8 John Bentley Mays, 'Phyllis Webb,' *Open Letter*, 2d ser. no. 6 (Fall 1973), 8–33

9 Leonard Cohen, *Flowers for Hitler* (Toronto: McClelland and Stewart 1961), 72

10 Leonard Cohen, *Beautiful Losers* (Toronto: McClelland and Stewart 1966), 16–17.

11 Stephen Scobie, *Leonard Cohen* (Vancouver: Douglas and McIntyre 1978), 96

12 Robert Kroetsch, 'For Play and Entrance: The Contemporary Canadian Long Poem,' in *The Lovely Treachery of Words* (Toronto: Oxford University Press 1989), 118

13 Ibid.

14 Cohen, *Beautiful Losers*, 167

SALTER The Idea of a National Theatre

This is a revised version of two interrelated papers read to the Association for Canadian Studies at the University of Windsor in May 1988 and to the Association of Canadian University Teachers of English at the University of Victoria in May 1990. I am grateful to the Faculty of Graduate Studies and Research at McGill University for financial support.

1 G., 'On the Influence of a Well Regulated English Theatre, in Montreal,' *Canadian Magazine and Literary Repository* 1, no. 3 (Sept. 1823), 221, 224

2 See Jean-Marc Larrue et al., eds., *Le Théâtre au Québec: Mémoire et appropriation* (Montreal: Société d'histoire du théâtre du Québec 1988–9).

3 Alice Rowe-Sleeman, 'A National Theatre for Canada,' *Canadians All* 3, no. 24 (1945), 24

4 Arthur L. Phelps, 'Canadian Drama,' *University of Toronto Quarterly* 9 (Oct. 1939), 84, 93

5 George Woodcock, 'Nationalism and the Canadian Genius,' *artscanada*, nos. 232–3 (Dec. 1979–Jan. 1980), 2–10. Woodcock suggests, following Orwell's example, that ' "Patriotism" is often no more than an unthinking love of the fatherland, but "national self-awareness" implies a consciousness not only of being involved in a community located in a particular

place or land but also of the historical and environmental implications of that involvement.' He finds the unqualified term *nationalism* unacceptable: 'But nationalism is fearful of the world outside; it is exclusive in sentiment and action; in its aggressive form it is unrelentingly imperialist, and in its defensive form it is always potentially xenophobic, as nationalist movements the world over have shown all too often since former colonial countries gained independence' (4). However, throughout this essay, I am using the term *nationalism*, though variously qualified, to refer to the kinds of 'national self-awareness' which Woodcock favours.

6 Ann Saddlemyer, 'Thoughts on National Drama and the Founding of Theatres,' in *Theatrical Touring and Founding in North America*, ed. L.W. Conolly (Westport, Conn.: Greenwood Press 1982), 209

7 See also Alan Filewod, 'Erasing Historical Difference: The Alternative Orthodoxy in Canadian Theatre,' *Theatre Journal* 41, no. 2 (May 1989), 201–10.

8 Robertson Davies, 'Mixed Grill: Touring Fare in Canada, 1920–1935,' in Conolly, ed., *Theatrical Touring and Founding in North America*, [41]. Davies is writing about Canadian theatre between the wars, but his observations also apply to earlier periods. Canada's long-standing preoccupation with Old World cultural values is detailed in Maria Tippett, *Making Culture: English-Canadian Institutions and the Arts before the Massey Commission* (Toronto: University of Toronto Press 1990).

9 Hector Charlesworth ['Touchstone'] in the Toronto *Evening News*, 5 June 1897. (I am grateful to Filewod, 'Erasing Historical Difference,' 209, note 11, for drawing my attention to this informative article.) Attribution of this article to Charlesworth is suggested by his book *Candid Chronicles* (Toronto: Macmillan 1925), 147, 165.

10 B.K. Sandwell, 'The Theatre: Little Theatre Festival,' *Saturday Night* 48, no. 22 (8 April 1933), 19. See also his 'The Annexation of Our Stage,' *Canadian Magazine* 38, no. 1 (Nov. 1911), 22–6, and 'Our Adjunct Theatre,' in *Addresses Delivered before the Canadian Club of Montreal: Season 1913–1914* (Montreal: n.p. [1914]), 95–104. See also Anton Wagner, 'A National or International Dramatic Art: B.K. Sandwell and *Saturday Night* 1932–1951,' *Canadian Drama / L'Art dramatique canadien* 12, no. 2 (Fall 1986), 345.

11 Laurence Irving, *Henry Irving: The Actor and His World* (London 1951; reprint, New York: Macmillan 1952). Some of Irving's ideas about a national theatre are quoted in Austin Brereton, *The Life of Henry Irving*, 2 vols. (London 1908; reprint, New York: Benjamin Blom 1969), 1: 257–9.

12 Hector Charlesworth, *Candid Chronicles*, 386–96, and *More Candid Chronicles* (Toronto: Macmillan 1928), 382–5; Wagner, 'A National or International Dramatic Art,' 342–3; B.K. Sandwell, 'There Are Still Some People Who Can Remember Irving,' *Saturday Night* 62 (17 May 1947), 37

13 The debate is partly summarized in John Elsom and Nicholas Tomalin, *The History of the National Theatre* (London: Jonathan Cape 1978). See

also Geoffrey Whitworth, *The Making of a National Theatre* (London: Faber and Faber 1951); Janet Minihan, *The Nationalization of Culture* (London: Hamish Hamilton 1977); and Loren Kruger, ' "Our National House": The Ideology of the National Theatre of Great Britain,' *Theatre Journal* 39, no. 1 (March 1987), 35–47. For a complete array of individual contributions to the debate, see William Archer, 'A Plea for an Endowed Theatre,' *Fortnightly Review*, n.s., 45, no. 269 (1 May 1889), [610]–26, Matthew Arnold, 'The French Play in London,' *Nineteenth Century* 6, no. 30 (Aug. 1879), 228–43; Frank R. Benson, 'The National Theatre,' *Nineteenth Century* 49 (May 1901), 772–80; Augustus Harris, 'The National Theatre,' *Fortnightly Review*, n.s., 44, no. 227 (1 Nov. 1885), 630–6; Henry Arthur Jones, *The Foundations of a National Drama* (New York: George H. Doran Company; London: Chapman and Hall, Ltd. n.d.); Bram Stoker, 'The Question of a National Theatre,' *Nineteenth Century* 63, no. 375 (May 1908), 734–[42]; William Poel, 'The Functions of a National Theatre,' *The Theatre* 22 (1 Sept. 1893), 162–6; [Sir John Martin-Harvey], *The Autobiography of Sir John Martin-Harvey* (London: Sampson Low, Marston and Co., Ltd. [1933]); [John] Martin Harvey, 'Canadian Theatres,' *University Magazine* 13, no. 2 (April 1914), [212]–19; William Archer and H[arley] Granville Barker, *A National Theatre: Scheme and Estimates* (London 1907; reprint, Port Washington, NY: Kennikat Press 1970); and Harley Granville Barker, *A National Theatre* (London: Sidgwick and Jackson 1930). The appearance of the Comédie-Française at the Gaiety Theatre in London in 1879 did much to stimulate the English debate; the French critic Francisque Sarcey gave a public lecture in London on the Comédie-Française which was published in the *Nineteenth Century* 6, no. 29 (July 1879), 182–200.

14 Even Shaw gave his support to the cause, although he was somewhat sceptical of certain aspects: see Kruger, ' "Our National House," ' 45–6; Elsom and Tomalin, *The History of the National Theatre*; and Whitworth, *The Making of a National Theatre*.

15 *Parliamentary Debates: Commons (Hansard)*, vol. 52 (23 April to 8 May 1913), 470. (This debate is quoted in Kruger, ' "Our National House," ' 47, with minor deviations from the *Hansard* text.)

16 H[arley] Granville-Barker, 'The Canadian Theatre,' *Queen's Quarterly* 43, no. 3 (Autumn 1936), [256]–67. His visit to Canada in 1915 is described in Arthur Beverly Baxter, 'The Birth of the National Theatre,' *Maclean's Magazine* 29, no. 4 (Feb. 1916), [27]–9.

17 See Phelps, 'Canadian Drama,' 88–94; W.S. Milne's annual review of drama in 'Letters in Canada,' *University of Toronto Quarterly*, from 1936 to 1941, especially 1936 (5, no. 3: 389–95), 1940 (9, no. 3: 301–7), and 1941 (10, no. 3: 300–5); John Edward Hoare, 'A Plea for a Canadian Theatre,' *University Magazine* 10, no. 2 (April 1911); [239]–53; Fred Jacob, 'Waiting for a Dramatist,' *Canadian Magazine* 43, no. 2 (June 1914), 142–6; John Coulter, 'The Canadian Theatre and the Irish Exemplar,' *Theatre Arts*

Monthly 22, no. 7 (July 1938), 503–9; Herman Voaden, 'Theatre Record, 1945,' *Canadian Forum* 25 (Nov. 1945), 184–7; Charlesworth, *Candid Chronicles* and *More Candid Chronicles*; Sandwell, 'Our Adjunct Theatre,' 96–104; and Vincent Massey, 'The Prospects of a Canadian Drama,' *Queen's Quarterly* 30, no. 2 (Oct. 1922), 194–212. In fact, all these men were playing a variety of roles in the development of Canadian theatre: Hoare, for example, was a playwright, critic, author, and supervising director from 1943 of the Montreal Repertory Theatre; Jacob was a novelist and the drama critic for the Toronto *Mail and Empire*; Voaden was a teacher, director, play anthology editor, and cultural activist. The reaction against this particular set of nationalistic ideas can be found in Tom Hendry, 'The Masseys and the Masses,' *Canadian Theatre Review*, no. 3 (Summer 1974), 6–10; Renate Usmiani, *Second Stage: The Alternative Theatre Movement in Canada* (Vancouver: University of British Columbia Press 1983); Alan Filewod, *Collective Encounters: Documentary Theatre in English Canada* (Toronto: University of Toronto Press 1987); Robert Wallace, *Producing Marginality: Theatre and Criticism in Canada* (Saskatoon: Fifth House 1990); Denis W. Johnston, *Up the Mainstream: The Rise of Toronto's Alternative Theatres, 1968–1975* (Toronto: University of Toronto Press 1991); and Richard Paul Knowles's article elsewhere in this volume.

18 Martin Harvey, 'Canadian Theatres,' 218. For additional comments on the importance of staging Shakespeare in Canada, see Frederic Robson, 'The Drama in Canada,' *Canadian Magazine* 31, no. 1 (May 1908), 59–61.

19 Carl F. Klinck, *Wilfred Campbell: A Study in Late Provincial Victorianism* (Toronto: Ryerson 1942); L.A. MacKay, 'Canadian Writers of the Past: William Wilfred Campbell,' *Canadian Forum* 14, no. 158 (Nov. 1933), 66–7; and Norman Shrive, *Charles Mair: Literary Nationalist* (Toronto: University of Toronto Press 1965). Charles Heavysege was also much influenced by Shakespeare: see Michael Tait, 'Playwrights in a Vacuum: English-Canadian Drama in the Nineteenth Century,' *Canadian Literature*, no. 16 (Spring 1963), 6–7. Campbell is a clear instance of how a classical writer like Shakespeare could be used to serve xenophobic interests. In his article 'Shakespeare and the Latter-Day Drama,' *Canadian Magazine* 30, no. 1 (Nov. 1907), 14–18, Campbell fulminates against Tolstoy, Cervantes, Shaw, and Ibsen, among others, in order to canonize Shakespeare as a symbol of 'the development of the best ideals of the British race' (18).

20 [John] Martin Harvey, 'First Impressions of Canada,' in *Addresses Delivered before the Canadian Club of Hamilton, 1913–1914* (Hamilton: Labor News Printing 1914), 91–2. See also Patrick O'Neill, 'The British Canadian Theatrical Organization Society and the Trans-Canada Theatre Society,' *Journal of Canadian Studies* 15, no. 1 (Spring 1980), 56–67.

21 See Robert G. Lawrence, 'John Martin-Harvey in Canada,' *Canadian Drama / L'Art dramatique canadien* 6, no. 2 (Fall 1980), 234–41; L.W. Conolly, 'Martin-Harvey in Canada,' in *Bernhardt and the Theatre of Her Time*, ed. Eric Salmon (Westport, Conn.: Greenwood Press 1984), [225]–42;

Robson, 'The Drama in Canada,' 58–61; and Sandwell, 'There Are Still Some People Who Can Remember Irving,' 37.

22 Hector W. Charlesworth, 'Some Modernisms of the Stage,' *Canadian Magazine* 1, no. 1 (March 1893), [43]–7; see also my article 'Ibsen in Canada: The Critical Reception, 1910–1980,' in *Canada and the Nordic Countries*, ed. Jorn Carlsen and Bengt Streijffert (Lund: Lund University Press 1988), 285–97.

23 Hoare, 'A Plea for a Canadian Theatre,' 249. Granville Barker's article, 'Two German Theatres,' appeared in the *Fortnightly Review*, n.s., 89 (2 Jan. 1911), 60–70. Horniman's Gaiety Theatre did in fact tour to Montreal and Toronto in 1912, and again in 1913, when they included the United States. They indirectly influenced the development of the Montreal Repertory Theatre. See Philip Booth, 'The Montreal Repertory Theatre, 1930–1961: A History and Handlist of Productions' (MA Thesis, McGill University, 1989), 12. Hoare also had in mind the example of the Abbey Theatre as an instrument of cultural nationalism (245). This comparison has been regularly made: see, for example, Coulter, 'The Canadian Theatre and the Irish Exemplar,' 503–9. The issue is expertly summarized in Saddlemyer, 'Thoughts on National Drama and the Founding of Theatres,' [193]–211.

24 Hoare, 'A Plea for a Canadian Theatre,' 250, 252

25 Ibid., 252

26 Massey, 'The Prospects of a Canadian Drama,' 199–201. The Aikins example is analysed in James Hoffman, 'Carroll Aikins and the Home Theatre,' *Theatre History in Canada / Histoire du théâtre au Canada* 7, no. 1 (Spring 1986), 50–70.

27 Mark Czarnecki, 'The Regional Theatre System' and 'Part II: Theatre and Drama across Canada,' in *Contemporary Canadian Theatre: New World Visions*, ed. Anton Wagner (Toronto: Simon and Pierre 1985), 35–48, and 96–174; Filewod, 'Erasing Historical Difference,' 202–10

28 Vincent Massey, ed., *Canadian Plays from Hart House Theatre*, 2 vols. (Toronto: Macmillan 1926), 1:vi. The playwrights included are Merrill Denison, Duncan Campbell Scott, Marian Osborne, H. Borsook, Isabel Ecclestone MacKay, Britton Cooke, Carroll Aikins, L.A. Mackay, and Leslie Reid.

29 Massey, 'The Prospects of a Canadian Drama,' 194–5, 206–8

30 Hon. Vincent Massey, 'Popular Address: Art and Nationality in Canada,' *Proceedings and Transactions of the Royal Society of Canada*, 3d. ser. 24 (1930), lxiii

31 Massey, 'The Prospects of a Canadian Drama,' 209

32 Claude Bissell, *The Young Vincent Massey* (Toronto: University of Toronto Press 1981) and *The Imperial Canadian: Vincent Massey in Office* (Toronto: University of Toronto Press 1986). See also Robertson Davies, 'Forum: Robertson Davies on the Young Vincent Massey,' *Theatre History in Canada / Histoire du théâtre au Canada* 3, no. 1 (Spring 1982), [97]–100.

33 Mair's imperialist ideas as they are developed in *Tecumseh* and elsewhere are discussed in Shrive, *Charles Mair: Literary Nationalist*, Carl Berger, *The Sense of Power: Studies in the Ideas of Canadian Imperialism 1867–1914* (Toronto: University of Toronto Press 1970), 50–77, and Dennis Duffy, *Gardens, Covenants, Exiles: Loyalism in the Literature of Upper Canada/Ontario* (Toronto: University of Toronto Press 1982), [55]–69; for Campbell, see his article, 'Shakespeare and the Latter-Day Drama,' 14–18, and Klinck, *Wilfred Campbell*. Much less attention has been devoted, of course, to a non-canoncial writer like Sarah Anne Curzon, who was attempting to take a revisionist approach to both dramatic conventions and patriarchal conceptions of Canadian history: see Heather Jones, 'Feminism and Nationalism in Domestic Melodrama: Gender, Genre, and Canadian Identity,' *Essays in Theatre* 8, no. 1 (Nov. 1989), 5–14.

34 The standard history of the DDF is Betty Lee, *Love and Whisky: The Story of the Dominion Drama Festival* (Toronto: McClelland and Stewart 1973).

35 Souvenir program, DDF / Theatre Canada Papers, National Theatre School / L'Ecole Nationale de Théâtre

36 Lee, *Love and Whisky*, 83–98

37 Malcolm Morley, 'Drama in Eastern Ontario,' *Saturday Night* 50, no. 46 (21 Sept. 1935), 12

38 Interview with Merrill Denison, broadcast in 'The Playwright on Our Theatre,' an instalment of Canadian Theatre: Fact and Fancy, CBC Radio, 1964. See also Denison's article 'Dramatic Brass Tacks,' *Saturday Night* 50 (6 July 1935), 5.

39 Malcolm Morley, 'Toronto Festival,' *Saturday Night* 51, no. 5 (7 Dec. 1935), 31. Four years later, in 1939, Phelps observed: 'Surely it is not healthy or respectable for nine Canadian drama festivals never to have evoked a single really important Canadian play, much less a significant body of Canadian drama ... That we enjoy European and American drama should indeed only raise the quality of our expectations as audiences for our own' ('Canadian Drama,' 88). The issue of adjudication is treated in my article 'Declarations of (In)dependence,' *Canadian Theatre Review*, no. 62 (Spring 1990), 11–18.

40 Minutes of the DDF executive meeting, Ottawa, 7 Nov. 1936, 6, Dominion Drama Festival / Theatre Canada Papers, National Archives of Canada.

41 Interview with Toby Ryan in Toronto, January 1988. I am grateful to Toby Ryan for kindly providing me with this opportunity.

42 Michel Saint-Denis, interview, in Dick MacDonald, 'The Drama in Canada,' *Canadian Commentator* 5, no. 6 (June 1961), 26

43 Saint-Denis is quoted in the Toronto *Evening Telegram*, 7 May 1937, 2d ed., 15. Sandwell was also worried when politics pre-empted art: see Wagner, 'A National or International Dramatic Art,' 345–7.

44 Toby Gordon Ryan, *Stage Left: Canadian Theatre in the Thirties* (Toronto: CTR Publications 1981), 131–3, 185. In fact, one could say that *any* kind of new play-writing, politically radical or otherwise, had a hard time of

it at the DDF. Robertson Davies has said of his own experience: '... the governors too often played theatrical grandees in a manner not substantiated by their experience. They were no use to a writer, and actually had a freezing influence on young playwrights' (Ann Saddlemyer, 'A Conversation with Robertson Davies,' *Canadian Drama / L'Art dramatique canadien* 7, no. 2 [1981], 116).

45 Granville Barker, 'The Canadian Theatre,' 260–3; Campbell, 'Shakespeare and the Latter-Day Drama,' 14–18

46 Arnold, 'The French Play in London,' 238–43

47 The possibility of creating a unifying theatrical focus for Canada still haunts the collective imagination; it's a myth that no amount of history seems able to dislodge: see Ray Conlogue, 'Cross Currents: National-theatre discussions provide insights on idea of nationhood,' *Globe and Mail*, 16 Oct. 1990; and Alan Filewod, 'National Theatre / National Obsession,' *Canadian Theatre Review*, no. 62 (Spring 1990), 9–10.

48 See Rota Herzberg Lister, 'What Is a Classic? The Case for Canadian Drama,' *Canadian Issues / Thèmes canadiens* 10, no. 5 (1988), 81–92.

KNOWLES Voices (off)

I would like to thank Harry Lane and Ann Wilson for commenting on an earlier draft of this essay.

1 Richard Perkyns, ed., *Major Plays of the Canadian Theatre 1934–1984* (Toronto: Irwin 1984); Richard Plant, ed., *Modern Canadian Drama* (Markham, Ont.: Penguin 1984); Jerry Wasserman, *Modern Canadian Plays* (Vancouver: Talonbooks 1985); Eugene Benson and L.W. Conolly, eds., *The Oxford Companion to Canadian Theatre* (Toronto: Oxford University Press 1989); W.J. Keith, *Canadian Literature in English* (London: Longman 1985); Eugene Benson and L.W. Conolly, *English-Canadian Theatre* (Toronto: Oxford University Press 1987); L.W. Conolly, ed., *Canadian Drama and the Critics* (Vancouver: Talonbooks 1987)

2 Perkyns, ix

3 Wasserman, 7, 9, 11

4 Ibid., 19

5 Chris Johnson, review of Perkyns and Plant anthologies, *Canadian Theatre Review*, no. 42 (Spring 1985), 148

6 Michael Scholar, 'A Plethora of Plays: Three New Anthologies of Canadian Drama,' *Canadian Drama / L'Art dramatique canadien* 11, no. 1 (1985), 280. This volume of *Canadian Drama* also includes the first version of Conolly's *Canadian Drama and the Critics*.

7 Plant, 26

8 See Perkyns, 3; Plant, 17; and Wasserman, 7–23.

9 Herbert Marcuse, *Negations: Essays in Critical Theory* (Boston: Beacon 1969), 88–133

10 Terry Eagleton, *Literary Theory: An Introduction* (London: Blackwell 1983), 11

11 Chris Brookes, *A Public Nuisance: A History of the Mummers Troupe* (St John's: Memorial University of Newfoundland 1988), 40

12 Marcuse, *Negations*, 85

13 Alan Sinfield, 'Give an account of Shakespeare and education, showing why you think they are effective and what you have appreciated about them. Support your comments with precise references,' in *Political Shakespeare: New Essays in Cultural Materialism*, ed. Alan Sinfield and Jonathan Dollimore (Ithaca: Cornell University Press 1985), 141

14 Jill Dolan, 'Bending Gender to Fit the Canon: The Politics of Production,' in *Making a Spectacle: Feminist Essays on Contemporary Women's Theatre*, ed. Lynda Hart (Ann Arbor: University of Michigan Press 1989), 320. This essay first appeared in an earlier version in Dolan's book, *The Feminist Spectator as Critic* (Ann Arbor: UMI 1988), 19–40.

15 Janet Staiger, 'The Politics of Film Canons,' *Cinema Journal* 35, no. 3 (Spring 1985), 10

16 See Barbara Godard, 'Ex-centriques, Eccentric, Avant-Garde,' *Room of One's Own* 8, no. 4 (1984), 57; and Rachel Blau DuPlessis, 'For the Etruscans,' in *The New Feminist Criticism: Essays on Women, Literature, and Theory*, ed. Elaine Showalter (New York: Pantheon 1985), 271–91.

17 Stanley E. McMullin, ' "Adams Mad in Eden": Magic Realism as Hinterland Experience,' in *Magic Realism and Canadian Literature: Essays and Stories*, ed. Peter Hinchcliffe and Ed Jewinski (Waterloo, Ont.: University of Waterloo 1986), 13

18 Barbara Herrnstein Smith, 'Contingencies of Value,' in *Canons*, ed. Robert von Hallberg (Chicago: University of Chicago Press 1984), 27

19 Kathleen Flaherty, 'Where's the Thrust? Putting Your Finger on the Conceptual Framework,' *Theatrum*, no. 14 (June/July/August 1989), 23

20 Max Horkheimer and Theodor Adorno, *Dialectic of Enlightenment*, trans. John Cumming (New York: Continuum 1972), 132–3

21 Dolan, 'Bending Gender,' 318–44

22 Ann Wilson, 'The Politics of the Script,' *Canadian Theatre Review*, no. 43 (Summer 1985), 174–9. Helene Keyssar also points out that 'feminist *scripts* are more subversive than the productions in which they are rendered in the large, commercial theatres' (*Feminist Theatre: An Introduction to Plays of Contemporary British and American Women* [New York: Grove 1985], 148).

23 Alan C. Golding, 'A History of American Poetry Anthologies,' in von Hallberg, ed., *Canons*, 301

24 Plant, in a letter to the author dated 30 November 1988

25 Wasserman, 19, 7

26 Perkyns adopts an historical perspective that Plant and Wasserman do not. Perkyns's selection of work by Voaden and Davies is in fact in line with 'received opinion,' including the judgments of Benson and Conolly, Keith, and others.

27 Scholar, 'A Plethora of Plays,' 280
28 Benson and Conolly, *English-Canadian Theatre*, 31, 32. See also Denis Salter's essay in this volume.
29 Ibid., 2
30 See von Hallberg's introduction to *Canons*, 3; articles in that collection by Bruns, Zetzel, Kerman, and Chandler; and Salter's essay in the present volume, on the connections between nationalism and canon-formation.
31 Wasserman, 15
32 Ibid., 9
33 Don Rubin, 'Celebrating the Nation: History and the Canadian Theatre,' *Canadian Theatre Review*, no. 34 (Spring 1982), 12–22
34 Greg Leach, 'Tarragon's Trademark Was Script Development,' *That's Showbusiness*, 28 Jan. 1976, 1–2; quoted in Chris Johnson, 'Is That Us?: Ray Lawler's *Summer of the Seventeenth Doll* and David French's *Leaving Home*,' *Canadian Drama / L'Art dramatique canadien* 6, no. 1 (Spring 1980), 30
35 See, for example, T.E. Kalem, *Time*, 17 Dec. 1973, reprinted in Conolly, ed., *Canadian Drama and the Critics*, 75.
36 Dolan, *The Feminist Spectator as Critic*, 84. Dolan quotes Catherine Belsey, 'Constructing the Subject: Deconstructing the Text,' in *Feminist Criticism and Social Change: Sex, Class and Race in Literature and Culture*, ed. Judith Newton and Deborah Rosenfelt (New York: Methuen 1985), 53.
37 The phrase 'male gaze' was brought into currency by E. Ann Kaplan, *Women and Film: Both Sides of the Camera* (New York: Methuen 1983), 23–35.
38 I have adapted this concept from Jonathan Culler, who talks in *On Deconstruction: Theory and Criticism after Structuralism* (Ithaca: Cornell University Press 1982), 43–64, about 'reading as a woman.'
39 Eagleton, *Literary Theory*; 187, citing Raymond Williams, *Drama from Ibsen to Brecht* (London: Hogarth 1987), 331–47
40 Richard Ohmann, 'The Shaping of a Canon: u.s. Fiction, 1960–1975,' in von Hallberg, ed., *Canons*, 387–90. Ohmann is here following Barbara Ehrenreich and John Ehrenreich, 'The Professional-Managerial Class,' in *Between Labour and Capitalism*, ed. Pat Walker (Boston 1979).
41 Benson and Conolly, *English-Canadian Theatre*, 64 (my italics)
42 Flaherty, 'Where's the Thrust?' 22
43 Perkyns, 3
44 See Michael Thompson, *Rubbish Theory: The Creation and Destruction of Value* (London: Oxford University Press 1979) for a valuable analysis of the relationship between classification and value.
45 Horkheimer and Adorno, *Dialectic of Enlightenment*, 131
46 Steve Barnet and Martin G. Silverman, *Ideology and Everyday Life* (Ann Arbor: University of Michigan Press 1979), 36
47 Frank Lentricchia, *Criticism and Social Change* (Chicago: University of Chicago Press 1983), 131
48 Godard, 'Ex-centriques, Eccentric, Avant-Garde,' 57

49 McMullin, ' "Adams Mad in Eden," ' 21

50 Benson and Conolly, *English-Canadian Theatre*, 1

51 Ibid., 2. The only widely distributed overview of drama by native peoples, Richard Courtney's 'Indigenous Theatre: Indian and Eskimo Ritual Drama,' in *Contemporary Canadian Theatre: New World Visions*, ed. Anton Wagner (Toronto: Simon and Pierre 1985), 206–15, is purely archaeological in focus and does not treat contemporary activity.

52 Keith, *Canadian Literature in English*, 192

53 Benson and Conolly, *English-Canadian Theatre*, 58 (my italics)

54 Alan Filewod, 'The Life and Death of the Mummers Troupe,' in *The Proceedings of the Theatre in Atlantic Canada Symposium*, ed. Richard Paul Knowles (Sackville, N.B.: Mount Allison University 1988), 127–41

55 Wasserman, 20

56 John Ripley, 'Plays That Tie,' *Canadian Literature*, no. 85 (Summer 1980), 117

57 Golding, 'A History of American Poetry Anthologies,' 301

58 Benson and Conolly, *English-Canadian Theatre*, 99

59 Eileen Thalenberg and David McCaughna, 'Shaping the Word: Guy Sprung and Bill Glassco,' *Canadian Theatre Review*, no. 26 (Spring 1980), 32–3

60 Brookes, *A Public Nuisance*, 163

61 Marcuse, quoted in Brookes, *A Public Nuisance*, 43

62 Diane Bessai finds that *Blood Relations* 'subsumes its issues entirely within personal character conflicts' and argues against considering Pollock's work to be feminist: 'what is taken for feminism is an aspect of this playwright's on-going response to new dramaturgical challenges.' See Diane Bessai, 'Sharon Pollock's Women: A Study in Dramatic Process,' in *A Mazing Space: Writing Canadian Women Writing*, ed. Shirley Neuman and Smaro Kamboureli (Edmonton: Longspoon/NeWest 1986), 126–7.

63 Flaherty, 'Where's the Thrust?' 21

64 Margaret Hollingsworth, 'Introduction: Margins,' in *Endangered Species* (Toronto: Act One 1988), 7

65 Patrice Pavis, 'Avant-Garde Theatre and Semiology: A Few Practices and the Theory behind Them,' in *Languages of the Stage: Essays in the Semiology of Theatre* (New York: Performing Arts Journal Publications 1982), 179–91

66 Flaherty, 'Where's the Thrust?' 24

67 Alain Martineau, *Herbert Marcuse's Utopia* (Montreal: Harvest House 1986), 83

68 Arthur Kroker, keynote address at the 'Literature and Values' Conference, Atlantic Universities Teachers of English, Halifax, 29 Oct. 1988

69 K.K. Ruthven, *Feminist Literary Studies: An Introduction* (London: Cambridge University Press 1984), 123

70 DuPlessis, 'For the Etruscans,' 287

71 Herbert Marcuse, *One-Dimensional Man: Studies in the Ideology of Advanced Industrial Society* (Boston: Beacon 1964), 11

72 I am referring here to post-Leninist Marxism, materialist feminism, and Derridean deconstruction. I recognize that this is a vexed theoretical issue, and that I am ignoring significant differences among widely divergent theoretical stances. I can only hope to scratch the surface here and to introduce some new ways of thinking about canonicity to what has been an exceptionally conservative discourse.

73 Michael Ryan, *Marxism and Deconstruction: A Critical Articulation* (Baltimore: Johns Hopkins University Press 1982), 211

74 Ibid., 80

75 Josette Féral, 'Writing and Displacement: Women in Theatre,' *Modern Drama* 27, no. 4 (Dec. 1984), 550

76 Ryan, *Marxism and Deconstruction*, 203

77 Ibid., 7

78 Mulgrave Road Co-op Theatre files

79 Interim report, Mulgrave Road Co-op's Long-range Planning Committee, prepared by Hugh John Edwards, revised and adopted by the general meeting of September 1988 (my italics)

80 There were problems for many years about how to define 'professional', and even why the restriction was necessary. The exclusion of 'non-professional' plays from the canon is an interesting topic in itself but is beyond the scope of this essay.

81 Richard Plant, letter to the author, 30 Nov. 1988

82 Ryan, *Marxism and Deconstruction*, 8

83 Barbara Johnson, *The Critical Difference: Essays in the Contemporary Rhetoric of Reading* (Baltimore: Johns Hopkins University Press 1980), 213

84 Smith, 'Contingencies of Value,' 14–15

ROBERT The New Quebec Theatre

1 For a discussion of the theoretical issues, see my book *L'Institution du littéraire au Québec* (Quebec: Presses de l'Université Laval 1989).

2 Michel Bélair, *Le Nouveau Théâtre québécois* (Montreal: Leméac 1973)

3 On this same subject, see Elaine F. Nardocchio, '1958–1968: Ten Formative Years in Quebec's Theatre History,' *Canadian Drama / L'Art dramatique canadien* 12, no. 1 (1986), 33–63; and Adrien Gruslin, *Le Théâtre et l'état au Québec* (Montreal: VLB Editeur 1981).

4 Laurent Mailhot, 'Prolégomènes à une histoire du théâtre québécois,' *Revue d'histoire littéraire du Québec et du Canada français* 5 (1983), 13

5 Don Rubin, 'Celebrating the Nation: History and the Canadian Theatre,' *Canadian Theatre Review*, no. 34 (Spring 1982), 16

6 Bélair, *Le Nouveau Théâtre québécois*, 27–8

7 Mailhot, 'Prolégomènes à une histoire du théâtre québécois,' 14

8 Pierre Lavoie, 'Bilan tranquille d'une révolution théâtrale,' *Jeu*, no. 6 (1977), 50

9 Bernard Dort, 'Sur le travail théâtral,' interview with Thérèse Arbic and Robert Chartrand, *Chroniques* 1, no. 4 (April 1975), 17

10 Mailhot, 'Prolégomènes à une histoire du théâtre québécois,' 14

11 Annie Brisset, 'Translation and Parody: Quebec Theatre in the Making,' *Canadian Literature*, no. 117 (Summer 1988), 92–106

12 Denis Saint-Jacques, 'Des Canadiens, des Québécois, une Acadienne ou de l'invisibilité du théâtre au théâtre,' *Etudes Françaises* 10, no. 2 (May 1974), 151–9

13 Laurent Mailhot and Jean-Cléo Godin, *Le Théâtre québécois* (Montreal: Hurtubise HMH 1970), 225

14 Fernand Villemure, 'Aspects de la création collective au Québec,' *Jeu*, no. 4 (Winter 1977), 57–71; Gérald Sigouin, *Théâtre en lutte. Le Théâtre Euh!* (Montreal: VLB Editeur 1982), 18, note 3

15 Gilbert David, 'Un Nouveau Territoire théâtral,' in *Le Théâtre au Québec, 1825–1980* (Montreal: VLB Editeur, Société d'histoire du théâtre au Québec, and Bibliothèque nationale du Québec 1988), 149

16 Laurent Mailhot, 'Le Théâtre québécois et la critique universitaire,' *Canadian Drama / L'Art dramatique canadien* 1, no. 1 (Spring 1975), 33

BAYARD Critical Instincts in Quebec

1 See Roland Barthes, *Essais critiques* (1964; reprint, Paris: Seuil 1981), 257: 'La critique n'est pas un hommage à la vérité du passé ... elle est construction de l'intelligible de notre temps.'

2 Peter Hyland, 'Introduction,' in *Discharging the Canon: Cross-Cultural Readings in Literature*, ed. Peter Hyland (Singapore: Singapore University Press 1986), 2

3 *L'Essai et la prose d'idées au Québec: Naissance et évolution d'un discours d'ici, recherche et érudition, forces de la pensée et de l'imaginaire*, ed. Paul Wyczinski, François Gallays, and Sylvain Simard (Montreal: Fides 1985), 276

4 'Nous avons tenté depuis la conquête de nous guérir par la parole littéraire, religieuse, politique. Par le discours. Nous nous sommes étendus sur le divan de l'Histoire et nous avons repris sans cesse le même récit. Nous avons essayé par les mots d'occuper une géographie' (Jacques Godbout, 'Le Réformiste,' *Liberté* 128 [March–April 1980] 109). The English translation is mine.

5 The term 'Quiet Revolution' was first coined by a *Globe and Mail* journalist to describe the changes taking place in Quebec after 1960. It was soon adopted by historians and journalists in Quebec, where it took on powerful and emotional connotations. For a detailed discussion of conflicting interpretations of this term, see Paul-André Linteau, René Durocher, Jean-Claude Robert, and François Ricard in *Le Québec Depuis 1930*

(Montreal: Boréal 1986), 394–403, and Gilles Bourque and Jules Duchastel, *Restons traditionnels et progressifs* (Montreal: Boréal 1988), 39–43.

6 A good assessment of their role and participation in this process may be found in the late René Payant's collection of essays entitled *Vedute: Pièces détachées sur l'art 1976–1987* (Montreal: Editions Trois 1987).

7 Gilles Marcotte, *Présence de la critique: Critique et littérature au Canada français* (Montreal: HMH 1966), 13.

8 Jean Fisette, 'De la description structurale à l'interrogation sémiotique,' forthcoming

9 On the 'nation-subject' and the subject of the nation, Ginette Michaud has written an article which documents Belleau's relationship to this problematic as well as that of the generation referred to as *la modernité*: 'On ne meurt pas de ne pas mourir: Réflexions sur le sujet-nation,' *Etudes Françaises* 23, no. 3 (Winter 1988), 113–34.

10 *Littérature: L'Imposture* (Montreal: Herbes rouges 1984), 205

BENNETT Conflicted Vision

1 The most obvious acts of canon-definition are anthologies – from early ones, such as Edward Dewart's 1864 *Selections from Canadian Poets* (which, in its introductory essay, protests the neglect of 'native literature'), to more recent ones, such as Dennis Lee's *New Canadian Poets*, that attempt to define the newest and not-yet-recognized generation of writers. Clearly surveys, which began in Canada with Archibald MacMurchy's early *Handbook of Canadian Literature* (1906) and have as a most recent example W.J. Keith's *Canadian Literature in English* (1985), are equally important in canon-formation. (Indeed, virtually all studies by critics are implicated in acts of canon-defining.) See also Lionel Stevenson's *Appraisals of Canadian Literature* (1926); E.K. Brown's *On Canadian Poetry* (1943); Desmond Pacey's *Creative Writing in Canada* (1952, 1961); Northrop Frye's 'Conclusion' to the *Literary History of Canada* (1965); D.G. Jones's *Butterfly on Rock* (1970); Margaret Atwood's *Survival: A Thematic Guide to Canadian Literature* (1972); and Gaile McGregor's *The Wacousta Syndrome* (1985).

2 Examples include Dorothy Livesay's argument about the 'documentary poem,' Desmond Pacey's consideration of 'the regional idyll,' Robert Kroetsch's discussion of the series novel, Barry Dempster's suggestion that the 'long poem' has a special place in Canadian literary history, and Rudy Wiebe's idea about the need for 'epic' novels as the inherent response to the Prairie sense of space.

3 Throughout this essay my use of *genre* as a term may seem larger or looser than that to which the reader is accustomed. I do not have the space here for a theoretical justification of that use (essentially my definition rests on genre as function rather than as fixed idea) but will simply note that I treat large literary forms as genres (e.g., novels, short stories,

lyric poems, epic poems) that contain smaller genres (e.g., the Gothic novel, the detective novel). Moreover, within these smaller genres, I would suggest other genres exist which are disguised by period terms or by our concept of literariness. Thus, for example, the literary novel is really a genre contained within the larger genre 'novel,' and the 'modernist novel' is a still smaller generic subdivision of the literary novel.

4 Donna Bennett, 'The Detective Story: Towards a Definition of Genre,' *PTL* 4, no. 2 (1979), 235

5 This notion of consensus is, of course, a difficult one, for no canon has received anything like a complete consensus from its culture. Perhaps the most useful way to think of consensus is in relative terms; that is, there must be a 'general' agreement among 'experts' with regard to how useful this construct is, as well as a knowledge of at least the rough shape of the canon by a larger population. Thus, for example, if there is a curricular agreement, accepted by faculty and taught to students, or if there exists a set of 'great books' that is published and sold to its expected market, then a canon can be said to have gained consensus.

6 This group is usually thought of as the literary or the critical 'establishment.' In most statements about the Canadian canon, those capable of bringing the canon into being are conceived of as academics who are professionally involved in Canadian literature in some way. But these are not the only potential canon-makers in Canada. Historically, religious representatives, 'men of letters,' and editors have played large roles in the construction of Canadian canons. (This issue deserves a fuller discussion than space affords. A consideration of the topic should look at the immediate pragmatic reasons for canon-making as an activity and at the shared backgrounds of members of the various institutions – see A.B. McKillop's *A Disciplined Intelligence* [1979] and *Contours of Canadian Thought* [1987] – and at the frequent amount of 'cross-over' in professional activities by members of the literary establishment.)

7 Faulty definitions of systems sometimes enumerate elements within the construct being defined as if membership were the complete description of a system. Such definitions ignore or gloss over the dynamics between those elements (and between them and the elements that lie outside), although it is these dynamic relationships that give shape to the system as a whole. In discussions of canons, there has been a tendency to focus upon the texts within each canon rather than to look also at the interactions between texts and between text and context. This emphasis on text overstates the role of texts in determining a canon and excludes extra-textual influences. In addition, most definitions of the canon do not take into consideration the constraints that the overall shape of the system itself places upon membership and function. The greatest variant affecting canon selection is not the texts or even the rules that govern selection but the determinants that show one how the rules may be applied.

8 Hugh Kenner, 'The Making of the Modernist Canon,' in *Mazes: Essays by Hugh Kenner* (San Francisco: North Point Press 1989), 40

9 Response to a canonical list is as much to the values that lie behind the list as to the texts themselves. For example, we accept, reject, or wish to modify A.J.M. Smith's selections for his anthologies, or the Halifax Board of Education's approved curriculum, or the choices for the New Canadian Library series, as much for the 'philosophy' that we believe governs inclusion and exclusion as for the list itself. We sense that the institutions and individuals 'shaping' a canon, particularly a national one, also control its literary values.

10 In the course of this paper I assume that non-aesthetic values – such as those that derive from nationality, ethics, and environmental contexts – not only help determine membership in a national canon, but also affect the aesthetic system itself.

11 They do have identity in one case, when the canon is looked upon as the genre of literary writing. Treated in this way, the canon becomes a resource for uncovering the history of a literature's controlling aesthetics.

12 Although it could be argued that Ross was attempting to construct only the subcanon of the Canadian novel, his inclusion of the category 'any genre' in his poll suggests that his goals were larger.

13 As the letter to the panellists made clear, they were to establish, at the conference, standards for determining canonicity: 'the purposes here are to provide a norm ... to suggest direction ... to establish selection criteria ... to provide a guide' (Charles Steele, ed., *Taking Stock: The Calgary Conference on the Canadian Novel* [Downsview, Ont.: ECW Press 1982], 156).

14 Or that the aesthetics of the speakers would be representative of all those polled. However, the structure of the sessions suggests that Ross did not really hold out much hope for this possibility.

The speakers at the conference had difficulties from the onset because their role was to define the standards behind the results of a poll that, in itself, was not formulated to yield a shaped national canon. Instead it produced something closer to a 'popular' list. Such popular lists tell us much about the group that has made the selections and its moment in time but tend to give us a distorted vision of the shape of a literature. An additional weakness in Ross's plan was that, prior to arriving at the conference, the panellists were not allowed access to the results of the poll. They had, therefore, to shape lists of their own, which, inevitably, were not consistent with the results of the poll or with those of other speakers. The unforeseen effect of this strategy was that it provided a significant record of the difference between the ideas of more prominent critics and what, according to the poll, the more 'ordinary' teachers and scholars seemed to think.

15 *Taking Stock*, 138

16 The division between Ross's assumptions about absolute, universal values determining canonicity and those more internal and culturally

relative goals of many of the panellists is a familiar feature of canon-making and one that occurs in many attempts to create a 'national' canon. We see this pattern repeatedly in debates about the nature of Canadian literature (the best-known example occurring in the exchange between A.J.M. Smith and John Sutherland). However, the argument is not a simple one, and those supporting indigenous traits as determiners of canonicity often see cultural characteristics as non-literary, overriding 'universal' literary rules.

17 Obviously a critic can define a genre rigidly and demand strict adherence to that definition – as, for example, Joseph Wood Krutch did in his well-known discussion of tragedy in *The Modern Temper* (1929). Such defini-tions are virtually useless because they exclude too many texts that most readers think of as part of the genre. Rigid genre definitions are actually attempts to form subcanons, defining generic excellence by making the typical an ideal quality – and often basing their notion of 'typical' in period (as Krutch locates all tragedy within the limits of Greek classicism). The rigidity of this sort of definition almost always derives from its function in an extra-generic argument, in which genre is in service to some larger ideal.

18 Genres do not have clear boundaries. A good way to understand both their internal gradation and the vagueness of their margins, tangent to other genres, is to see their structure in terms of fuzzy sets. For more information, see Bennett, 'The Detective Story,' 233–66.

19 One dealt with region directly; one, with thematicism, which is seen by many to be chiefly a Central-Canadian issue; and one, with the compari-son between the writing of English and French Canada. Because my subject is the English-Canadian canon, I have ignored this last section.

20 Obviously a number of other ways of thinking have influenced our notions about canon-making, including literary and non-literary state-ments in American culture, the theories brought over by the Scottish thinkers, neo-classicism's rigid grid of genre definition, and Romanti-cism's thematic narration both of nature and of literary forms. Never-theless the Victorian literary models were the dominant ones in the English-Canadian literary establishment throughout the nineteenth century and most of the twentieth.

21 English Canadians had a particularly good opportunity to create and maintain a culturally stable continuity with England. For a time, its French underclass and then its waves of settlers from other cultures (such as the Scots, Irish, Ukrainians, and Chinese) delayed the English settle-ment's having to adapt its social and political structures to deal with the requirements of frontier life or with the exploration of new territory. However, by the end of the first decade of the twentieth century the political assimilation of its immigrants, the development of a distinct Western society, and changes in urban life all began to challenge the Victorian sensibility that controlled English-Canadian culture.

22 Smith published a second volume to complement this book, *The Canadian Century: English-Canadian Writing since Confederation*, but not until 1973, at which point prose had finally secured a place in the Canadian canon.

23 Discussing 'realism' is always a difficult problem because the term has no stable meaning and because the techniques employed to produce 'realist' writing also vary widely.

24 These 'realistic' values generally intersect with those sought for Canadian poetry; however, poetry was always expected to achieve a literarily 'technical' excellence as well.

25 While the 'reality' of these novels is almost antithetical to that in nineteenth- and early twentieth-century idealized realism, it does have earlier roots: consider, for example, Sara Jeannette Duncan's writing or even D.C. Scott's pictures of French-Canadian life.

26 This is a large topic that deserves further discussion. Essentially the morally correct writing of the late nineteenth and early twentieth centuries took the form of fictionalized tracts (e.g., Nellie McClung's *Sowing Seeds in Danny* or Ralph Connor's novels), which subordinated the aesthetics of the literary text to that of the ethical lecture.

27 One suspects that the multiple literary traditions which Western and rural Canadians inherited from their immigrant backgrounds serve as resource for the techniques and aesthetics visible in Prairie realism.

28 This form of realism also appeared in rural poetry of the 1920s and 1930s, in the work of Dorothy Livesay, Raymond Knister, W.W.E. Ross, Anne Marriott and others. Their poetry is characterized by a movement away from the techniques traditionally associated with poetry.

29 I hope by this point that my neglect of Maritime writing and its relative invisibility in the English-Canadian canon has become obvious. For much of this century many Maritime writers have adopted, not the two possibilities sketched out in this essay, but a third reaction to the changes of twentieth-century life and the values that have evolved out of them – rejection and an adherence to a characteristically Maritime form of Victorian 'literary' ideals. Perhaps Pratt's early work is the most successful example of this kind of writing, for it modified nineteenth-century concepts about poetry in a way particular to the Maritime culture, in terms not only of subject matter but also of technique. However, when we look at twentieth-century Maritime writing, we can also find work the values of which are consistent with those that evolved out of Prairie and rural Ontario aesthetics. Thus writers such as Ernest Buckler and David Adams Richards give us a realist fiction related in kind to other Canadian realist writing of their period. This kind of realism remains relatively unpopular in Maritime anthologies and Maritime publishers' lists, which continue to show as canonical to the region a somewhat ornate style, an idealized realism, and a tendency to accept moral and formula writing (elsewhere more frequently associated with 'popular' literature) as 'literary.' This divergence in basic aesthetics and cultural

perspectives has kept Maritime writers a marginalized group in terms of the whole of Canadian literature.

30 The idea of 'everyday' language is a relative one. Obviously Eliot in England and Smith in Canada both thought of themselves as adopting a diction more ordinary than that of their predecessors. However, their notion of everyday language is more elevated than that of writers who identified their work with working-class or Bohemian styles.

31 It could well be argued that Montreal was the ideal location for English Canadians to produce this kind of poetry, since only there could be found both the urban conditions that motivated such writing and a small enough English middle class as to make its older Victorian sense of 'reality' relatively invisible and unimportant.

32 National canons have frequently excluded sizeable segments of the nation's cultural production, cutting out whole areas of writing, as well as omitting work by members of society who are disenfranchised. However, it is relatively unusual for writing by members of the privileged groups (white, male) to be ignored, and it is a significant event when that occurs. As well as in the marginalization of Prairie writers, we can see examples of this phenomenon in the treatment of Southern writers in the United States.

33 It is important to note, however, that Prairie realism never had and continues not to have the pessimistic core that the urban perspective developed. While Grove, Sinclair Ross, W.O. Mitchell, and Kroetsch all write about the loss of a vision, what we as readers experience is not, necessarily, the marking of the end of standards but rather the chronicle of a void that can be filled. There is in Prairie writing a belief in rebirth that runs counter to the more ironic, later modernist vision.

MATHEWS Calgary, Canonization, and Class

1 Charles Steele, ed., *Taking Stock: The Calgary Conference on the Canadian Novel* (Downsview, Ont.: ECW Press 1982), 150. This work is hereafter cited as *TS*.

2 Robert Lecker, 'The Canonization of Canadian Literature: An Inquiry into Value,' *Critical Inquiry* 16 (Spring 1990), 664. All further references to this work (Lecker) appear in the text.

3 Note the wording of 'Letter with the Ballot' (*TS*, 158).

4 Richard Ohmann, 'The Shaping of a Canon: U.S. Fiction, 1960–1975,' in *Canons*, ed. Robert von Hallberg (Chicago: University of Chicago Press 1984), 377–401. All further references to this work (Ohmann) appear in the text.

5 W.J. Keith, 'The Function of Canadian Criticism at the Present Time,' *Essays on Canadian Writing*, no. 30 (Winter 1984–5), 2

6 Dick Harrison, *Unnamed Country: The Struggle for a Canadian Prairie Fiction*

(Edmonton: University of Alberta Press 1977), 181. All further references
to this work appear in the text.

7 T.D. MacLulich, *Hugh MacLennan* (Boston: Twayne 1983), 91–2

8 J.M. Kertzer, 'Margaret Laurence,' in *Canadian Writers and Their Works*,
ed. Robert Lecker, Jack David, and Ellen Quigley, Fiction Series, Vol. 9
(Toronto: ECW Press 1987), 295

9 Robin Mathews, *Canadian Literature: Surrender or Revolution* (Toronto:
Steel Rail 1978), 216

SIMON Culture and Its Values

1 See Anthony Purdy, ' "Ceci n'est pas un roman." A la recherche d'un
vraisemblable: discours et contrat dans le roman canadien-français du
XIXe siècle,' in *Prefaces and Literary Manifestoes / Préfaces et manifestes
littéraires*, ed. E.D. Blodgett and A.G. Purdy (Edmonton: Research Institute for Comparative Literature, University of Alberta 1990), 18–28.

2 Marcotte's preface to his book establishes the inaugural tone: 'I leave
others to wait for the great book, the undisputed masterpiece, before
they admit to the existence of French-Canadian literature. I don't have
the time. Books, works, exist – some imperfect, mere documents; some
verging on greatness – and I wish to engage in dialogue with them now'
(*Une littérature qui se fait* [Montreal: HMH 1962]).

3 André Belleau, *Le Romancier fictif* (Montreal: Presses de l'Université du
Québec à Montréal 1980)

4 Michel van Schendel, 'L'Amour dans la littérature canadienne-française,'
Recherches sociographiques 5, nos. 1–2 (Jan.–Aug. 1964), 156. See also Gilles
Marcotte, *Une littérature qui se fait* (Montreal: HMH 1968), 76.

5 Most of this debate was aired at the conference whose proceedings were
published as 'Littérature et société canadiennes-françaises,' a special
issue of *Recherches sociographiques* (5, nos. 1–2 [Jan.–Aug. 1964]). Pierre
Nepveu gives an excellent overview of the question in 'A (Hi)story that
Refuses the Telling: Poetry and the Novel in Contemporary Québécois
Literature,' *Yale French Studies*, 65 (1983), 90–105.

6 André Brochu and Gilles Marcotte, *La Littérature et le reste (livre de lettres)*
(Montreal: Quinze [prose exacte] 1980), 12. Brochu delivers this judgment as bait to Marcotte but scrupulously avoids the question.

7 Roger Dragonetti 'Dante face à Nemrod,' *Critique* (1979), 691

8 'Bakhtin assigns the term "novel" to whatever form of expression within
a given literary system reveals the limits of that system as inadequate,
imposed, or arbitrary' (K. Clark and M. Holquist, *Mikhail Bakhtin* [Cam-
bridge: Harvard University Press 1984] 276–7). Henri Meschonnic has
criticized the facile binary opposition between the novel and poetry
which he attributes in part to the reception of Bakhtin in France. He
accuses Kundera of falling into this 'modernist cliché.' Meschonnic argues

that any form of writing can have a critical function. See Henri Meschonnic, 'Littérature et oralité,' *Présence francophone* 31 (1987), 19–24.

9 *La Mort du genre*, Parts 1 and 2 (Montreal: La Nouvelle Barre du jour 1988–9)

10 Pierre Nepveu, *L'Ecologie du réel* (Montreal: Boréal 1988); Patricia Smart, *Ecrire dans la maison du père* (Montreal: Québec/Amérique 1988). All further references to these works appear in the text.

11 René Payant, 'Le Postmodernisme selon le cinéma,' in *Vedute: Pièces détachées sur l'art 1976–1987* (Montreal: Editions Trois 1987), 599

12 The history of the term 'realism' lends itself readily to such indetermination. In his review of the critical debates over realism and modernism during the 1930s, R.S. Livingstone remarks that 'both Brecht and Lukács can claim the term "realism" for widely differing practices' (R.S. Livingstone, 'Ernst Bloch,' in *1936: The Sociology of Literature [Volume 1 – The Politics of Modernism]*, ed. Francis Barker et al. [Essex: University of Essex 1979], 4). Smart's conflation of realism and modernism is very much in the tradition of Virginia Woolf and very much opposed to that of Raymond Williams.

13 Louise Dupré's study of the poetry of Nicole Brossard, Madeleine Gagnon, and France Théoret takes an opposite attack, seeking rather to exploit the differences among these writers – especially their differing questioning of subjectivity. See Louise Dupré, *Stratégies du vertige* (Montreal: Remue-ménage 1989).

14 For example: the work of historian Robert Linteau, sociologist Micheline Labelle, philosopher Pierre Anctil, and art critic Esther Trépanier; the research program and publications of the Institut québécois de recherche sur la culture.

15 Jean Larose, 'Nationalisme et culture: Les campagnes référendaires,' in *La Petite Noirceur* (Montreal: Boréal 1987), 45–6; François Ricard, 'Marcel Rioux entre la culture et les cultures,' *Liberté* 31, no. 2 (April 1989), 3–13

16 Ricard, 4

17 In a recent encyclopaedic and perceptive overview of modern Quebec criticism, Barbara Godard discerns in recent criticism a return to the social concerns which, according to André Belleau, belong to a kind of 'traditional sociocritique,' a general sociologizing discourse practised by journalists, writers, and professors 'who tend to consider each important work that appears as a moment, successful or not, in a literary evolution inseparable from national and political evolution' (André Belleau, 'La Démarche sociocritique au Québec,' *Voix et images* 8, no. 2 [1983], 300). The current prominence of socio-criticism, the impressive body of research devoted to the 'literary institution,' and a return to subjectivity and emotion are so many indications, according to Godard, of a flight from formalism and the renewed centrality of what has in various forms been a distinguishing characteristic of criticism in Quebec. See Barbara Godard, 'Critical Discourse in/on Quebec,' in *Studies on Canadian Litera-*

ture: Introductory and Critical Essays, ed. Arnold E. Davidson (New York: Modern Language Association of America 1990), 271–95.

18 For instance Jacques Michon uses Bourdieu's popular concept of the 'literary market-place' and the ideological expectations of readers to define literary value: 'The value or importance of a genre or technique at a certain time is not due to intrinsic formal qualities but to the conformity of its structure to the needs and ideological expectations of the receiving society' (J. Michon, *Structure, idéologie et réception du roman québécois de 1940 à 1960* [Sherbrooke: Département d'études françaises, Université de Sherbrooke 1979], 9).

19 Suzanne Lamy, *d'elles* (Montreal: L'Hexagone 1979); and *Quand je lis je m'invente* (Montreal: L'Hexagone 1985). See also the special issue of *Voix et images* (37 [Autumn 1987]) devoted to her work.

20 See especially Belleau's remarkable essay 'Code social et code littéraire dans le roman québécois,' in *Surprendre les voix* (Montreal: Boréal 1986), 175–92.

21 See, for instance, two important recent publications which present two very different versions of Quebec culture and identity: Simon Harel, *Le Voleur de parcous: Etrangeté et cosmopolitisme dans le roman québécois* (Longeuil: Editions du Préambule 1989) and Micheline Cambron, *Une société, un récit: Discours culturel au Québec (1967–1976)* (Montreal: L'Hexagon 1989).

   Nonetheless, even if canon-formation is considered in its institutional form as a process of transmission of valorized works and therefore necessarily also a process of exclusion, it must be noted that 'la littérature québécoise,' – though increasingly open to writers born elsewhere but writing in French – remains inaccessible to Anglo-Quebec writers. Will an anthology of Quebec literature one day contain work in translation by Richler or Cohen?

22 Régine Robin is perhaps the writer who (both in her fictional and theoretical works) has most articulately and extensively promoted the definition of the linguistic and cultural marginality of the writer. See, in particular, her recent *Kafka* (Paris: Editions Belfond 1989).

23 Suzanne Lamy, 'Du privé au politique: *La Constellation du Cygne* de Yolande Villemaire,' *Quebec Studies* 5 (1987), 17–28; Caroline Bayard, 'Serait-ce cela inspire l'Amérique?: *La Constellation du Cygne* de Yolande Villemaire,' *Quebec Studies* 6 (1988), 112–20

24 Janet Paterson, though defending the novel as the record of a culture seeking its self-transformation, wondered whether *La Vie en prose* would seem by the end of the century to be an example of narcissism and neo-mannerism. And Suzanne Lamy, though as impressed as Paterson and other critics by the sheer virtuosity and energy of the novel, concludes her perceptive article on the work with the cryptic envoi: 'In the end, this pink is a ethic, an art de vivre. What more can be said for the seriousness of writing?' See Janet M. Paterson, 'A Poetics of Transforma-

tion: Yolande Villemaire's *La Vie en prose*,' in *A Mazing Space*, ed. Shirley Neuman and Smaro Kamboureli (Edmonton: Longspoon/NeWest 1986), 315–23; and Suzanne Lamy, 'Subversion en rose,' in *Féminité, Subversion, Ecriture*, ed. Suzanne Lamy and Irène Pagès (Quebec: Remue-ménage 1983), 107–18.

25 On this question see, for instance, Barbara Godard, S. Simon, and P. Smart, 'Feminism and Postmodernism: The Politics of the Alliance,' *Quebec Studies* 9 (Fall 1989–Winter 1990), 131–50, and discussions among Quebec feminist writers in the journal *Tessera*, nos. 5 and 6 (1989).

26 See, for instance, Robert Schwartzwald, '(Homo)sexualité et problématique identitaire,' in S. Simon, P. L'Hérault, R. Schwartzwald, and A. Nouss, *Fictions de l'identitaire au Québec* (Montreal: xyz Editeur 1991).

WEIR Normalizing the Subject

1 Linda Hutcheon, *The Canadian Postmodern: A Study of Contemporary English-Canadian Fiction* (Toronto: Oxford University Press 1988). This work is hereafter cited as TCP.

2 Linda Hutcheon, *A Poetics of Postmodernism: History, Theory, Fiction* (New York: Routledge 1988); hereafter cited as PP. Note Frank Davey's claim that 'the chief assumption' of such guidebooks 'is that criticism is an act of mediation – a facilitator of easy consumption' (*Reading Canadian Reading* [Winnipeg: Turnstone Press 1988], 14).

3 Academic manuscripts on Canadian (and other) subjects are frequently submitted to this program (ASPP) for a subsidy to meet a portion of publication costs. Manuscripts are sent to area experts selected by the president of each of the Canadian 'learned societies' which together comprise the Canadian Federation for the Humanities. Since these experts are typically very senior members of the profession and since theory is a relatively new addition to the humanities in Canada, manuscripts appear frequently to be referred to those whose competence does not extend to theoretical materials which they are nonetheless asked to assess. To my knowledge, there are few theorists in Canada whose files do not include assessments from those whose purpose has been to censor technical vocabulary and berate speculative thought whether deconstructive or new historicist, semiotic or feminist. Such oppressive working conditions, compounded by the resistance at the departmental level in many Canadian universities, more than any other factors serve to thwart the development of theory in this country, whether focused on Canadian or other materials.

4 Fredric Jameson, 'The Politics of Theory: Ideological Positions in the Postmodernism Debate' (1984), reprinted in *Contemporary Critical Theory*, ed. Dan Latimer (San Diego: Harcourt Brace Jovanovich 1989), 374

5 Robert Kroetsch et al., 'Present Tense: The Closing Panel,' in *Future*

Indicative: Literary Theory and Canadian Literature, ed. John Moss (Ottawa: University of Ottawa Press 1987), 244

6 From 'Postcoloniality, Resistance, the Gendered Subaltern: Mahasweta Devi's "The Hunt," ' a lecture by Gayatri Spivak at the International Summer Institute for Semiotic and Structural Studies, University of British Columbia, 12 Aug. 1988

7 Jean-Pierre Lyotard's phrase, from *The Postmodern Condition: A Report on Knowledge*, trans. Geoff Bennington and Brian Massumi (Minneapolis: University of Minnesota Press 1984); quoted in TCP, 15

8 Umberto Eco, *Semiotics and the Philosophy of Language* (Bloomington: Indiana University Press 1984), 163

9 Hugh Kenner, 'Reflections on the Gabler Era,' *James Joyce Quarterly* 26, no. 1 (Fall 1988), 19

10 Lorraine Weir, 'The Discourse of "Civility": Strategies of Containment in Literary Histories of English Canada,' in *Problems of Literary Reception / Problèmes de réception littéraire*, ed. E.D. Blodgett and A.G. Purdy (Edmonton: Research Institute for Comparative Literature, University of Alberta 1988) 24–39; ' "Maps and Tales": The Progress of *Canadian Literature*, 1959–87,' in *Questions of Funding, Publishing and Distribution / Questions d'édition et de diffusion*, ed. I. McLaren and T. Potvin (Edmonton: Research Institute for Comparative Literature, University of Alberta 1989), 141–59

11 Robert Kroetsch, 'A Canadian Issue,' *Boundary* 2 3, no. 1 (1974), 1

12 Andreas Huyssen, *After the Great Divide: Modernism, Mass Culture, Postmodernism* (Bloomington: Indiana University Press 1986), 53–4

13 Huyssen, 60. Compare Frank Davey's curious exclusion of the avant-garde from international modernism (*Reading Canadian Reading*, 119).

14 See Lorraine Weir, *Writing Joyce: A Semiotics of the Joyce System* (Bloomington: Indiana University Press 1989). The inscription of Joycean intertexts in Canadian and Québécois literature typically coincides with semantic/ideological dissent. Consider, for example, A.M. Klein, Sheila Watson, Nicole Brossard, and Hubert Aquin. On Klein and Joyce, see Lorraine Weir, 'Portrait of the Poet as Joyce Scholar,' *Canadian Literature*, no. 76 (Spring 1978) 47–55; on Brossard and Joyce, see Lorraine Weir, 'From Picture to Hologram: Nicole Brossard's Grammar of Utopia,' in *A Mazing Space: Writing Canadian Women Writing*, ed. Shirley Neuman and Smaro Kamboureli (Edmonton: Longspoon/NeWest 1986), 345–52.

15 Roman Jakobson, 'The Dominant' (1935), reprinted in *Readings in Russian Poetics: Formalist and Structuralist Views*, ed. Ladislav Matejka and Krystyna Pomorska (Cambridge: MIT Press 1971), 82. All further references to this work appear in the text.

16 Jurij Tynjanov, 'On Literary Evolution' (1927, 1929), reprinted in Matejka and Pomorska, eds., *Readings in Russian Poetics*, 72 (Tynjanov's italics)

17 Boris M. Ejxenbaum [Eichenbaum], 'The Theory of the Formal Method,' in Matejka and Pomorska, eds., *Readings in Russian Poetics*, 33

18 Ibid., 27
19 M.M. Baxtin [Bakhtin], 'Discourse Typology in Prose,' reprinted in Matejka and Pomorska, eds., *Readings in Russian Poetics*, 176. All further references to this work appear in the text.
20 Ferdinand de Saussure, *Course in General Linguistics*, ed. Charles Bally and Albert Sechehaye with Albert Riedlinger, trans. Wade Baskin (New York: McGraw-Hill 1966), 78; Eco, *Semiotics and the Philosophy of Language*, 83–4
21 M.A.K. Halliday, *Language as Social Semiotic: The Social Interpretation of Language and Meaning* (London: Edward Arnold 1978)
22 Saussure, *Course in General Linguistics*, 78
23 Julia Kristeva, *Desire in Language: A Semiotic Approach to Literature and Art*, ed. Leon S. Roudiez, trans. Thomas Gora, Alice Jardine, and Leon S. Roudiez (New York: Columbia University Press 1980), 131
24 Kristeva, *Desire in Language*, 47
25 Emile Benveniste, *Problems in General Linguistics*, trans. Mary Elizabeth Meek (Coral Gables: University of Miami Press 1971), 236
26 Benveniste, *Problems in General Linguistics*, 237 (Benveniste's italics)
27 Jurij Lotman, *The Structure of the Artistic Text*, trans. Gail Lenhoff and Ronald Vroon, Michigan Slavic Contributions, no. 7 (Ann Arbor: University of Michigan 1977), 9. See also Jurij Lotman, 'The Dynamic Model of a Semiotic System,' trans. Ann Shukman, *Semiotica* 21, nos. 3–4 (1977), 193–210. Note the title of chapter 2 of *A Poetics of Postmodernism*: 'Modelling the Postmodern ... ,' which leads to 'limiting,' 'decentering,' 'contextualizing,' and 'historicizing' it in subsequent chapters.
28 See, for example, Paul Ricoeur on Aristotelian process theory in Study 1 of *The Rule of Metaphor: Multidisciplinary Studies of the Creation of Meaning in Language*, trans. Robert Czerny with Kathleen McLaughlin and John Costello, S.J. (Toronto: University of Toronto Press 1977) and Louis Zukofsky, *Prepositions: The Collected Critical Essays*, expanded ed. (Berkeley: University of California Press 1981), 12–23 and 57–64. See also chapter 5 of Weir, *Writing Joyce*, on Joyce and Zukofsky.
29 Linda Hutcheon, 'History and/as Intertext,' in Moss, ed., *Future Indicative*, 171
30 Huyssen, *After the Great Divide*, 54
31 Compare Hutcheon's interrogation of the 'extremes' of surfiction (and modernism): 'Can language and literature *ever* be totally non-mimetic, non-referential, and still remain understandable as literature?' (*PP*, 52). Thus Hutcheon's razor, less acute than Ockham's, measures literariness in terms of reader response and limits the literary to the response patterns of those already, by definition, acculturated to specific forms.
32 D.E. Schleiermacher, '*The Hermeneutics*: Outline of the 1819 Lectures,' trans. Jan Wojcik and Roland Haas, *New Literary History* 10, no. 1 (Autumn 1978), 14
33 Wilhelm Dilthey, 'The Development of Hermeneutics' (1900), in

W. *Dilthey: Selected Writings*, ed. and trans. H.P. Rickman (Cambridge: Cambridge University Press 1976), 259

34 Saint Augustine, *On Christian Doctrine*, trans. D.W. Robertson, Jr (New York: Liberal Arts Press 1958), 45

35 Stanley Fish, *Is There a Text in This Class? The Authority of Interpretive Communities* (Cambridge: Harvard University Press 1980), 321, 340 (Fish's italics)

36 Davey, *Reading Canadian Reading*, 79

37 See Pierre Macherey, *A Theory of Literary Production*, trans. Geoffrey Wall (London: Routledge and Kegan Paul 1978), 66–8 and passim.

38 In this context consider, for example, Atwood. See Lorraine Weir, 'Atwood in a Landscape,' in *Margaret Atwood: Language, Text and System*, ed. Sherrill E. Grace and Lorraine Weir (Vancouver: University of British Columbia Press 1983), 143–53.

39 Toronto: New Press 1972

40 Consider the *Oxford English Dictionary* on *compromise*: '1. to adjust or settle (differences, etc.) between parties ... 4. to expose ... to risk or danger, to imperil, to involve in a hazardous course, to commit (oneself).'

41 See Frank Kermode, *The Genesis of Secrecy: On Interpretation of Narrative* (Cambridge: Harvard University Press 1979), 53. 'Why,' Kermode asks, 'does it require a more strenuous effort to believe that a narrative lacks coherence than to believe that somehow, if we could only find out, it doesn't?' (53).

42 It is a tragic irony that in English Canada, communitarian models have typically been, in practice, anti-communitarian, using the rhetoric of community and mutuality in order to exclude nonconformists (Hutcheon's 'ex-centrics') from literary, political, and social canons of 'good taste' and 'equality.' For some literary-critical variants see Weir, 'The Discourse of "Civility," ' 26–9 and passim.

43 Jameson, 'The Politics of Theory,' 375

44 Huyssen, *After the Great Divide*, 54. Compare Huyssen's comments on 'the recent neoconservative attempt to reinstate a domesticated version of modernism' (185), parallel to similar attempts during the 1950s to integrate modernism into the 'liberal-conservative consensus of the times' (190). Thus the revolt of artists during the 1960s 'sprang precisely from the success of modernism, from the fact that in the United States, as in West Germany and France ... modernism had been perverted into a form of affirmative culture' (190).

45 Consider, for example, Huyssen's claim that 'poststructuralism is primarily a discourse of and about modernism ... [I]f we are to locate the postmodern in poststructuralism it will have to be found in the ways various forms of poststructuralism have opened up new problematics in modernism and have reinscribed modernism into the discourse formations of our own time' (207).

46 Consider, for example, Hutcheon's assertion that in postmodern litera-

ture 'there has been a general (and perhaps healthy) turning from the expectation of sure and single meaning ... ' (*TCP*, 23), her discovery in Cohen's *Beautiful Losers* of 'perversion (in official terms)' and 'perhaps shocking language' (*TCP*, 34), and her assertion that postmodern metafictions like Cohen's 'suggest the need to examine (or even change) reading habits – and maybe also living habits' (*TCP*, 35).

47 Compare the belated attempts of another Canadian champion of postmodernism to preserve it, together with post-structuralist theory, for humanism. See Moss, ed., *Future Indicative*, 141, where Bakhtinian dialogism is saved for humanism; and 123, where 'the system of an author's *oeuvre*' is one focus of an attempt to 'illuminate' texts.

48 Jacques Derrida, *Memoires for Paul de Man*, trans. Cecile Lindsay, Jonathan Culler, and Eduardo Cadava (New York: Columbia University Press 1986), 73

Index